HIKING RUINS
OF SOUTHERN
NEW ENGLAND

HELP US KEEP THIS GUIDE UP TO DATE

Every effort has been made by the author and editors to make this guide as accurate and useful as possible. However, many things can change after a guide is published—trails are rerouted, regulations change, techniques evolve, facilities come under new management, etc.

We appreciate hearing from you concerning your experiences with this guide and how you feel it could be improved and kept up to date. While we may not be able to respond to all comments and suggestions, we'll take them to heart and we'll also make certain to share them with the author. Please send your comments and suggestions to the following email address:

FalconGuides
Reader Response/Editorial Department
Falconeditorial@rowman.com

Thanks for your input, and happy trails!

HIKING RUINS
OF SOUTHERN
NEW ENGLAND

A GUIDE TO 40 SITES IN CONNECTICUT,
MASSACHUSETTS, AND RHODE ISLAND

Nick Bellantoni and Barbara Ann Kipfer

FALCONGUIDES

ESSEX, CONNECTICUT

To Angela Bellantoni and Paul Magoulas,
our favorite hiking partners.

FALCONGUIDES®

An imprint of Globe Pequot, the trade division of
The Rowman & Littlefield Publishing Group, Inc.
4501 Forbes Blvd., Ste. 200
Lanham, MD 20706
www.rowman.com

Falcon and FalconGuides are registered trademarks and Make Adventure Your Story is a
trademark of The Rowman & Littlefield Publishing Group, Inc.

Distributed by NATIONAL BOOK NETWORK

Title page photo: Stone wall enclosure, Tunxis Trail, Caseville, Barkhamsted, CT.
Photos by Nick Bellantoni unless otherwise noted.
Maps by Melissa Baker and The Rowman & Littlefield Publishing Group, Inc.
Front cover photo: Stone stairway into the lower level of historic Coogan Barn, Mystic, CT. Back
cover photo: The collapsed stone chimneys from Revolutionary War huts at Putnam State Park.

British Library Cataloguing in Publication Information available

Library of Congress Cataloging-in-Publication Data available

Names: Bellantoni, Nick, author | Kipfer, Barbara Ann, author.
Title: Hiking ruins of southern New England : a guide to 40 sites in Connecticut, Massachusetts,
   and Rhode Island / Nick Bellantoni and Barbara Ann Kipfer.
Description: Essex, Connecticut : Falcon Guides, [2024] | Includes bibliographical references. |
   Summary: "Hiking Ruins of Southern New England is a guide to hiking archaeological sites in
   Connecticut, Massachusetts, and Rhode Island"—Provided by publisher.
Identifiers: LCCN 2023033350 (print) | LCCN 2023033351 (ebook) | ISBN 9781493068548
   (paperback) | ISBN 9781493068555 (epub)
Subjects: LCSH: New England—Antiquities—Guidebooks. | New England—Archaeological sites—
   Guidebooks. | Hiking—New England—Guidebooks. | Trails—New England—Guidebooks.
Classification: LCC F6 .K56 2023 (print) | LCC F6 (ebook) | DDC 917.404—dc23/eng/20231114
LC record available at https://lccn.loc.gov/2023033350
LC ebook record available at https://lccn.loc.gov/2023033351

∞™ The paper used in this publication meets the minimum requirements of American National
Standard for Information Sciences—Permanence of Paper for Printed Library Materials, ANSI/
NISO Z39.48-1992.

The authors and The Rowman & Littlefield Publishing Group, Inc. assume no liability for accidents
happening to, or injuries sustained by, readers who engage in the activities described in this
book.

CONTENTS

THE HIKES

Connecticut

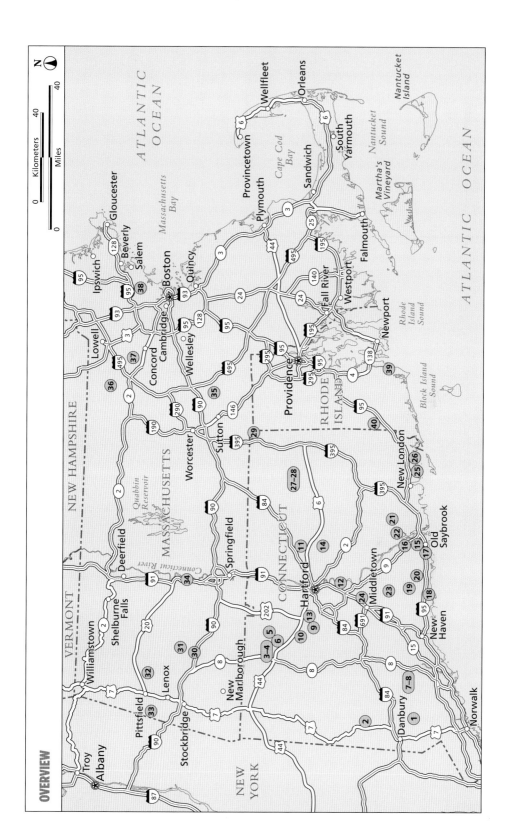

ACKNOWLEDGMENTS

During our careers, we have spent a lot of time hiking wooded areas and identifying archaeological sites often comprised of stone ruins throughout southern New England. Yet, we hadn't seen all that these states offer for the interested hiker. As a result, we are indebted to experienced trekkers throughout the region who have come upon stone ruins in their journeys and have assisted us in compiling this book.

Archaeologist Marc Banks and historian Paul Hart shared their knowledge and identifications of stone ruins along trails in the Barkhamsted, CT, area, including the Henry Buck, Walt Landgraf, Lighthouse, and Tunxis (Caseville) Trails.

We thank archaeologist Kenneth Feder for his support, extensive research, and establishment of the Lighthouse Village Trail, Peoples State Forest, Barkhamsted, CT.

Ed Chiucarello, President of the Rocky Hill Historical Society, gave us a tour of Dividend Park Archaeological Preserve and shared his knowledge of the park's industrial ruins.

Abbie Cadman, Natural Resources Conservation Service, imparted stone ruins she recognized during her stewardship of Connecticut farmland.

We benefited from our discussions with Glenda Rose, President of the Friends of the Office of State Archaeology, an experienced and knowledgeable Connecticut hiker.

Our dear and longtime friends, Robert (Bob) and Mary-Jo Young, shared site information on Israel Putnam State Park and Lovers Leap Trails in western Connecticut.

Marina Englund toured Putnam State Park with us, pointing out significant Revolutionary War stone works.

Peter and Barbara Rzasa introduced us to several historical features along trail systems in New Haven County, including the Laurel Lime Kiln and Keith Mitchell Trails. They are great tour guides, and our hikes together are always informative and fun.

Lee and Carol West are dear friends and longtime colleagues who turned us on to the Tri-State Trail and journeyed up the mountain to the Eyrie House Ruins and Dividend Park. Lunch afterward is always as enjoyable as the hikes themselves.

A tip of the hat to Dale Geslien, CT Chapter of the Appalachian Mountain Club, for rounding up their membership to assist. Dale set up a virtual meeting with experienced hikers who shared their knowledge of trails in the region. Valuable information was gleaned from Gene Grayson, John Grasso, June Powell, Mike Cunningham, Steve Braciak, and Phil Wilsey. Phil hiked with us to the abandoned community of Caseville along the Tunxis Trail and located the Mount Higby plane crash site. We are appreciative of AMC members for their enthusiasm, support, and trail expertise.

In Avon, Terri Wilson, Director of the Avon Historical Society, and Janet Conner put us in touch with Fran Gurman and Norm Sondheimer, who gave us a personal tour of the Farmington Canal Trail. Also, Carl E. Walter shared his immense knowledge of the Farmington Canal.

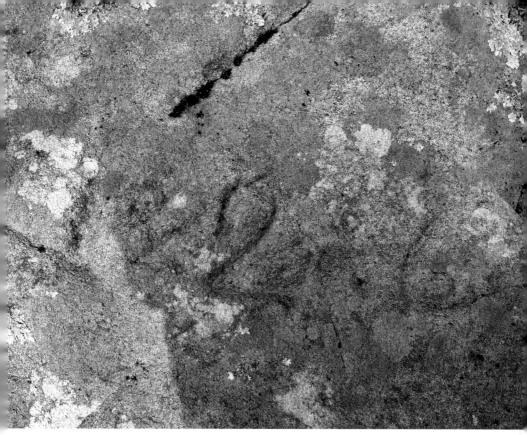

Dates carved into Townline Boulder, Canfield Woods Trail, Deep River–Essex, CT.

Donna Dufrense shared her extensive research into Ashford Woods in Natchaug State Forest, and the awe-inspiring history of African American and Nipmuc tribal members eking out a living in northeastern Connecticut. Donna's research has opened new interpretations of stone ruins and the families that built them.

Sarah Atwell and John Ertle, Durham Historical Society, aided in relocating the Durham Pest House ruin and provided a tour of the site.

Finally, we acknowledge our FalconGuides editor, Mason Gadd, for his total support, guidance, and flexibility and for piloting this book through to completion.

We apologize to any individuals we may have missed in this acknowledgment. Without their expertise, the extent and variety of stone ruins from southern New England presented in this book would not have been possible. We thank all for their support and enthusiasm toward the project.

MEET YOUR GUIDES

Nick Bellantoni, PhD, is emeritus Connecticut State Archaeologist and an adjunct associate research professor in the Department of Anthropology at the University of Connecticut. He
served as state archaeologist with the Connecticut State Museum
of Natural History at the University of Connecticut. He earned
his BA in anthropology at the Central Connecticut State College
in 1976 and his doctorate in anthropology from UConn in 1987,
shortly thereafter appointed state archaeologist. He retired from
that position in 2014.

Bellantoni is co-editor of *In Remembrance: Archaeology and
Death,* and he has also contributed to journals such as the *Journal of Forensic Science, Journal of Archaeological Science*, and *American
Journal of Physical Anthropology*. He most recently has authored
The Long Journeys Home: The Repatriations of Henry 'Opukaha'ia and Albert Afraid of Hawk
and *"And So the Tomb Remained": Exploring Archaeology and Forensic Science within Connecticut's Historical Family Mausolea.* He has been excavating in Connecticut for forty years.

Barbara Ann Kipfer, PhD, is the author of nearly seventy books,
including: *Hiking Is Fundamental* (FalconGuides), *Archaeologist's
Fieldwork Guide 2nd Edition, Encyclopedic Dictionary of Archaeology
Second Edition, 14,000 Things to Be Happy About, Natural Medita-
tion*, and *1,001 Ways to Live Wild*.

Dr. Kipfer holds a PhD in archaeology (Greenwich University), BS in physical education (Valparaiso University), PhD and
MPhil in linguistics (University of Exeter), and MA and PhD in
Buddhist studies (Akamai University). She is a Registered Profes-
sional Archaeologist. Visit her at https://www.thingstobehappy
about.com.

INTRODUCTION

REGION OVERVIEW

All archaeological ruins in Connecticut, Massachusetts, and Rhode Island have a cultural tale to tell, though most sites are not available to the public or associated with hiking trails. The ones included in this book are, though they may be unfamiliar to the experienced hiker who has seen these ruins but has little idea of their purpose or origin. Hence, we offer the hiker an insider's look at places archaeologists have investigated as part of the region's cultural development. Like an archaeologist, you will become familiar with the history of the sites and the people who lived on the land. You will see stone features left behind by Native Americans, Colonial European settlers, and later industrialists and entrepreneurs.

We invite you to speculate on the stories of these places by observation of the ruins, though always remembering that they were built by people living, working, and worshiping, attempting to raise healthy, prosperous, and happy families with whatever technologies were available. Be sure to imagine the people as your mind's eye reconstructs the past based on the vestiges of their lives observed in ruins.

This compilation of stone ruins takes you to places where southern New England's history can be experienced via hiking trails. We are confident that you will be puzzled by some of the stone features encountered and may speculate beyond the explanations offered in this book as to other origins to the stone-built environment you observe. If so, remember that all these ruins have historical, archaeological, and oral traditions behind their interpretations. And if primary records are lacking, scientists fall back on the problem-solving principle of Occam's razor, which basically states that when all things are equal and you have two or more theories with the same predictive outcome, the best explanation is the simpler one; that is, the one that requires the least number of assumptions and complications is usually the correct one.

Enjoy hiking these ruins seldom seen. Appreciate that hiking trails help preserve southern New England's cultural past.

WEATHER

The climate of New England varies greatly across its 500-mile span from northern Maine to southern Connecticut, but the states of southern New England are similar. The coastline of Connecticut and Rhode Island can be a bit milder in the summers and winters due to the ocean's effect.

Most of interior Massachusetts and upland interior Connecticut have a humid continental climate. The summer months are moderately warm to hot and humid. Annual rainfall is spread evenly throughout the year. In Massachusetts and northern Connecticut, the winters may include snows that are heavy. Cities like Boston, Hartford, and Providence receive an average of 35–50 inches of snow in winter.

In eastern Massachusetts, northern Rhode Island, and northern Connecticut, a hot-summer version of the humid continental climate prevails. Coastal Rhode Island and southern Connecticut are the broad transition zone from continental climates to the north, to temperate climates to the south. Summers can be quite humid, with tropical air masses common between May and September. In the lower Connecticut River valley of southern Massachusetts and Connecticut, summer temperatures range between 80–90 degrees F on a regular basis during June, July, and August. Convective thunderstorms are common in these months as well, some of which can become severe.

The coast of Connecticut through to Westerly and Newport, Rhode Island, is usually the mildest area of New England in winter. Winter precipitation in this area frequently falls in the form of rain or a wintry mix of sleet, rain, and wet snow. Seasonal snowfall averages 24–30 inches. Cold snaps in this far southern zone also tend to be shorter and less intense than points north. Winters also tend to be sunnier and warmer in southern Connecticut and southern Rhode Island compared to northern and central New England.

Summers are getting longer, hotter, and more humid with climate change. Fall is drier than summer and an inspiring time to hike the area. Winter can bring chilly rains, snow, and some subfreezing temperatures. Spring has variable weather, and it is the time to once again beware of ticks.

GEOLOGY OF NEW ENGLAND

New England is a mountainous area of significant relief. There are mountain ranges, forests, countryside, rivers and lakes, and coastlines. Much of the region is composed of volcanic arcs formed during prehistoric times. Volcanic arcs are curved chains of volcanoes in the overriding tectonic plate of a subduction zone, which form as the result of rising magma formed by the melting of the descending tectonic plate.

The area is made up of highly deformed Precambrian (4,600 million years ago -541 (+/- 1) million years ago) and Paleozoic (541 (+/- 0.4) million years ago -251.902 (+/- 0.024) million years ago) metamorphic rocks including gneisses, schists, slates, quartzite, and marble. The Precambrian rocks occur primarily to the west and south, with Paleozoic sedimentary and metamorphosed sedimentary rocks making up the rest of the region. In some areas, erosion has exposed large masses of coarsely crystalline Paleozoic granite. New England was glaciated during the Pleistocene (2,580,000–11,700 years ago) and shows both depositional and erosional effects of glacial ice.

Marble, granite, and slate are all widely distributed in New England. Talc, asbestos, and zinc (from the minerals franklinite, willemite, and zincite) are also in the region.

FLORA AND FAUNA

Connecticut was a forested region prior to its settlement by Europeans. The southern two-thirds were largely oak forest, and the northern region contained the northern hardwood region of birch, beech, maple, and hemlock. Higher elevations and sandy sections support coniferous forest cover. Virtually all the primeval forest has been cut, however, and, although some of the original speciation still exists, the woodland that now covers nearly two-thirds of the state more closely resembles a mixed forest of evergreen forests of spruce, pine, and balsam.

Deer are still abundant but in general the populations of larger animals (bears, moose, wolves, foxes) have been severely reduced. There are smaller mammals such as raccoons, muskrats, porcupines, weasels, and beavers. Coyotes may also be seen, especially in early morning or after dark.

More than 300 species of birds are often seen in the state. The wild turkey, missing from the state since the early 19th century, is abundant again after having been reintroduced in the 1970s. Shorebirds, waterfowl, and seabirds abound along the coast.

Lyme disease, a potentially debilitating bacterial infection spread by ticks, was first identified in the southeastern town of Lyme, CT. Please use protective caution when hiking in grassy, bushy, and wooded areas. Consider EPA-approved tick repellent and clothing, walk in the center of trails when possible, and check your clothing and body carefully for ticks after every hike (any ticks found should be removed), and we recommend showering within two hours after coming indoors, washing all hiking clothes in hot water and tumble drying for at least 10 minutes set at high heat.

Massachusetts has preserved many of its forests, and there are now nearly 150 state forests, reservations, and parks. About a dozen national wildlife refuges and the Cape Cod National Seashore allow further contact with nature. Though few large animals remain in the wild, an occasional bear or moose is sighted. Other animals seen in the woods include deer, beavers, muskrats, minks, otters, snowshoe hares, red foxes, woodchucks, raccoons, and chipmunks. Along the shores, sandpipers, blue herons, American egrets, sanderlings, and turnstones can be seen. Waterbirds include gulls, scoters, cormorants, and loons; those most often seen on land are kingfishers, warblers, bobwhites, brown thrashers, sparrow hawks, falcons, owls, yellow-shafted flickers, woodpeckers, and whippoorwills. Game birds include ruffed grouse, wild turkeys, and pheasant.

Rhode Island is more than three-fifths forested with secondary tree growth. White pine grows in scattered locations and several varieties of oak are abundant. Ash, hickory, and maple are widely dispersed, with some birch, black walnut, and hemlock also found in mixed woodlands. Swamp maple grows in wet places, while cedar, juniper, and poplar fill in abandoned fields and pastures. Spruce, fir, and pine are grown on tree farms. Wildflowers are found throughout New England.

Small animals such as rabbits, woodchucks, raccoons, skunks, opossums, red and gray squirrels, minks, and beavers are distributed widely outside urbanized areas. Red and gray foxes are increasingly common, while white-tailed deer are found on Prudence and Block Islands, in the western woodlands, and in suburban areas. The eastern coyote and the wild turkey are found in growing numbers all over the state.

LEAVE NO TRACE

Plan and Prepare: Know the regulations and special concerns for the area you will visit. Prepare for extreme weather, hazards, and emergencies. Schedule your trip to avoid times of high use.

Planning includes visiting in small groups or splitting larger groups into smaller groups. Repackage food to minimize waste. Use a map and compass to eliminate the use of marking paint, rock cairns, or flagging.

Travel and Camp on Durable Surfaces: In popular areas, concentrate use on existing trails and campsites. Camp at least 200 feet from lakes and streams. Keep campsites small and focus activity in areas where vegetation is absent. Walk single file in the middle of the trail, even when it is wet or muddy.

In pristine areas, disperse use to prevent the creation of new campsites or trails. Avoid places where impacts are just beginning.

Dispose of Waste Properly: For everything from litter to human waste to rinse water, pack it in and pack it out. Leave a place cleaner than you found it. Carry water 200 feet away from streams or lakes and use small amounts of biodegradable soap to wash yourself or dishes. Scatter drained dishwater.

Deposit solid human waste in catholes dug 6–8 inches deep, at least 200 feet from water, camp, and trails. Cover and disguise the cathole when finished. Pack out toilet paper and hygiene products. Some areas require that human waste be packed out, too.

Minimize Campfire Impacts: Make fires where they are permitted and use established fire rings, fire pans, or mound fires. Keep fires small and use only sticks from the ground that can be broken by hand.

Burn all wood and coals to ash. Put out campfires completely. Scatter the cooled ashes. Do not bring firewood from home. Buy it from a local source or gather it there if and where it is allowed.

Leave What You Find: Take only pictures and leave only footprints. You can look at, but not touch, cultural or historic structures and artifacts. Leave rocks, plants, and nature in general as you find them.

Avoid introducing or transporting non-native species. Clean shoe and boot soles, bike tires, and boat hulls between trips. Do not build structures or furniture or dig trenches.

Respect Wildlife: Do not approach animals. Observe from a distance and do not follow them or feed them. Avoid wildlife during sensitive times such as mating, nesting, raising young, or in winter.

Protect wildlife—and your food—by storing your rations and trash securely. If you bring pets, leash and control them at all times.

Be Considerate of Others: Respect other visitors and treat them as you would like to be treated. Be courteous.

Yield to other users on the trail. Step to the downhill side of the trail when encountering horses or other pack animals.

Take your breaks and camp away from the trails and other visitors. Manage any pet you bring.

Let the sounds of nature prevail. Avoid using loud voices, making loud noises, or talking a lot.

ETIQUETTE AT ARCHAEOLOGY SITES

Archaeology is everywhere people have lived, represented in historic and cultural sites. At home or traveling to other communities, be respectful of the people and history there.

Be a good steward of the past. It is everyone's responsibility to protect archaeological sites for the future. If you find a structure or artifact, please leave it in place. You can record the location and alert the state archaeologist.

Remember to leave artifacts where they are. Archaeological sites tell the stories of past people's lives. Moving artifacts takes away from those stories. Admire, draw, or photograph them instead.

Be careful where you walk at an archaeological site. Stepping, leaning, sitting, or climbing on stone structures could damage them. Pay close attention to signs and paths in parks or heritage areas.

Think about what you leave behind. Leaving your own materials at archaeological sites could spoil the experience for others. Trash, food, and campfires can contaminate sites, making it harder to learn about the past.

ARCHAEOLOGY SITES AND THE LAW

Archaeological sites contain important and irreplaceable information about the past. Unfortunately, climate change, development, vandalism, and looting destroy sites at an alarming rate. Site protection is not only the responsibility of law enforcement officials or archaeologists. The past belongs to everyone, and it is everyone's responsibility to help protect and preserve it.

Laws in the United States on federal and state lands protect archaeological sites. People who violate these laws can and will be prosecuted. Laws pertaining to private lands distinguish between surface collecting (picking up objects laying on top of the ground) and any ground-disturbing activities, like digging for artifacts. Laws pertaining to state and federal lands do not distinguish between surface collecting and digging for artifacts. In other words, removing artifacts from state and federal lands is illegal.

In 1906, President Theodore Roosevelt signed the Antiquities Act into law. This established the first broad legal protection of cultural and natural resources in the United States. Since then, there have been other laws passed for preservation on federal lands.

It is illegal to surface collect, metal detect, or dig on any federal lands without a federal permit. Federal lands include lakes and lands managed by the Army Corps of Engineers or the Bureau of Land Management. It also includes US Forests, National Parks, National Wildlife Refuges, and military bases, as well as public land at the state and municipal levels.

Native American tribes in the Northeast have viewed many stone mounds as a part of their heritage and refer to them as sacred ceremonial landscapes. There is active debate as to which clusters of stone mounds are sacred or part of Euro-American farming activities. No matter the interpretation, these are all significant stone-built cultural resources. Do not disturb these stone features in any way. We emphasize not to touch, move, or climb on stone ruins or take any artifacts. These stone features are for you and future generations to enjoy and learn about the historical past.

It is illegal to disturb human skeletal remains or burials no matter where they are. It is also unlawful to receive, keep, own, or dispose of any human body part (including bones), knowing it to have been removed from a grave unlawfully.

To surface collect, metal detect, or to legally dig on any state property, you should check the permitting requirements in your state. State property includes state parks, historic sites, wildlife management areas, and state forests. It also includes state highway rights-of-way, navigable river and stream bottoms, and some coastlines. The State Historic Preservation Office, State Archaeologist, or Department of Natural Resources can offer more information.

WILDERNESS/LAND USE RESTRICTIONS AND REGULATIONS

The hikes in this book are primarily in city, state, and federal parks as well as national forests and wildlife refuges. Each has its own rules and hikers are responsible for knowing those rules. Since these hikes are in historical destinations, there is a mix of recreation and preservation.

HOW TO USE THIS GUIDE

This guide contains most of the information you will need to choose, plan for, and enjoy a hike through southern New England's archaeology. This book features forty mapped and cued hikes.

Since ground vegetation can be extremely thick during the summer months of southern New England, plant cover can often hide low-lying stone ruins from view, so we recommend hiking these trails from November through April to provide the most visual appreciation of the complexity of historical ruins.

Hiking to view some of the stone ruins requires shorter walks than the overall trails, so consider going beyond the ruins and take in the beauty of what the entire trail has to offer. As a result, we not only provide maps on how to get to the ruins but include additional trails to enjoy a longer hiking experience.

In addition, many trails noted in this book are relatively close together. For example, there are two trails in the Natchaug State Forest in Eastford, CT, and four trails in Barkhamsted, CT. Hiking them in a day or two allows a variety of historical stone features and experiences.

Many of these trails offer picnic areas, so consider bringing your lunch and enjoy recreational facilities while discovering stone ruins throughout southern New England.

Each hike starts with a short summary. These overviews give a taste of the hiking adventures and the archaeology contained within. There is information on terrain and what each route has to offer. Hike specs, the details of the hike, including GPS positioning of trailheads, total distance, degree of hiking difficulty, trail surface, canine compatibility, land status, contact information, nearest town, and fees or permits required are also listed.

Note that the mileage indicators are estimates and may or may not be exact. You are encouraged to explore the stone ruins, taking your time, and walking around historical features to get a better appreciation of their construction. While mileage markers will vary based on individual survey, they will provide a relative gauge of distances.

Our hopes are that this book will give you experience on how to recognize historical stone features: mill ruins, house foundations, quarries, barns, and stone mounds. With your new knowledge of stone ruins and what to look for, keep your eyes open for any stone-built environment as you hike trails not listed in this book. It may be important to report your observations to the respective State Archaeologist and/or State Historic Preservation Office.

Overview map: This map shows the location of each hike in the area, by hike number.

Route map: This is the primary map for the trails and roads of the hike, archaeological features and sites, landmarks, historical points, and geographical features. It distinguishes trails from roads, paved roads from unpaved. The hiking route is highlighted, and directional arrows point the way.

Start: Name of trailhead

Distance: The total distance of the recommended route.

Hiking time: The average time it will take to cover the route based on total distance, elevation gain, condition, and difficulty of the trail. Be sure to figure in your fitness level.

Difficulty: The rating system's levels have been researched and corroborated but are still meant as a guideline. Some trails will prove easier or harder for different people depending on ability and physical fitness.

Easy: Defined as 5 miles or less trip distance in one day, minimal elevation gain, paved or smooth-surfaced dirt trail.

Moderate: Defined as up to 8 miles trip distance in one day, moderate elevation gains, and potentially rough terrain.

Difficult: Defined as more than 8 miles trip distance in one day, strenuous elevation gains, and rough and/or rocky terrain.

Trail surface: What to expect underfoot.

Seasons: What seasons trails are open and best time of the year to observe ruins.

Other trail users: Animals, other types of exercisers.

Canine compatibility: Whether dogs are allowed and trail regulations.

Land status: City, state, federal.

Nearest town: For other needs, such as food, fuel, lodging.

Fees and permits: Alerts hikers to whether they need to carry money or get a permit.

Schedule: When park is open to public.

Maps: Maps to supplement those in this book.

Trail contact: Location, phone number, website for the management of the trail.

Finding the trailhead: Driving directions and geographic coordinates.

The History and Ruins: History and background of the ruins.

The Hike: Detailed, researched description of the trail and the archaeological sites encountered along it.

Miles and Directions: Mileage cues identify the turns and trail name/color changes as well as points of interest. Options are also offered for some hikes to make them shorter or longer. Remember this guide is just that—a guide. Maps are provided so you can make your own routes and adventure.

MAP LEGEND

Municipal

≡95≡ Interstate Highway

≡202≡ US Highway

≡107≡ State Road

—— Local Road

= = = = Gravel Road

⊢—+—⊣ Railroad

·· — ·· State Boundary

Trails

------ Featured Trail

------ Trail

Water Features

◯ Body of Water

Marsh/Swamp

River/Creek

Symbols

✗ Airport

≍ Bridge

▪ Building/Point of Interest

✝ Cemetery

⫯ Gate

🗼 Tower

🅿 Parking

🏳 Scenic View/Overlook

○ Town

① Trailhead

❓ Visitor/Information Center

Land Management

State/Regional Park

Preserve/Woods/Open Space

Reservation

CONNECTICUT

Civilian Conservation Corps–built stone stairs, Tunxis Trail, Cassville, Barkhamsted, CT.

1 PUTNAM MEMORIAL STATE PARK TRAIL

A hike through Revolutionary War history. During the winter of 1778–1779, Major General Israel Putnam was ordered by George Washington to develop encampments protecting Danbury while providing military access to Long Island Sound and the Hudson River should troops be needed to repel British attacks against West Point. There are eight archaeological sites associated with Putnam's Brigades along the trail and the ruins are visible to the hiker.

Start: Putnam State Park, junction of CT 58 and 107, Redding, CT
Distance: 1.43-mile loop
Hiking time: About 1 hour
Difficulty: Easy
Trail surface: Gravel
Seasons: Mar through Nov
Other trail users: Biking, service vehicles
Canine compatibility: Dogs on leash
Land status: Connecticut State Park

Nearest town: Redding, CT
Fees and permits: None
Schedule: Year-round
Maps: USGS Bethel, CT, Quadrangle
Trail contact: Connecticut Department of Energy and Environmental Protection, http://www.ct.gov/deep/putnammemorial; deep.stateparks@ct.gov; Visitor Center: (203) 938-2285

FINDING THE TRAILHEAD

Putnam Memorial State Park is located at the junction of CT 58 and 107. From the south, take US 7 north to CT 107; from I-84, take exit 3, following US 7 south to CT 107; from CT 15 (Merritt Parkway), take exit 44, following CT 58 north. The trailhead begins by the main visitors' parking lot. **GPS:** 41.338889, -73.380833

THE HISTORY AND RUINS

In April 1777, British forces garrisoned in New York City under the command of Major General William Tyron marched inland through western Connecticut from their ships anchored in Long Island Sound. The British armies exploded an important Patriot arsenal and burned seventeen houses in the "Raid of Danbury." General George Washington mobilized a series of encampments in western Connecticut, south-central New York, and northern New Jersey to keep the British contained. The Connecticut encampment was under the direction of Major General Israel Putnam, commanding general of the Connecticut militia, veteran of the French and Indian War and the Battle of Bunker Hill.

During the harsh winter of 1778–1779, Putnam organized three Continental Army encampments in Redding, Connecticut, with the main camp positioned at the foot of rocky, east-facing bluffs. Log huts were built along an avenue extending for over a quarter of a mile. A mountain brook furnished plenty of fresh water and powered a forge for the manufacturing of musket balls and rifle parts.

While the troops arrived at the winter camp in good spirits, privations soon led to insubordinations and desertion. The militias were forced to endure many physical

Revolutionary War Memorial at Putnam Park.

hardships, including frigid temperatures, bad bread and salted beef, and lack of blankets, shirts, and other clothing. Winter snow was deep and spring thaws muddied the roads so thick that flour and bread stored in Danbury could not reach the camps. Joseph Plumb Martin, who endured winter camps at Redding and Valley Forge the previous year, wrote in his 1830 narrative *Private Yankee Doodle* that he suffered more in the winter conditions at Redding than he had with Washington at Valley Forge.

When the army finally dispersed to other strategic locations in the spring of 1779, the deserted camp, as was the custom then, was ravaged: huts were burned, chimneys fell into heaps of stone, and the forge dismantled. After a few generations, the hillside

Firebacks to enlisted men's huts.

became overgrown with vegetation and the location of the campground was practically unknown. However, in 1887, the Connecticut legislature purchased properties containing traces of the encampment's stone ruins to create a monument to the Revolutionary War soldiers who suffered to help secure our Independence. Putnam Memorial State Park was established.

Unfortunately, some of the encampment's stone ruins were disturbed in restoration efforts. Landscaping, tree removal, and grading had an impact on stone firebacks (back walls of fireplaces) that were cleaned out with their artifacts removed. Reconstructions of camp buildings at the turn of the 20th century were built directly over ruins of the guardhouse and some log and stone barracks, causing further impact to stone foundations. Nonetheless, thanks to modern conservation and cultural resource protection plans, many portions of the park maintain archaeological and historical integrity.

Archaeological excavations have been conducted at the Putnam encampments over a span of many decades, beginning in the 1970s and continuing into the 21st century. One of the most dramatic discoveries was encountered during initial excavations (1974) by University of Connecticut archaeologists who identified butchered horse bones in one of the firebacks. It is one thing to read about the hardships and sufferings at Putnam's "Valley Forge," but quite another to handle the physical evidence, offering a vivid perspective of the troop's ordeals and their sacrifice for our emerging nation.

THE HIKE
Begin at the main entrance to the park. The road is gravel, wide, and easy to walk. Proceed up the hill to the monument dedicated to Revolutionary War soldiers.

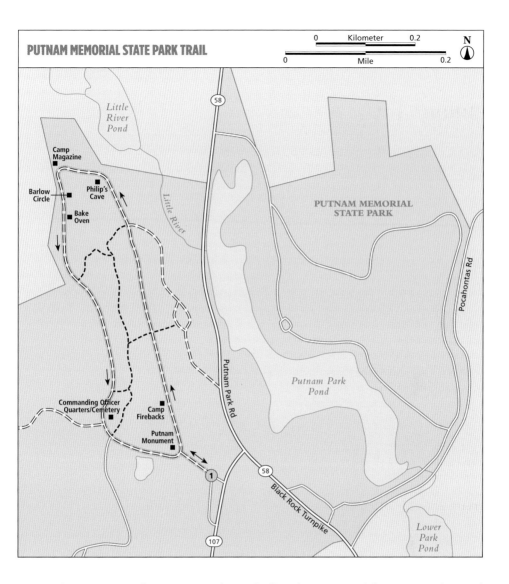

As you come to the monument, the road splits—bear to your right. However, do spend time at the monument as it incorporates hut firebacks (ruins from collapsed chimney stacks) and other features of interest. As you proceed on the gravel road to the right, there are another series of firebacks associated with the enlisted men's huts. The huts were burned, and the chimneys dismantled when the camp was deserted.

Continue along the road through two trail intersection. On your left upslope, you will see stone ruins that are the enlisted men's barracks. Look closer and step off the road to the edge of the wooded area to get a better view of the barracks' ruins.

As the road bends upslope to the left, an outcropping of bedrock with a small ledge, known as Philip's Cave, can be seen through the vegetation. According to local legend, a "Mr. Philips," one of the soldiers who served with Putnam at the camp, returned after the war and lived a hermit's life in his small cave. Unfortunately, to support himself, Mr.

Philips stole chickens and produce from local farmers. Soon, Philips was "permanently removed" from his rocky residence by the locals. The museum, up some stairs on the right at the first intersection, has a beautiful collection of archaeological finds. Do go there as part of your visit.

Upslope on your right is a reconstructed officer's quarters/magazine. The stone ruins were reassembled from the 1778 foundation in 1890, shortly after the park was established. However, recent archaeological excavations associated with the ruin suggest that the stone structure was a magazine storing kegs of gunpowder, not an officer's residence.

As you continue uphill along the gravel road, locate a kiosk and a circle of stones. This is a memorial to Joel Barlow, a prominent resident of Redding and the chaplain to the Continental Army. Barlow graduated from Yale College the same year that Putnam developed the Redding camps. Barlow visited the camp often, hence this dedication to one of Redding's local heroes.

Just beyond Barlow's Circle to your left are piled stone ruins. These are the remains of oven foundations used to cook food (what little they had) for Putnam's troops.

Also, on your left a bit downhill from the ovens is a kiosk identifying a "Burial Monument." Step onto the dirt path and approach a carved stone dedicated to the "Memory of the Unknown Heroes Buried Here." However, look to the back left and the front right and you will see a couple of low-lying stone piles. Archaeological excavation has demonstrated that these features were firebacks of officer's quarters, not a burial ground!

From the Burial Monument area, continue on the gravel road to your left and proceed downhill. Stay on the gravel road to the left as you approach a cutoff taking you back to the monument and the main entrance.

There is a reconstructed guardhouse and a Visitor Center to your left. The Visitor Center houses exhibits from the many archaeological digs conducted at the park. Putnam Park was designated a State Archaeological Preserve, hence, digging, metal-detecting, moving of stones, and collecting are strictly prohibited; violators will be prosecuted. So, enjoy the historical sites, but please respect the ruins and their historical significance.

MILES AND DIRECTIONS

0.0   Start at the main entrance trailhead. Proceed up the steep gravel road to the monument area.

0.03   At the monument, the road forks. Bear right along an avenue of stone ruins.

0.37   Ruins of the enlisted soldiers' hut structures will be seen on your left extending for two-thirds of a mile.

0.76   Look through vegetation upslope on your left for ruins associated of the enlisted soldiers' barracks.

0.88   Kiosk and Philip's Cave on the left.

0.96   Magazine and reconstructed officer's quarters are on the right.

0.97   Officer's barracks are ahead as the road veers to the left.

1.0   Barlow's Circle.

1.13   Oven foundations.

1.30   Burial Monument—take the dirt path on the left to the monument off the road.

1.43   Arrive back at the main entrance trailhead.

2 LOVERS LEAP STATE PARK TRAILS

Within a single hike and five trails you will encounter a set of fabulous stone ruins, including a "castle" built on a high ridge over the confluence of the Shepaug and Housatonic Rivers, the Hurd Family Tudor Mansion and Tea House, Indian Spring House, and the industrial remains of the Bridgeport Wood Finishing Factory. A diversity of historical stone ruins are amid a gorge and beautiful Lake Lillinonah.

Start: Park entrance, 178 Short Woods Rd., New Milford, CT 06776
Distance: 1.85-mile loop and out-and-back
Hiking time: About 1.45 hours
Difficulty: Easy, though one steep hill to climb
Trail surface: Dirt, paved
Seasons: Best in late fall/early spring
Other trail users: None
Canine compatibility: On leash
Land status: State of Connecticut Park, Department of Energy and Environmental Protection, Parks Division
Nearest town: New Milford, CT
Fees and permits: None
Schedule: Year-round
Maps: USGS New Milford, CT, Quadrangle
Trail contact: Department of Energy and Environmental Protection, State Parks Division, 79 Elm St., Hartford, CT 06106-5127; (860) 424-3000; Friends of Lovers Leap State Park, 61b Park Ln., New Milford, CT 06776

FINDING THE TRAILHEAD

From Danbury and I-84 take US 202/7 northbound to New Milford. After crossing the town line, turn right onto Still River Drive. Stay straight through the traffic rotary and the park entrance will be on your right. Southbound on US 202 at the intersection of US 202/7, turn onto Grove Street, which will turn into Lower Grove Street. Cross the Housatonic River and the park entrance will be on the left. **GPS:** 41.542935, -73.408156

THE HISTORY AND RUINS

With the melting of the last glaciation and warming conditions, the first people entered the Housatonic River Valley—most likely following herds of caribou and other big game. The meltwaters created lakes and drainage paths re-aligning the landscape. This environmental shift from a spruce–park tundra to a mixed deciduous forest teemed with abundant wildlife ranging from post-Pleistocene megafauna to smaller, more solitary animals of the Holocene Period. Based on radiocarbon dates, Indigenous People occupied Connecticut by at least 12,500 years ago.

In response to these environmental and topographical changes, the gorge at "Great Falls" on the Housatonic River became an ideal place for faunal and floral exploitation by Native Americans 8,000 years ago. Fish migrating upriver were trapped at the base of the falls, providing abundant shad and salmon.

Sachem Waramaug, the leader of the Wepawaugs, attempted to live in peace by accommodating English settlers. But by the mid-18th century, the tribe was displaced, moving

Bridgeport Wood Finishing Company foundation.

farther up the Housatonic River joining the Schaghticoke in Kent, CT. Waramaug died in 1735 and is believed to be buried somewhere in the river gorge area.

Both the lake and the park get their name from Waramaug's daughter, Lillinonah. Legend has it, Lillinonah was distraught over losing her English lover and canoed into the Great Falls, plunging to her death, hence, the title "Lovers Leap." Romantic fancy for sure.

By the late 19th century, Great Falls became an important source for harnessing waterpower. Great Falls Bridge, built by the Berlin Iron Bridge Company in 1895, linked opposite sides of the river above the gorge, providing access for factory workers housed on the east side and employed at the Bridgeport Wood Finishing Company on the west bank.

The water-powered Bridgeport Wood Finishing Company (1881–1927) manufactured high-quality paint products for almost fifty years. Large water supplies from the Housatonic River were heated to high temperatures producing steam, which powered large grinding machines breaking quartz and other minerals into powder to be mixed into paints. While the company used both water and coal to operate the grinding machines, the ready abundance of water saved money on the high cost of transporting coal from Pennsylvania enabling higher profits for a lucrative business operation.

The availability of water was not the only attraction of the gorge area for the paint industry. The Great Falls district provided access to local quartz quarries and proximity to the Housatonic Railroad, transporting raw materials for manufacture and conveying finished paint products to outside markets.

The stone ruins of the Bridgeport Wood Finishing Company were listed on the National Register of Historic Places in 1976 and two decades later selected as a State of Connecticut Archaeological Preserve.

Even before the closing of the paint factory in 1927, the area became home to wealthy families who built large summer homes overlooking Great Falls. In 1889, architect Frank W. Hurd and his wife, Emily Adeline (Sanford), purchased 50 acres of land that eventually became much of Lovers Leap State Park. Their daughter, Catherine Judson Hurd (born on May 9, 1894), was orphaned by the time she was 15 years of age, inheriting the family estate and Hurd Castle, a Tudor-style mansion that her father designed and built. Though Catherine lived in New York City during the winter, the castle offered a perfect summer escape.

Catherine studied drama in hopes of an acting career. She worked with and befriended Bob Hope, among other show business acquaintances, and Cole Porter stayed at her New Milford "castle," enjoying the mansion with its panoramic views of the gorge and waterfall.

The budding actress called the Tudor mansion the "Yellow Cat Tea House," which she named after her treasured collection of angora cats. Catherine died in 1971, bequeathing the country estate as a public park to Connecticut. Over time, Lovers Leap expanded to 160 acres by acquiring adjacent properties. Sadly, two fires destroyed the abandoned majestic buildings: the castle in 1988 and the Tea House in 1995.

The 144-foot high Shepaug Dam constructed downriver in Southbury, CT, in 1955, created Lake Lillinonah below the falls. With it, the drop of Great Falls was greatly reduced. From the perspective offered by the trails, one can appreciate the magnitude of the gorge, the Great Falls locale, and its influence on the history of the area.

THE HIKE

Lovers Leap State Park offers a series of trails exclusively for the hiker and each has associated historical stone ruins. The hike we recommend starts at the Lovers Leap Trail, switches onto the Castle Loop and Tea House Trail, the Waramaug Loop, and concludes with the Old Factory Trail.

Leaving the parking lot, follow a dirt path behind the trailhead, to an old, paved roadbed downhill toward the Housatonic River and the Iron Bridge. Interpretive signage line the left side of the trail providing histories and photographs of the ruins ahead.

Cross the red Berlin Iron Bridge. Be sure to enjoy the views of the Housatonic River below and get a sense of the gorge leading to the falls and Lake Lillinonah.

After crossing, take the Lovers Leap Trail on your right uphill for about one-third of a mile. This will be a long, straight ascending climb that was once the private driveway leading to the Hurd family mansion. When you reach the top, the road will bend left and split. The short path to the right will lead downslope to a scenic overlook of Lake Lillinonah; on the left is a path leading uphill toward the "castle." After enjoying the view, proceed uphill (Red Trail).

When the Red-blazed trail splits, stay right. (The footpath will get a bit steep here.) At a second split, bear right again onto the Castle Loop Trail. The "castle" will appear upslope on the right at a third split in the trail. The tall brick chimney stack and foundation of the Hurd mansion will be on your left.

Explore the two ruins, then take the trail that travels between them farther back into the hill. The trail will even out and lead to the stone ruins of the mansion's Tea House on your left. This is a large stone foundation and is best seen during times with less ground vegetation. (In your mind's eye, picture Catherine Judson Hurd entertaining Cole Porter while enjoying a lovely view of the gorge and falls below.)

Bridgeport Wood Finishing Company basement.

After the Tea House ruins, follow the trail leading downhill on the right. This is the Tea House Trail that will loop you back to where you diverted off Lovers Leap Trail. Once there, turn right and return to the iron bridge.

Recrossing the bridge, note the fence line on your left. At the end of the fence, turn left on the Waramaug Loop (Blue) Trail, which leads south along the top of the gorge. This high, flat area was once the home of Native Americans, utilizing the natural resources of the gorge and river for thousands of years. The Shepaug Valley Archaeological Society conducted excavations here in the 1970s.

Take the first trail split on your right (Yellow Trail) and look for stone embankment ruins. The stone foundations served as office buildings for the Bridgeport Paint Factory. After viewing, bear to the left and rejoin the Blue Trail; turn right continuing along the gorge ridge. There is a scenic overlook within a tenth of a mile.

Just beyond the viewpoint as the trail bends to the right is the Indian Spring House perched on the side of the cliff to the left. There is a natural spring coming out of the hill used as a source of potable fresh water by Native Americans, factory workers, and residents.

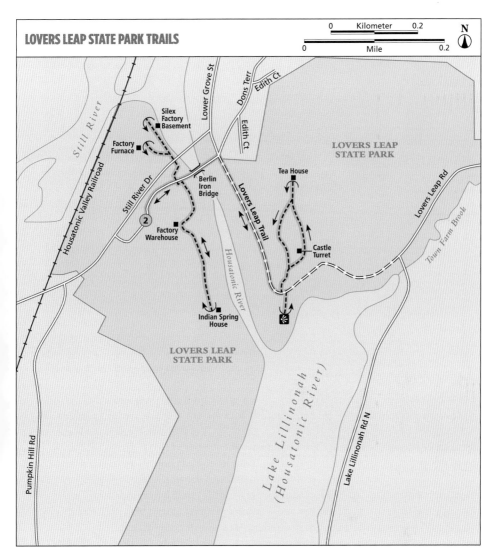

Turn back retracing your steps toward the old iron bridge. Upon returning, cross the paved road to the Old Factory (White) Trail. Stone steps lead steeply downhill toward the underside of the current bridge over the Housatonic River.

The trail descends rapidly until you cross under the bridge. Continue to the other side and take the first small path on the left. You will only be on this trail a short distance, but it will provide you with a perspective of the basement and foundation of the Bridgeport Wood Finishing Company ruins below and leads to the furnace providing power for the machinery. This is a must-see stone ruin perched high above the workplace, standing like a Mayan ruin.

Turn back toward the bridge. When you reunite with the trail, turn left, and descend a short, but rather steep, drop, placing you into the basement workstations of the factory. The trail runs through the guts of the work area with stone blocks on both sides that once supported grinders all connected through a series of gears and belts. This is a most

Indian Spring House, Lovers Leap State Park.

unique set of industrial stone ruins, so walk slowly through the area and carefully explore the work stations.

As the trail bends to the left away from the river, there are no further stone ruins to view. You can continue the Old Factory Trail and loop back, or retrace your steps under the modern bridge up to the main trail. There, turn right, pass the kiosks, and proceed uphill to the parking lot and trailhead.

MILES AND DIRECTIONS

0.0   Start at the trailhead by the parking lot. Take gravel path downslope.

0.01 Turn right on old paved roadbed.

0.04 Approach signboards on left.

0.10 Historic iron bridge. Cross bridge over the Housatonic River gorge.

0.14 Turn right onto gravel road (Lovers Leap Trail) upslope on the opposite side of the river.

0.36 Arrive at the two-way split in the trail: head right to see scenic view of lake, then return to this point.

0.37 Take path uphill (Red Trail) leading to the "castle" and mansion ruins.

0.40 Split in trail. Bear to the right and hike steeply uphill onto the Castle Loop.

0.44 Second trail intersection. Bear right again.

0.48 "Castle" stone turret will appear upslope on your right side. Left is the brick fireplace and foundation of the mansion. Take the trail between the turret and fireplace farther back into the hill.

0.57 Bear left, going slightly downhill.

0.58 Another path appears on your left (Tea House Trail). Stay straight for now, but return to this intersection.

0.60 Tudor Mansion/Tea House stone foundation will appear on your left. Explore. Then return to the last intersection.

0.62 Take trail to your right (Tea House Loop).

0.64 Intersection with the Red Trail. Continue straight.

0.74 Rejoin the beginning of the "loop" trail and turn right downslope to the gravel roadway (Lovers Leap Trail) by the lookout.

0.77 Turn right and retrace your steps down gravel trail to the iron bridge.

0.99 Reach iron bridge. Turn left and cross bridge.

1.06 Take Blue Trail on left at end of red iron fence.

1.12 Turn right on the Yellow Trail.

1.14 Stone ruins associated with Bridgeport Finishing Company offices. Proceed to your left and continue Yellow Trail.

1.20 Reconnect with Blue Trail, turn right along the ridge with the river below on your left.

1.25 Lookout over the gorge and Lake Lilinonah. Continue the Blue Trail.

1.27 Indian Spring House on your left. Make an about-face and return to the iron bridge along the Blue Trail.

1.48 Reach the old, paved road by the iron bridge. Start the Old Factory (White) Trail across road.

1.52 Cross under the modern road bridge.

1.53 Take small path on your left.

1.55 Large stone furnace and brick fireworks on your left. Return toward bridge.

1.61 Back at the trail turn left. Bridge underpass will be on your right. Be careful as the trail descends steeply downhill and is often eroded.

1.63 The finishing factory ruins. Note the large stone slabs serving as foundations for machinery.

1.67 Reach the end of the factory. Retrace your steps back to the beginning of the White Trail and paved road.

1.77 Return up stone steps to paved road. Turn right passing kiosks uphill toward Trailhead.

1.85 Arrive back at the trailhead.

3 HENRY BUCK TRAIL

This rugged trail includes archaeological sites associated with the Civilian Conservation Corps (CCC) and a unique stone mill ruin where cheese boxes were manufactured in the 19th century. The mill site seems suspended at the top of a high, steep hill. This is a less-traveled trail very much fitting the title of "ruins seldom seen." Worth the effort.

Start: West River Road, Barkhamsted, CT
Distance: 2.4 miles out-and-back
Hiking time: About 1 hour
Difficulty: Moderate to difficult
Trail surface: Dirt and stone
Seasons: Best in late fall/early spring
Other trail users: None
Canine compatibility: On leash
Land status: American Legion State Forest

Nearest town: Barkhamsted, CT
Fees and permits: None
Schedule: Year-round
Maps: USGS New Hartford, CT, Quadrangle
Trail contact: Department of Energy and Environmental Protection, State Parks Division, 79 Elm St., Hartford, CT 06106-5127; (860) 424-3000

FINDING THE TRAILHEAD

Traveling on US 44 in Barkhamsted, CT, turn onto CT 318 east. Follow winding road to the village of Pleasant Valley. Turn left at the stop sign onto West River Road and drive for 2.4 miles. The Farmington River will be on the right and the state forest on your left. The signpost for Henry Buck Trail will be on your left though no kiosk is present. There is a dirt pull-off area by the sign. **GPS:** 41.941306, -73.012670

THE HISTORY AND RUINS

It started with a change in weather during early 19th century New England. Meteorological fluctuations brought increased precipitation, creating heightened yields of grazing grasses, which benefited the region's cows increasing dairy productivity. Farms in Litchfield County and along the Farmington River delivered incredible amounts of milk, butter, and cheese.

Cheese could be transported and sold to the developing western states and territories via the Erie Canal, developing economic markets beyond local needs. According to Howard Russell in his study of New England farming, Barkhamsted alone produced over 103,000 pounds of cheese in 1845. Previously, the town of Goshen produced an incredible 380,000 pounds of cheese in 1811 alone. Since cheese needed to be packed and shipped to distant markets, wooden boxes were necessary. The response was the development of the cheese box industry in the region.

Cheese boxes were round and usually made of basswood lumber that could be cut into thin sheets and molded into shape. Barkhamsted provided access to trees and sawmills where logs could be sliced into lumber, transported to workshops for shaping, then sent out to local farms for packing.

Local oral tradition suggests that the stone ruins along the Henry Buck Trail are associated with cheese box manufacturing. The mill would have been powered by water

Left: CCC-built stone stairs on Henry Buck Trail.
Right: Stone water channel into turbine pit.

streaming from a millpond that can be seen along the trail at the top of the slope. A wooden sluiceway transported the water through a stone "stairway" in the foundation. The workshop would have been powered by a turbine to operate the wood-shaping machines used to finish the product. The workshop floor would have sat over the still visible water turbine pit.

THE HIKE

After parking along the road at the Henry Buck Trailhead, take a moment to look toward the Farmington River on your right. Visible are stone pillars that supported a bridge once crossing the river. The former bridge would have connected the East and West River Roads near the site of the Lighthouse Village.

The Henry Buck Trail in American Legion State Forest starts in relatively flat terrain. The trail is delineated with blue blaze on adjacent trees.

Proceeding along the trail, take the time to look downslope on your left to a lower level plain. Sharp eyes will perceive remnants of a Civil Conservation Corp (CCC) Camp White. The CCC was one of the Franklin Roosevelt administration's alphabet soup of federal relief agencies in the 1930s, employing young men during the Great Depression for improving state and federal lands throughout the country. The CCC constructed bridges and trails (including the Henry Buck Trail), cleared forests, made roads, and created other development projects that can still be viewed today. However, the

Top: Cheese box mill stone ruins.
Bottom: Henry Buck Trailhead.

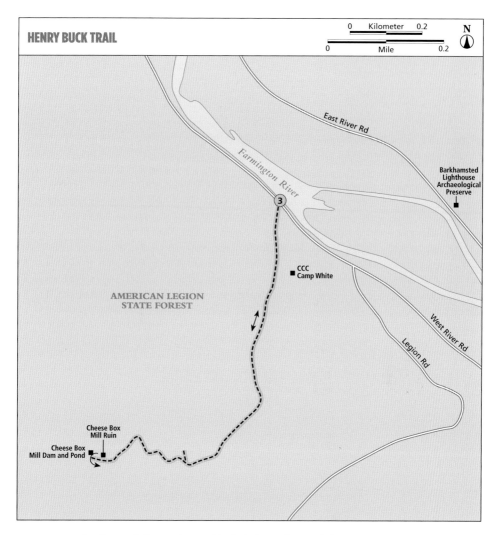

camps that housed the workers with their barracks, workshops, and parade grounds have long since been abandoned leaving their archaeological evidence behind.

Downslope to your left is a water pump and well, roadbeds and remnants of buildings associated with Camp White. There are no stone ruins, but you can explore these Depression-era features by coming off the trail and descending to the "ghost camp." Be careful since there are no marked paths and be sure you return to the Henry Buck Trail where you disembarked.

Proceeding west on the trail, trek along the base of a high hill on your right. The trail here is an easy walk, though it crosses a couple of streams. Be careful of slippery conditions, especially if it has rained prior to your hike or during the winter when ice can form.

The trail swings to the north climbing a steep slope. The ascent is made easier by a series of "stone steps" placed by CCC workers creating a "stairway" for hikers. These stone features are unique, testifying to the steepness of the trail grade and the hard work and ingenuity of the CCC employees.

The last leg of the hike is steep and rugged, switchbacking to ascend. But, once there, the exertion is well worth it! Stone ruins of the cheese box mill will appear on both sides of the trail. The first obvious structure is a large high stone divider—the upper sidewall of the mill. Below the sidewall is a circular stone formation which housed the turbine for powering machinery. The upslope end of the circle has a small stone-lined channel from which water flowed from the upper millpond supplying power to the turbine.

Explore further by following the trail upslope to the millpond dam. The trail extends across the dam, so you are hiking on top of the stone and earthen feature. Take a moment and observe the terrain behind the dam and consider how much water would have been impounded and how it could provide power for the mill's manufacturing requirements. Water from the dam would have been transported by a wooden sluiceway and gravity-fed directly into the circular turbine pit to power the workshop. While the wooden sluiceway has long since decomposed (or, been removed), see if you can trace its path down to the mill.

The turbine and other metals were retrieved during the scrap iron drives of World War I and World War II, so only stone ruins are left for us to interpret the mill operation.

From the cheese box ruins, either return to the trailhead by reversing your hike, or continue along the Henry Buck Trail, which will also terminate on West River Road about a half mile north of where you parked your vehicle and entered the trail.

MILES AND DIRECTIONS

0.0   Start at the Henry Buck Trail sign on West River Road.

0.3   Remnants of CCC Camp White downslope to your left.

0.6   Stone steps constructed by CCC.

1.1   Arrive at stone ruins of the former cheese box mill.

1.2   Reach the millpond dam.

2.4   Arrive back at the trailhead.

4 LIGHTHOUSE VILLAGE AND JESSIE GERARD TRAILS

Two trails take you through some of the most significant archaeological sites in the region and accessed by an easy, short hike. Well-written kiosks offer historical and archaeological information that will enhance your experience and knowledge of the "Village of Outcasts."

Start: East River Road Trailhead
Distance: 0.41-mile loop
Hiking time: About 40 minutes
Difficulty: Easy
Trail surface: Dirt
Seasons: Best in Oct through Dec
Other trail users: Hikers only
Canine compatibility: Dogs on leash
Land status: Peoples State Forest, CT

Nearest town: Barkhamsted, CT
Fees and permits: None, except for overnight stay in the camping area
Schedule: Year-round
Maps: USGS New Hartford, CT
Trail contact: Department of Energy and Environmental Protection, State Parks Division, 79 Elm St., Hartford, CT 06106-5127; (860) 424-3000

FINDING THE TRAILHEAD

Traveling on US 44 through Barkhamsted, CT, turn onto CT 318 East. Follow the winding road to the village of Pleasant Valley. Continue straight at the stop sign and over the iron bridge spanning the West Branch of the Farmington River (combined CT 318 and 181). Upon crossing the river, turn left (north) onto East River Road for 2.4 miles and there will be a long-paved pull-off on your left for parking. The trailhead is directly across on your right. A kiosk at the trail entrance will provide historical background and maps for the Lighthouse Village. **GPS:** 41.942731, -73.006957

THE STORY AND RUINS

Legend has it that in the mid–1700s, Mary (Molly) Barber, a prominent young woman from Wethersfield, CT, was exceedingly upset with her demanding father, Peter, over the fact that he considered any suitors asking for her hand in marriage as unacceptable. Distraught that she might end up an old maid, and in retaliation to her father's stubbornness, Molly vowed to marry the first man walking through the door of their residence. The man turned out to be a Narragansett Indian from Block Island by the name of James Chaugham. True to her vow, Molly and James married and absconded to the unsettled and rugged terrain of the upper Farmington River, living in hiding from her father. There, they built a small house on a terrace above the river and below Ragged Mountain in today's town of Barkhamsted, CT.

While historical documents pertain to James Chaugham, there are no extant records of a Mary (Molly) or Peter Barber having ever resided in Wethersfield. The story of their elopement is most likely fanciful. Nonetheless, land and church records show that in 1782, James purchased 49 acres in Barkhamsted on Ragged Mountain and there he and Molly sired eight children. Soon, they were joined by other families, including African and Native Americans as well as disenfranchised European Americans, establishing an "outcast community" at their remote outpost.

Jessie Gerard and Lighthouse Village Trailhead.

Chaugham's village grew with each subsequent generation and eventually became widely known within the region. As settler populations increased and pushed their way up the Farmington River, the old narrow road downslope from the village was improved for stagecoach passage. The Farmington River Turnpike was a tributary of the Albany Turnpike connecting Hartford with the New York capital. Stagecoach drivers would anticipate the Chaugham village on their nightly travels through the heavily forested area and the lights from this outcast community's houses became a beacon alerting the teamsters that the town of New Hartford, an important waystation for resting horses and passengers, was only a few miles down the road. The village became known as the "Lighthouse," and can even be found on late 19th-century county maps.

James died in his nineties in 1790. Molly reached the astonishing age of 104 years, dying in 1818. Their descendants and other families continued to occupy the Lighthouse Village through the 19th century when the village was finally abandoned.

In 1986, Central Connecticut State University archaeologist Kenneth L. Feder began multi-year field seasons conducting archaeological investigations at the Lighthouse Site. Dr. Feder and his students uncovered the physical evidence of the Chaughams' community, consisting of the ruins of 10 stone house foundations, five quarries, four charcoal hearths, and a cemetery. Artifacts included ceramics, buttons, smoking pipes, firearms, coins, and food remains. In addition, Coni Debois, genealogist and Lighthouse community descendant, has compiled extensive genealogical research. Her work eventually united other descendants of the village's former residents, who have handed down family stories that creates a cultural continuity to the present. The Lighthouse Site was listed as a State Archaeological Preserve in 2008.

THE HIKE

Park on East River Road across from the trailhead. Take time to read the trailhead kiosk detailing the history and archaeological significance of the site.

Your first house ruin is directly beside the trailhead—an oval depression in the ground that is the cellar hole of one of the Lighthouse residences.

The hike starts uphill on the Jessie Gerard Trail that quickly intersects with the Falls Cut-Off Trail on your left. Be sure to stay on the Gerard, continuing upslope where the trail bends to the right onto the first terrace leading to the Lighthouse Village Cemetery. Behind the cemetery kiosk, search for small standing, unengraved fieldstones serving as burial markers—there are over 50 of them. Somewhere in the cemetery James and Molly Chaugham are buried. CCC workers surrounded the cemetery with a wooden stockade fence and gate entrance. The stockade is gone, but if you walk carefully behind the kiosk, look for a shallow, linear depression in the soil that denotes the position of the fenced area. Step prudently so as not to disturb the stones and be respectful that you are walking on sacred ground.

Leaving the cemetery, the Lighthouse (Yellow) Trail separates uphill on your left from the Jessie Gerard Trail. Ascend to the next set of kiosks on your right. The first stand describes the house cellar hole in front of you, one of ten found in the village. The dwellings were small and may have been covered as "wigwams"—a typical New England Native American house structure, as opposed to colonial plank construction. Hence, the houses were built as a composite of traditional Indigenous techniques above

Top: Lighthouse dwelling foundation.
Bottom: Lighthouse Village Cemetery unengraved tombstone.

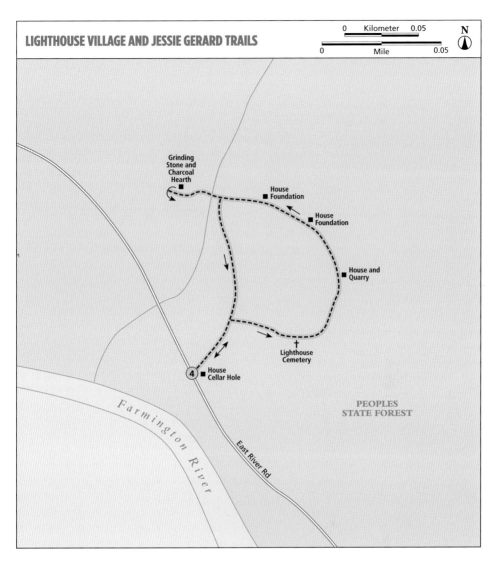

an English-style cellar. These dome-shaped house structures were very efficient in maintaining heat during the cold winter months on the west side of the mountain.

Look carefully behind the stone foundation. Two big boulders exhibit evidence of traditional stone quarrying. Step behind the house along the edge of the stones to see a series of drilled holes splitting the rock. These were made by quarry workers pounding a steel rod into the stone every 10 inches or so in a straight line with a mallet producing cracks that eventually cleaved the rock. An iron wedge was found during the archaeological excavations that perfectly fit into one of the holes.

Continue along the Lighthouse Trail for additional house ruins—one will be readily apparent on your right before you approach a gulley. The next trail kiosk will alert you to a grinding stone used by the community to pulverize seeds and dried corn kernels. Villagers cultivated land below the terrace west of East River Road that land records note as "James Chaugham's plow land" and "Molly Chaugham's garden." This grinding stone may have been used to process their agricultural produce.

In the same area are the remnants of charcoal hearths. The Lighthouse community was involved in several subsistence activities: agriculture, hunting, stone quarrying, and charcoal production.

Prior to the advent of the railroads and coal production, large charcoal blocks were valuable as fuel for the big iron furnaces in the northwestern corner of the state. Colliers felled and cut trees, stacked them into mounds, and slowly burned the wood in kilns that averaged 20–30 feet in diameter. Four flat circular terraces are the remains of charcoal hearths. Due to the slope, the downhill sides of the hearths had to be built up leveling the kilns. Look closely for a shallow trough encircling each hearth permitting air to enter into the hearth, controlling the burning process and operating as a firebreak.

Continuing northward, the Lighthouse Trail will intersect with the Falls Cut-Off Trail. You can either turn left and go downhill back to the trailhead, or should you wish a longer hiking experience, turn right going upslope to see a seasonal waterfall and Chaugham's Lookout. The Falls Cut-Off Trail is strenuous, requiring the ascent of 299 stone steps to the upper level of Ragged Mountain, but you will be rewarded with a picturesque vista.

MILES AND DIRECTIONS

0.0   Start at the Jessie Gerard Trailhead on East River Road. There is a house cellar hole on your right as you begin.

0.02   Intersection of Falls Cut-Off Trail on the left. Stay straight on Jessie Gerard Trail bending uphill to the right.

0.10   The Lighthouse Village Cemetery is on your right.

0.11   Follow the Lighthouse (Yellow) Trail uphill on your left.

0.18   Arrive at another house cellar hole ruin.

0.19   Stone quarry site is located off the trail immediately behind the cellar hole.

0.23   Unmarked on your right will be another small house structure.

0.27   Grinding stone.

0.28   Four charcoal hearths in this area.

0.34   Intersection of Lighthouse Trail and Falls Cut-Off Trail. Turn left downslope.

0.41   Arrive back at the trailhead.

5 TUNXIS TRAIL, CASEVILLE

A short out-and-back hike with several stone ruins associated with a historical community known as "Caseville." Once you shift from the access trail and onto the Tunxis (Blue) Trail, houses, barns, and animal enclosure ruins will appear in abundance, ending at "Indian Council Caves" where, according to legend, local Native Americans convened and traded with European settlers in the region.

Start: Intersection of Legeyt Road and CT 179, Barkhamsted, CT
Distance: 2.08 miles out-and-back
Hiking time: About 1.5 hours
Difficulty: Easy
Trail surface: Dirt
Seasons: Year-round
Other trail users: None
Canine compatibility: On leash
Land status: State of Connecticut Forest, Eversource, Inc.

Nearest town: Barkhamsted, CT
Fees and permits: None
Schedule: Year-round
Maps: USGS New Hartford, CT, Quadrangle
Trail contact: Connecticut Department of Energy and Environmental Protection, State Parks Division, 79 Elm St., Hartford, CT 06106-5127; (860) 424-3000

FINDING THE TRAILHEAD

From US 44 in Canton, turn north onto CT 179 (Cherry Brook Road) passing Canton Center and North Canton. CT 179 connects with CT 219; turn right (north), staying on CT 179 to Legeyt Road on the right. Pull-off parking is available on the right. From US 20 West, turn right onto CT 219 and follow until it merges with CT 179. Turn left and Legeyt Road will be your first right. **GPS:** 41.951573, -72.915667

THE HISTORY AND RUINS

Historical records regarding the town of Barkhamsted's east side "Caseville" are limited to land deeds and oral accounts. Sylvester and Jason Case built and operated an up-and-down sawmill along Roaring Brook, which led other families to settle the area of rich wetlands and hillside pastures. By the early 1800s, a road was established, and a community developed.

The earliest land records show that on or before 1800, Richard Case III purchased the land, which was handed down through three generations of his sons who, in turn, sold the tract to William and Daniel Beers (Biers) in 1832. While the Case and Beers families seem to have been the primary residents of Caseville throughout the 19th century, it is unclear which clan built the houses and barns that comprise the stone ruins on the trail. Records do indicate that the main house by the wetlands, closest to the sawmill that was dismantled in 1932, is associated with the Case family.

According to the Town of Barkhamsted's Centennial History (1879), the Case family was so numerous in the eastern section of Barkhamsted and bordering towns that if one were to pass a stranger on the road and bid, "Good morning, Mr. Case," they were probably correct.

Top: Barn foundation at Caseville.
Bottom: Stone foundation and center stack of the Truman Allyn House.

The large house foundation upslope on the right of the Tunxis Trail heading south may have been built by either Truman Allyn, John Beers, or Daniel Beers. An 1873 map indicates that the property was owned at that time by Daniel Beers.

The house foundation on the left with a water well inside the structure is not listed in town records but is assumed to have been occupied and built by either the Case or Beer families. Based on the foundation, this structure would have been erected later in the 19th century than some of the earlier buildings.

On the other side of the road from this stone ruin is the site of "Indian Rock," or "Indian Council Caves." There are no documentary sources for the name, though it may have been the site of a Native American settlement. Though unsubstantiated, it may explain why English settlers did not establish Caseville until the 1800s.

And, of course, Indian Council Caves is not a cave, but rather a glacial erratic deposited by the receding ice, scouring the bedrock, breaking off and tumbling rock. Hence, the "caves" are simply a maze of large, toppled boulders.

THE HIKE

There are many options for entering the Tunxis Trail, most of which provide longer hikes to the stone ruins. We recommend the shortest and easiest approach but do feel free to expand your hike along this well-marked trail.

Start your hike at the T-intersection of Cherry Brook (CT 179) and Legeyt Roads where there is limited, pull-off parking along both roads. Directly across from Legeyt Road, toward the west side of CT 179, is a yellow gate closing the road to motorized traffic serving as the trailhead. The gravel/dirt access drive is historically a continuation of Legeyt Road to the west.

Please stay on the roadway as you proceed downhill to join the Tunxis Trail since the property on your left is owned by the Metropolitan District Commission (MDC). MDC has graciously allowed access for hikers to use the roadway link to the Tunxis Trail, so be respectful and remain on the trail.

Though improved, the roadway dates to at least the early 19th century and bends south as it joins the Tunxis (Blue) Trail. Your search for stone ruins will be entirely along the north/south Tunxis Trail, passing numerous house and barn ruins associated with the Caseville community.

As you approach the Tunxis Trail, the northern side of a millpond near the headwaters of Roaring Brook will be on your left. Although stone ruins are no longer visible, this is the site of Sylvester and Jason Case's up-and-down sawmill.

After passing the pond, the roadway intersects with the Tunxis (Blue) Trail. Turn right for a brief hike uphill to view a possible animal enclosure on the left. Return downhill back to the intersection and continue the trail south.

The stone ruins on your left are most likely the Richard Case house (c. 1800). In 1832, the property was purchased by Daniel Beers, though it is not certain whether it was Case or Beers who built the house.

A stone foundation is built into the side of the hill on the right side. Note the iron pin drilled into the bedrock that adjoins the stone wall. This is most likely the remnants of a barn structure.

Another stone ruin appears on your left—a three-sided foundation that may have been another barn and most likely part of the Richard Case or Daniel Beers farms.

Top: Stone foundation of the Abel Beers House with the well inside the structure.
Bottom: Indian Council Caves.

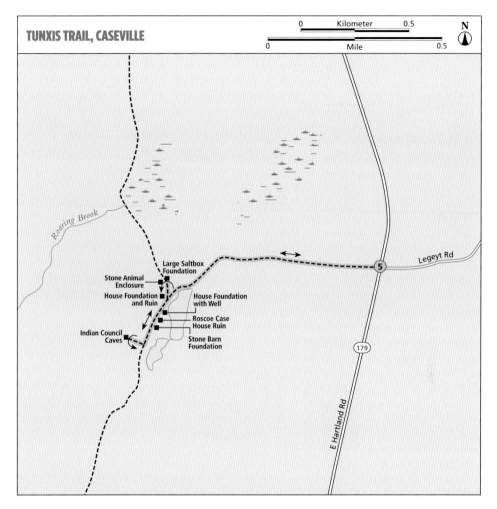

On the right behind a stone wall lies a stone foundation. It is upslope and not visible from the trail, so climb up beyond the stone wall. Barkhamsted land records associate this parcel with Truman Allyn, who purchased the land in 1814. The cellar hole and base of the chimney are clearly visible. By the size of the stone foundation, this was the largest saltbox house built in Caseville.

Continue to a trail loop on the left where there is a three-sided stone foundation (barn) and house cellar hole. These structures appear to have been erected later than some of the other ruins, possibly by Abel Beers in 1873. Pay particular attention to the cellar hole and look for the water well dug inside the foundation walls. There are few examples of 19th-century houses with wells inside, making this ruin unique. After you explore the area, continue along the cutoff loop until it rejoins the main trail.

The Tunxis (Blue) Trail turns right toward "Indian Council Caves." Local legend has it that the prominent rock marked a meeting ground where Native Americans convened and traded with English settlers. Whether the legend is true or false, the "caves" are extraordinary and so conspicuous that one wants to believe that they held special significance for both cultures.

To the left, the trail climbs a steep ridge on flat stone steps constructed by the Civilian Conservation Corps (CCC) in the 1930s to assist hikers scaling the rocky slope. You can take the stairwell to the top of the ridge for an overview of the area or retrace your steps back to the trailhead.

MILES AND DIRECTIONS

0.0 Enter gravel/dirt roadway via yellow gate across from Legeyt Road.

0.65 Connect with Tunxis (Blue) Trail after passing a small millpond on your left. Turn right to observe stone enclosure, then back downhill and continue southbound on Tunxis Trail.

0.67 To the left (toward the pond) is a stone house foundation.

0.70 Stone foundation uphill on right built into the slope. Note iron pin drilled into the bedrock. Explore, then continue the trail.

0.75 Three-sided stone foundation (barn) on left. Note cellar hole overlooking the pond, stone walls.

0.82 On the right, climb the slope to view a large cellar hole with a mound of stone indicating the base of the center chimney. Return to trail and continue right.

0.93 Bear left when road splits. A house ruin with the water well in the foundation stone. Note that this is a partial cellar with the full house extending to the left.

1.0 Reconnect with the road/trail.

1.02 Tunxis (Blue) Trail turns right.

1.04 Arrive at the Indian Council Caves. Stone steps to the left ascending the hill, placed by the CCC in the 1930s. Repeat steps northward on the Tunxis Trail and access road.

2.08 Return to the parking area.

6 WALT LANDGRAF AND ELLIOT BRONSON TRAILS

Walt Landgraf Trail, Peoples State Forest, will transport you back 4,000 years. In a time when Native American craftsmen were utilizing geological features for shelter and quarrying raw soapstone into bowls and other artifacts.

Start: Elliot Bronson Trailhead on Park Road
Distance: 1.14 miles out-and-back
Hiking time: About 1 hour
Difficulty: Easy/moderate
Trail surface: Dirt
Seasons: Best in Oct through Dec
Other trail users: Hikers only
Canine compatibility: Dogs on leash
Land status: Peoples State Forest, CT

Nearest town: Barkhamsted, CT
Fees and permits: No fees or permits required.
Schedule: Year-round
Maps: USGS New Hartford, CT
Trail contact: Department of Energy and Environmental Protection, State Parks Division, 79 Elm St., Hartford, CT 06106-5127; (860) 424-3000

FINDING THE TRAILHEAD

Traveling on US 44 in Barkhamsted, CT, turn onto CT 318 East. Follow winding road to the village of Pleasant Valley. Continue straight over the iron bridge spanning the Farmington River and uphill on combined CT 318 and 181. When CT 318 turns right at Saville Dam Road, continue straight along CT 181 (Center Hill Road), turning left onto Park Road. The Elliot Bronson Trailhead is 50 yards ahead on the left. **GPS:** 41.920649, -72.971435

THE HISTORY AND RUINS

Based on archaeological evidence, the extensive outcropping of bedrock along this trail provided shelter for Native Americans during at least two time periods: 4,000 years, and 2,000–1,000 years ago. Locally referred to as the "Indian Caves," state site files note it as "Ragged Mountain Rockshelter Site." Amateur archaeologists first excavated the ledge in 1901. Recognizing the significance of the site, they invited Yale University to conduct further scientifically controlled excavations led by William Fowler.

While concentrating excavations under the rock ledge, Fowler was unaware that a soapstone quarry site worked by Indigenous Peoples was in close proximity. His team found evidence of soapstone artifacts, including quarry picks and fragments of soapstone vessels, under the rock ledge, but he hadn't realized that the source of these materials was in the immediate area.

In 1995, amateur archaeologist Andrea Rand and naturalist Walt Landgraf (namesake of the trail) discovered two large, round-shaped pieces of soapstone protruding from the ground. Thinking it might be an intact stone bowl, they attempted to lift the artifact. Unable to do so, they realized that the vessel was still connected to a larger core of soapstone beneath the surface. In other words, the vessel had not been completed and remained attached at its source—the original quarry.

Underside of an unfinished steatite bowl.

Beginning in 2011, Dr. Kenneth L. Feder, Central Connecticut State University, began multi-year archaeological field schools at the quarry site greatly enhancing our understanding of the soapstone bowl-making process. Feder found over 10,000 artifacts associated with quarrying activities: chisels and scrapers made from local geological materials such as quartzite, schist, and granite, as well as projectile points, knives, and soapstone pieces. Radiocarbon dates yielded age ranges from 2,870 to 2,760 BP (Before Present) and 930 to 800 years ago, dates supporting William Fowler's initial study.

THE HIKE

From the Elliot Bronson Trailhead on Park Road, follow the trail entering the forest on your right—a blue marker with a red center. The trail climbs upslope and intersects with the Walt Landgraf (Red) Trail on the left, and ends at the soapstone quarry, so you will go out and come back to the Bronson Trail after viewing the archaeological ruins.

The Walt Landgraf Trail winds through a steep gradient, then to a more gradual ascent. At a bend in the trail, look for a charcoal hearth on your left and a dug-out portion of the hill on your right. The excavated materials were used as fill, packing the downslope side to level the hearth.

Continue on the trail to a field of stone boulders. Be observant and just off the Red Trail to the downward left side, search for a rounded, smooth chisel-shaped stone appearing like the rounded underside of a bowl. (There is a tree with a red ribbon tied around it serving as a marker.) The bowl, sculptured on a soapstone boulder, never completed, remains unfinished.

Marker at the intersection of the Walt Landgraf and Elliot Bronson trails.

Return upslope to the Red Trail, and turn left continuing eastward. A high rock wall will emerge on your right. The trail follows the ledge to a place where the rock overhangs the slope providing shelter underneath. Connecticut has few (if any) natural caves, but has numerous bedrock overhangs, which Native Americans and colonists camped, seeking protection from the elements during hunting and, in this case, quarrying activities.

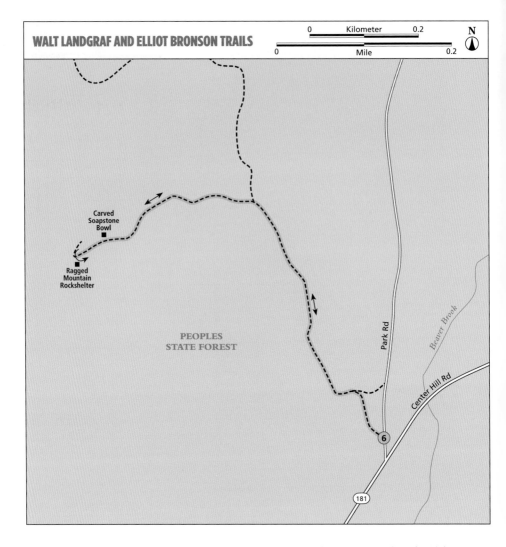

As you stand along the trail by the "Indian Cave" rock shelter site, note the talus debris piled along the slope. This was created by back dirt excavated from under the ledge. Archaeologists used hardware mesh screens to sift the soil to recover artifacts, resulting in the talus pile. Likewise, the depressions under the ledge are from excavation units that have never been backfilled. The entire shelter has been excavated.

The soapstone quarry is downslope from Ragged Mountain. Follow the trail as it bends left to the newly placed kiosk.

The trail terminates at the kiosk. Retrace your steps back to Elliot Bronson Trail, where you can either turn right and return to the trailhead, or left for an extended hike into the interior of Peoples State Forest.

Ragged mountain rock shelter.

MILES AND DIRECTIONS

0.0 Start at the Elliot Bronson Trailhead on Park Road—follow blue blaze with red center marker.

0.33 Intersection of the Bronson and Walt Landgraf (Red) Trails. Turn left.

0.41 Circular charcoal hearth on left. Excavated area on right was used to provide soil to level the downside slope side of the hearth.

0.48 On your left (downslope) look for a small tree with a red ribbon. In front of the tree lies an unfinished steatite bowl.

0.51 A high rock ledge appears on your right (upslope).

0.56 Arrive at "Ragged Mountain Rockshelter."

0.60 Arrive at Quarry Kiosk; trail ends.

0.84 Bronson Trail; turn right to the trailhead.

1.20 Arrive back at the trailhead.

7 FALLS TRAIL, KEITH MITCHELL PARK

Falls Trail, an out-and-back hike, remains unfinished to its proposed terminus at Great Hill Reservoir. Nonetheless, the currently completed section of the trail offers three stone dams and associated mill ruins. There is also a unique opportunity to see a keystone arch bridge before setting out on the trail.

Start: Trailhead at the intersection of CT 188 and 34, Seymour, CT
Distance: 0.82 miles out-and-back
Hiking time: About 45 minutes
Difficulty: Easy
Trail surface: Dirt
Seasons: All seasons
Other trail users: Mountain bikes
Canine compatibility: On leash
Land status: Town of Seymour, CT

Nearest town: Derby, CT
Fees and permits: None
Schedule: Year-round
Maps: USGS Long Hill, CT, Quadrangle
Trail contact: Town of Seymour Parks and Recreation, 1 First St., Seymour, CT 06483; (203) 888-0406; www.seymourct.org

FINDING THE TRAILHEAD

Trailhead and parking are located on the northeast corner of the intersection of Squantuck Road (CT 188) and CT 34 at Keith Mitchell Park. The gravel parking area has a gazebo for picnics, with the trail starting on its east side. There is a public kayak launch for access to the Housatonic River. **GPS:** 41.364873, -73.140028

THE HISTORY AND RUINS

As local Native Americans were pushed off their homelands by the increased numbers of British colonists migrating to Connecticut during the 1600s, Indigenous Peoples sought land away from European settlement where they could maintain traditional subsistence patterns. Such was the case when tribal members living at the confluence of the Housatonic and Naugatuck Rivers removed themselves upriver and inhabited an area they called Wesquantuck. (English settlers shortened the placename to "Squantuck.") Before long, the Wesquantuck villagers were once again forced off the land, removing farther up the Housatonic River to reside with the Schaghticoke Tribe at Kent, CT.

By 1850, the Squantuck area became incorporated into the town of Seymour, accommodating a small community of farmers, fishermen, and early industrialists. The broad Fourmile Brook offered an excellent source of free-flowing water cascading a gorge from atop Great Hill down to the Housatonic River—perfect topography and hydrology for water-powered industries. The first mills appeared in the early 1700s.

The most prominent mill operators along Fourmile Brook were R. S. Treat, a resident of Squantuck, and J. W. Tomlinson, from nearby Great Hill. Treat owned a gristmill and sawmill near the brook's confluence with the Housatonic River, and shared the waterway with Tomlinson, who focused on a sawmill operation farther upstream. Both mills are highlighted in the 1868 Beers map of the district.

Tomlinson's Sawmill stone dam. PETER J. RZASA

Unfortunately, there are few historical references to Squantuck or the operating mills along Fourmile Brook; however, extensive stone ruins indicate successful economic enterprises. To erect such high dams and mills, whose stone foundations line the trail, demonstrates flourishing businesses and creative uses of the land by these early industries.

THE HIKE

Before starting out on the Falls Trail, walk toward the park entrance on CT 34, making a V-turn downslope on a dirt driveway to the kayak launch area. CT 34 will be above you on the right and a keystone bridge will be on your left. This dry-laid stone bridge was the original road designed to carry horses and oxen-pulled wagons over Fourmile Brook. The advent of automobiles in the early 20th century increased the weight load traveling over the bridge, so, in 1934, the Connecticut Highway Department shifted the road by replacing the old stone bridge with the current metal overpass used today. The keystone bridge stands as a distinctive stone ruin of a bygone era.

Return to the parking area, and pick up the trail on the east side of the gazebo. There is no trailhead sign, but a clear path leading inland along the brook serves as the beginning of Falls (White) Trail.

The first stone ruin will promptly appear. A high dam impounded water for R. S. Treat's grist- and sawmills. The massive stone edifice resides prominently on a hill with the mill situated directly below in front. Take a small path off the main trail to your left to view the ruins of the gristmill foundation, including the waterwheel well. Try to reconstruct how the wheel operated. Over-shot or undershot wheel? Treat also operated

Top: R. S. Treat's grist and sawmill foundation. PETER J. RZASA
Bottom: Stone arch bridge at Keith Mitchell Park. PETER J. RZASA

a sawmill near the site, but the stone ruins of that structure have been lost to subsequent development of the area.

Return to the trail, and continue uphill to the face of the dam. You get a good impression of its size by standing beside the façade. The trail curves to the right following the

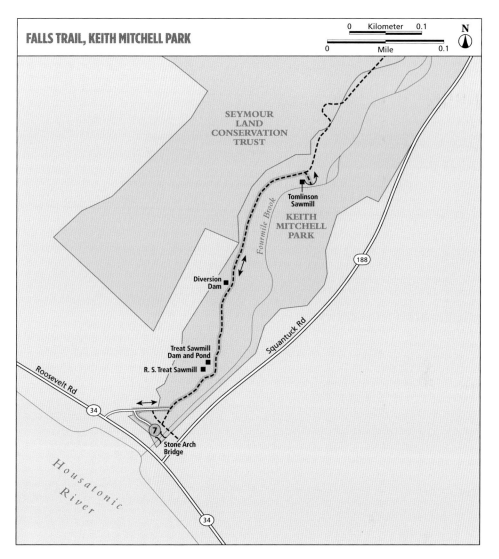

dam, providing various perspectives of this amazing stone feature. Note the curvature on the right to contain the millpond along its lower side above the brook. This is a unique feature not seen in many New England mill dams.

Proceed up the slope, looking left toward the large ground depression of the drained millpond. Usually, once the dam is breached and water no longer fills the basin vegetation growth will obscure its appearance. In this case, the depression remains relatively free of undergrowth, allowing a wonderful opportunity to visualize the pond.

Continue to a White Trail marker and pause to observe the ground. Look for a series of small stones lined in a zigzag formation crossing the trail. We are not sure what this pattern represents, but they may have served as foundations to small sheds or outbuildings associated with the mill operation.

Cross what appears to be a stone wall—the second stone dam. We believe this was a diversion dam that filtered water to a wooden sluice filling the millpond.

Since trails remain unfinished, there is a sign to hike upslope to the left. You will be taking this route soon, but for now, stay straight and follow the trail beyond the diversion dam. Be careful, as there are iron rods protruding from the ground which once supported machinery. Note stone foundations that would have supported the mill's workshops. Retrace your steps returning to the second stone dam and follow the White Trail upslope on your right.

Ascend the hill. When the trail crosses a stone wall, look downslope on your right toward the brook below. There you will see the remains of Tomlinson's Sawmill, including the dam, mill, and a series of stone foundations and culverts, most of which are on the opposite bank of the brook. Fourmile Brook flows over and through the breached stone dam, creating a delightful little waterfall, thus giving the trail its name.

The Tomlinson Mill operated into the 20th century and went through various phases of modernization, resulting in the extensive stone foundations observed.

Our trail ends here. However, there are two more dams and mills farther upstream, as well as stone retaining walls supporting an early road. Though currently unsafe to hike out to these additional stone ruins, it will give us something to look forward to when Falls Trail is completed.

MILES AND DIRECTIONS

Note: Before setting out on Falls Trail, walk back toward the Keith Mitchell Park entrance near the street and take the dirt road on your left leading down to Fourmile Brook and a kayak launch. Note the stone retaining wall on your left that supported the old CT 34 roadbed, Over the brook, a unique keystone arch bridge straddles Fourmile Brook. Return and begin the trail left of the gazebo. There is no trailhead sign but take the path that proceeds down along the brook.

- **0.0** The trail starts on the east side of the gazebo.

- **0.04** R. S. Treat's mill and dam. Take a moment to look across Fourmile Brook and view the stone ruins of another mill structure on the opposite (south) bank. Take a small path on the left leading to the mill and waterwheel well. Return to the trail and turn left uphill toward the dam.

- **0.07** Reach the rise at the stone dam. On the right the dam curves to maintain water in the millpond. Continue the trail, and look left toward the dried remnants of the millpond.

- **0.14** Trail Alignment (White) Sign. Note a zigzag pattern of stones on the ground.

- **0.20** The trail is marked going uphill on your left. However, for a moment, continue and cross through what appears to be a stone wall but is another stone dam.

- **0.25** Passing through the stone dam, be sure to look out for iron pegs sticking out of stone bases and a small stone foundation, most likely a mill workshop. Reverse your steps, then turn uphill to your right and follow the White Trail signs.

- **0.41** Cross a stone wall. Downslope on your right is Tomlinson's Sawmill. Explore. Note the small waterfall as Fourmile Brook flows through the breached dam. On the far side of the brook, look for numerous building foundations and other stone features. This was a large sawmill complex. The remainder of the White Trail up to Great Hill Reservoir remains closed and unfinished. Reverse your travels to return to the trailhead.

- **0.82** Arrive back at the trailhead and parking area.

8 LITTLE LAUREL LIME RIDGE TRAIL

This easy-to-moderate trail offers several archaeological ruins: one of the best-preserved historical lime kilns in New England and three marble quarries, the earliest of which dates to the late Colonial Period, and 19th-century charcoal-making hearths. Part of the trail follows old mining roads heightening the historical experience.

Start: Little Laurel Lime Ridge Park, Seymour, CT
Distance: 2.21-mile loop
Hiking time: About 3 hours
Difficulty: Moderate
Trail surface: Dirt and stone
Seasons: Best in late fall/early spring
Other trail users: ATVs and dirt bikes at times
Canine compatibility: On leash
Land status: Town of Seymour/ Seymour Land Trust

Nearest town: Seymour, CT
Fees and permits: None
Schedule: Year-round
Maps: USGS Naugatuck, CT, Quadrangle
Trail contact: Town of Seymour Parks and Recreation, 1 First St., Seymour, CT 0648; (203) 888-0406; Seymour Land Trust, 13 Chatfield St., Seymour, CT 06483; (203) 464-4345

FINDING THE TRAILHEAD

Traveling CT 8 northbound from Bridgeport take exit 19 (CT 334). Turn left on Wakelee Avenue, and follow CT 334, traveling west up Great Hill Road. Turn left on Laurel Lane, which leads into Tibbets Road, and park at the cul-de-sac. Coming southbound on CT 8 from Waterbury, take exit 20 (Derby Avenue) and follow straight for 3 miles, turning right onto Great Hill Road (CT 334). **GPS:** 41.359091, -73.127123

THE HISTORY AND RUINS

The geological history that enticed the colonists to explore the Naugatuck and Housatonic River Valleys begins 200 million years ago. Hard to imagine, but Connecticut was under a vast ocean then, part of a coral sea with a volcanic island emerging from its depths. This ancient reef compressed and metamorphosed into marble creating small natural caves and an economic product that would be mined into the 20th century.

Colonial and Early Republic farmers baked marble in fiery kilns at 2,000 degrees F for days turning the ore into lime, which was applied over their cultivated fields to reduce soil acidity. Lime was also used to deodorize outhouses, make paint, plaster, and cement as well as remove impurities from iron ore production.

The exact date of the Laurel Park lime kiln is unknown, but the oven probably started its operation in the late 1700s. The kiln was constructed alongside an outcropping containing enough marble to burn into lime. Marble was quarried and broken into smaller pieces by hand with a sledgehammer, then transported by horse-pulled carts to the kiln where the crushed stone was dumped into a fire "hopper" through an opening at the top of the kiln. Wood and charcoal kept the combustion hot for several days, resulting in

Laurel Lime Kiln foundation. PETER J. RZASA

burnt lime, which would be raked out from the lower front doorway, cooled, barreled, and carted to the farm or market.

Once the manufactured lime was extracted from the kiln doorway, the process would start again. The kiln was maintained in a broiling, burning condition without allowing it to cool before reloading with additional marble ore. "Lime burners," who maintained the kiln, carefully controlled the process by keeping the oven at a constant temperature over time. If the kiln got too hot, the melting limestone could turn into unwanted slag.

THE HIKE

Start from the Tibbets Road cul-de-sac taking the path leading back into the woods. The Blue Trail will start about 500 feet into the hike on your left. However, continue straight ahead, then take the Blue Trail when it turns right. Bear to the left, staying on the Blue Trail, which will swing to the right and downhill along an old mining road. At this point, you will be starting a counterclockwise loop leading to several historical features.

As you proceed, notice three historical landscapes: a small marble quarry on the right (oval pit in the bedrock), a second quarry, and the Laurel Lime Kiln. Explore but do not climb on the stone foundation as it is very fragile.

After exploring the kiln, continue the Blue Trail, turning left at the bottom of the swale. The terrain will flatten before the trail rises on an outcropping bedrock. As you climb over the bedrock, look for scratch marks on the surface on the rock. These are glacial striations created by advances and recessions of massive ice scraping the substratum.

Stone wall on Little Laurel Lime Ridge Trail. PETER J. RZASA

If you have a compass, line it up along the scratch marks to determine the direction of the glacier's movement. At the apex of the outcropping is a magnificent view of the Housatonic River below.

From the overlook, the trail descends, twisting through areas of small semi-open fields. A brook will mark the intersection of the Blue (turns downslope to the right) and White Trails (straight ahead). Cross the brook onto the White Trail.

Turn left at the second Blue/White Trail intersection and the land opens from dense vegetation to largely cleared former pastures. Stone and retaining walls will line the landscape and the hike will soon become steep climbing to the marble quarries. Note an old 1980s Ford Escort abandoned behind the stone wall to your right.

Continue on the Light Blue Trail to the right and uphill where a large marble quarry becomes visible. Hike to and along the face of the quarry. Search for talus piles (rock debris), drill holes, and cave openings. Explore the quarry face, returning downhill back to the trail. Stay straight on the Blue Trail and pay attention to "holes" on the right side of the trail. These are old prospecting pits dug in search of marble veins.

Soon there is another intersection with the White Trail. Look for the remains of a circular charcoal hearth with a draft channel dug around the circumference allowing air to seep into the kiln. There are a total of ten historic charcoal hearths on this trail. Colliers (coal/charcoal miners) built these cooking mounds to fuel the Naugatuck and Housatonic River Valley's brass and steel mills. Enter the White Trail at this point and proceed uphill.

When you see what looks like a small cave upslope on your right, leave the trail. The cave is another marble quarry. Explore along the quarry face leading to a gorge. This

Lime Kiln Hopper. PETER J. RZASA

was purposely cut to gravity-feed ore down to oxen-pulled carts waiting to transport the marble to the kiln for processing. Return to the White Trail and turn right to continue.

Along with these quarrying operations, some natural caves do exist that were created by the breakdown of their marble veins. In August 2013, two members of the Central Connecticut Caving Club entered the quarry caves at Little Laurel Lime Ridge Park and explored more than 50 feet into the largest and most recent of the caves. Please know that these were experienced cavers. Please do not enter these caves during your hike as they can be very dangerous.

The White Trail returns you to the Blue Trail near the lime kiln, completing the counterclockwise loop. Turn right and retrace your steps back to the parking lot on Tibbets Road.

MILES AND DIRECTIONS

0.0 Start at the end of Tibbets Road.

0.04 Blue Trail enters on left—bear right.

0.07 Turn right onto Blue Trail.

0.16 Alternative entrance onto trails will be on your right—bear left staying on Blue Trail.

0.29 Trail intersection. Bear right remaining on Blue Trail.

0.34 First quarry hole on right.

0.39 Second quarry also on right.

0.41 Explore Laurel Lime Kiln on right. Continue trail to your right, downslope.

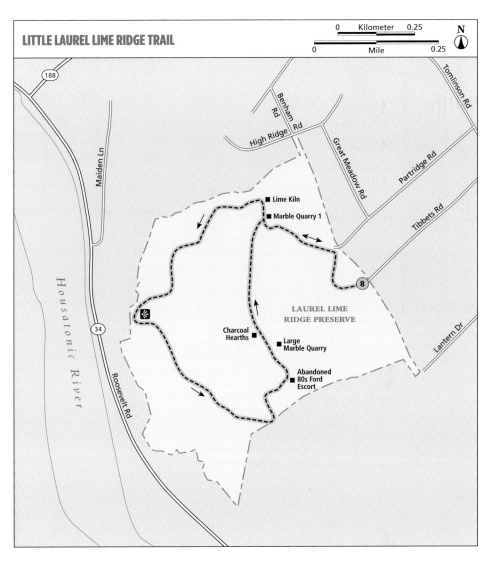

0   Kilometer   0.25

0   Mile   0.25

N

188

Tomlinson Rd

Benham
Rd

High Ridge   Rd

Great Meadow Rd

Partridge Rd

Tibbets Rd

Maiden Ln

■ Lime Kiln

■ Marble Quarry 1

LAUREL LIME
RIDGE PRESERVE

8

Housatonic River

34

Roosevelt Rd

Charcoal
Hearths ■

■ Large
Marble Quarry

Abandoned
■ 80s Ford
Escort

Lantern Dr

0.44 Turn left staying on Blue Trail.

0.51 Trail fork. Bear right. To the left is an old mining road.

0.62 Trail veers to the right, creating a U-turn.

0.73 Granite outcropping. Search rock surface for glacial scratch marks.

0.74 Arrive at scenic overlook with north-facing aspect of the Housatonic River. Continue Blue Trail to your right.

0.94 Trail turns sharply to the right.

1.10 Cross stream onto the White Trail. (*Note:* Blue Trail goes to the right and downslope for a longer loop.)

1.21 Reunite with the Blue Trail. Turn left, uphill.

1.31 Abandoned car on right.

1.36 Blue Trail veers to the right uphill to large quarry.

1.39 Third (largest) quarry on left. Hike along the face of the quarry. Return to Blue Trail when completed. Stay straight with Light Blue Trail markers.

1.49 Take the road on the left, downhill.

1.52 Cross White Trail and note the charcoal hearth ahead. Look for circular rise with draft channel surrounding hearth. Stay on White Trail uphill.

1.60 Turn right (off the trail) toward a marble quarry. Walk along quarry face.

1.67 Gorge created for removing ore, gravity-feeding the stones to waiting wagons below. Return to quarry and proceed back downhill to the old road. Turn right on to the combined White and Light Blue Trails.

1.75 Another charcoal hearth is on the left of the trail as you climb the hill.

1.85 Turn right onto the Blue Trail at the first quarry you initially passed. You have completed a loop and will retrace your steps back to the parking lot.

1.91 Blue Trail veers left but stay to the right.

2.12 Turn left to the trailhead.

2.21 Arrive at trailhead and parking lot.

9 SUBURBAN PARK TRAIL

Suburban Park, an abandoned late 19th- and early 20th-century amusement park, offers a short, though hilly, hike to stone and wooden ruins of an ice cream parlor, water fountain, dance pavilion, and carousel rides. Geology buffs will enjoy glacial kettles (hollows formed by ice shearing off the glacier). If the wind is whistling through the trees, you can still hear ghostly laughter and dance music.

Start: Lions Memorial Park, end of Cottage Road
Distance: 2.02 miles out-and-back
Hiking time: About 50 minutes
Difficulty: Easy to moderate at times
Trail surface: Dirt
Seasons: Best in late fall/early spring
Other trail users: None
Canine compatibility: On leash
Land status: Town of Farmington

Nearest town: Unionville, CT
Fees and permits: None
Schedule: Year-round
Maps: USGS Collinsville, CT, Quadrangle
Trail contact: Unionville Historic District and Properties Commission, Town of Farmington, 1 Monteith Dr., Farmington, CT 06032; (860) 675-2300; www.farmington-ct.org

FINDING THE TRAILHEAD

From I-84, take exit 36 for Farmington, CT 4. Stay westbound on CT 4 for approximately 5 miles into Unionville. Turn right on CT 167 and make a quick left onto Cottage Street. The road will bend to the right and end at Lions Memorial Park. **GPS:** 41.75941, -72.88090

THE HISTORY AND RUINS

Unionville was the terminus of the Hartford Suburban Trolley Line connecting this mill village with the city of Hartford at the end of the 19th century. The trolley line followed Farmington Avenue and today's CT 4 along the Farmington River. To entice city inhabitants aboard the trolley and venture out to the suburbs, the company purchased land and constructed a small amusement park in 1895. The park increased ridership on evenings and weekends contributing to the economic development of the village.

However, the amusement park was short-lived, closing ten years later, though the trolley continued to run until 1933. Competition from other Hartford area amusement parks and the increasing availability of the automobile put an end to the festivities at Suburban Park.

In its heyday, the amusement park had a swimming pool, punting pond (for boating), electric-run water fountain, carousel, dance pavilion, ice cream parlor, and restaurant. People were also allowed to bring their own provisions and picnic on the grassy lawns overlooking the kettles. It was quite a draw for city folks at the time.

Once the park closed, the property changed hands numerous times, though most of the ruins were never dismantled. A housing development was proposed but never built. The dance pavilion was converted to a cottage in 1907, winterized with a partial cellar, and occupied year-round by the Hawley family until it was destroyed by fire in the 1960s.

Stone and cement foundation of the dance pavilion at Suburban Park.

The stone ruins of one of the first electrified water fountains (most streets and homes were still using gas for lighting) have survived. Although the park was illuminated by the trolley line's power station on CT 4, the entertainment area still used an underground cold storage cellar for refrigeration.

The punting pond, named after the type of flat-bottom wooden boats used in the late 19th century, was created to allow visitors to enjoy summer boat rides. In the winter the pond froze and was used for ice skating and hockey games between rival high schools.

The park's natural resources include glacial kettles. These are deep hollows in the ground, usually circular and developed when chunks of ice calved off the glacier and melted, creating bowl-shape depressions in the sandy soil.

Today, Suburban Park, maintained by the town of Farmington, is a wonderful public open space used for passive recreation. Signboards assist the hiker in direction and provide historical photographs to reconstruct the abandoned amusement park. Glacial features provide a beautiful up-and-down landscape and hiking challenge.

THE HIKE

There are two entrances to Suburban Park. We recommend Lions Memorial Park on Cottage Road with ample parking and easy access to the ruins. Hike through the open woodland to the beginning of the Yellow Trail.

The first kiosk tells of the canals or sluices built to divert water providing power to several mills downstream. Notice a shallow linear depression on the ground by the sign,

Top: Stone ruins of the electrified water fountain.
Bottom: Stone foundation of the ice cream parlor.

an earthen berm on the left, and a stone retaining wall on the right. This is the remnant of the canal (headrace) to the waterwheels.

Follow the trail uphill as it bends to the left. When you reach the first intersection, turn right, and climb farther uphill. The underground cold-storage cellar used to keep produce and food refrigerated at the park during the summer months faces you. The trolley offices were located in this area until 1897, when they were relocated to Hartford.

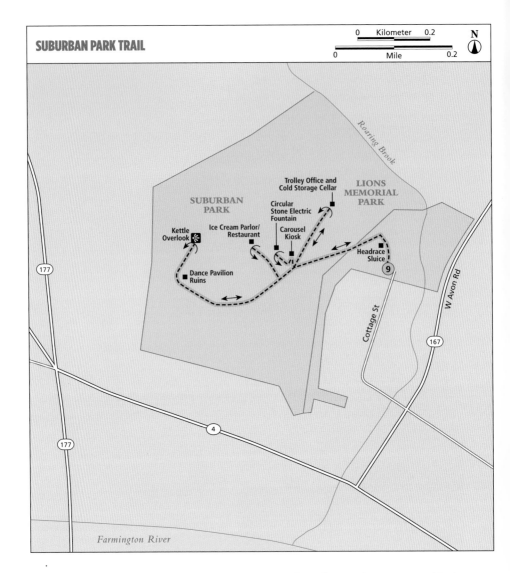

After viewing the storage cellar, retrace your steps downslope and reconnect with the Yellow Trail. Follow to the base of the hill and do a horseshoe turn to the kiosk describing the carousel location. Come back and turn right, toward the stone ruins of the electrified water fountain. Another kiosk will provide historical photos.

Return to the Yellow Trail and continue uphill to your right. Notice the patches of macadam on the ground surface. When the Hawley family obtained the property and built their cottage on the foundation of the dance pavilion, they paved their driveway. Follow the trail to the stone and cement foundation of the dance pavilion on your right. The old radiator used by the Hawley family to heat the cottage can be seen in the cellar hole.

From there, proceed farther uphill around the left side of the foundation for a wonderful view of the glacial kettles below. Return downhill around the dance pavilion and continue the Yellow Trail, retracing your steps.

Downslope on the left will be another path. Follow to a kiosk—the site of the park's restaurant and ice-cream parlor. No below-ground foundation here, simply stones set up as supports for the buildings.

This is the last of the stone ruins on the hike, but you can explore side trails through a maze of cultural and natural features. From the Yellow Trail keep left, downslope, to the parking lot.

MILES AND DIRECTIONS

0.0 Start at the trailhead entrance at Lions Memorial Park. Walk straight back through an open area to the first kiosk and Yellow Trail.

0.10 Kiosk for water canal.

0.14 Divert from the Yellow Trail to the right and hike uphill.

0.20 Underground cold-storage cellar. Return downhill to the Yellow Trail.

0.26 Turn right toward the carousel kiosk.

0.29 Return to the Yellow Trail, and turn right to the fountain ruins.

0.32 Return to the Yellow Trail and proceed uphill, right.

0.38 Dance pavilion/Hawley cottage.

0.41 Go around the ruins to the left hiking upslope for a view of the glacial kettles.

0.44 Return to the dance pavilion and retrace your steps downslope.

0.60 Turn left onto side path to the restaurant/ice cream parlor.

0.75 Return to main trail, and turn left downslope toward the trailhead.

2.02 Arrive back at the trailhead and parking lot.

10 SWEETHEART MOUNTAIN TRAIL

No stone ruins, but rather industrial and wooden ruins of a mid-20th-century ski club. The abandoned Canton Ski Club property is managed for hikers by the Canton Land Conservation Trust. Strap on your hiking shoes (not skis) and enjoy a short, but steep trail—after all it is a ski slope.

Start: 76-80 Dunne Ave. entrance
Distance: 0.5-mile loop
Hiking time: About 50 minutes
Difficulty: Moderate to strenuous
Trail surface: Dirt
Seasons: Best in late fall/early spring
Other trail users: None
Canine compatibility: On leash
Land status: Canton Land Conservation Trust, Inc.

Nearest town: Collinsville, CT
Fees and permits: None
Schedule: Year-round
Maps: USGS Collinsville, CT, Quadrangle
Trail contact: Canton Land Conservation Trust, Inc., PO Box 41, Canton Center, CT 06020; www.cantonlandtrust.org

FINDING THE TRAILHEAD

From I-84, take exit 36 for Farmington, CT 4. Stay westbound on CT 4 for approximately 7 miles continuing straight onto CT 179 north for Collinsville. Turn left onto Bridge Street, then merge right onto Dunne Avenue. The entrance to the trailhead is a driveway between houses. Stay straight with the trailhead ahead. Dunne Avenue is a one-way street, so when leaving turn left to Torrington Avenue, turn right, and return to Bridge Street. **GPS:** 41.81067, -72.92945

THE HISTORY AND RUINS

After World War II, an avid cadre of skiers organized the Canton Ski Club. The club's first ski slope was located on CT 179, but in 1948 they switched to larger Dunne Hill, named after the family owning the land.

Encouraged by the record-breaking snows of the winter of 1947–1948 (3 feet accumulation), the club decided to install their first towline the following year. For power, the towline was wrapped around the rear wheel hub of a car and attached to a pulley at the top of the slope. Skiers would hold on to the rope to be transported uphill. Two trails were developed with a small wooden ski jump.

Expansion brought a new tow house with a steel frame gearing the rope tow. This gave more security to the towline and the club members were able to grade the hill for better and safer runs. Success followed by the construction of a second towline with a gentler slope for novices.

The ski club flourished into the 1960s and at one point had one hundred adults and 500 children as members, enough traffic to require a ski patrol and allow the operation to stay open seven days a week, weather permitted.

Then, a major setback occurred in the 1970s when a young girl got her hair caught on the towline. While the safety gate stopped the rope, a mix-up in communication between the operators turned frightful when the towline started up again and ripped the girl's hair off her head. She was lucky to survive though her hair never grew back.

Top: Tow-rope pulley at the base of Sweetheart Mountain.
Bottom: Towline gears and pulleys at the top of Sweetheart Mountain.

Two trees grow around the pulley.

The ski club, however, did not endure the accident as insurance costs skyrocketed and attendance dwindled. With the opening of Ski Sundown in New Hartford, the Canton Ski Club closed in 1975. The Canton Land Trust eventually obtained the property and has maintained hiking trails through the old ski slopes. Most of the towline mechanisms are still in place, along with old tow shacks and light poles. You are not likely to see an industrial ruin like this elsewhere.

THE HIKE

The hike starts by the lower rope tow gear, advancing uphill along the towline path, past towers with light fixtures for night skiing, leading to machinery at the summit.

The concrete and metal ruins of the lower ski tow rope are on your right in a wooded area just a few steps from the trailhead. Follow the Yellow Trail upslope. Since the trail follows the old towline, it's a steep, but a short hike to the summit. If you find the hike too difficult, take the Red Trail avoiding the steeper portions. If you do, you will overshoot the summit machinery, so turn left (downslope) when the Red Trail reconnects with the Yellow Trail. Another option if the trek is too difficult is to take the White Trail loop,

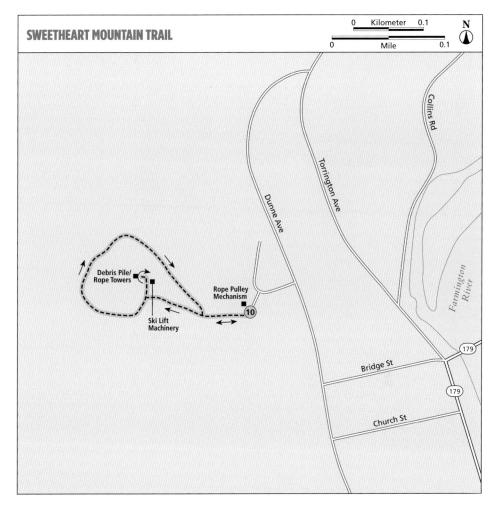

which skirts the steepest parts of the Yellow Trail. The White Trail will take you to the gears at the summit.

If you choose to stay on the Yellow Trail, you will come to the engine and gears of the ski slope within a quarter mile. Turn right onto the White Trail to inspect the ski towline gears and engine.

Can you figure out how the ski operation worked? Take the path beyond the machinery, to wooden poles holding light fixtures, ropes, and additional pulleys. Explore a small (unmarked) path on your left before the trail bends downslope to the right. Stone removed to create a smoother downhill slope for the skiers are piled on your left.

Return to the summit engine and the Yellow Trail. This represents the last of the ski club ruins, so either take the Yellow Trail downhill back to the parking lot, or proceed uphill taking the Yellow Loop Trail through the rest of Sweetheart Mountain. When you finish the loop and head back, turn left onto the Red Trail for a nice view of Collinsville. The Red Trail will return to back to the Yellow Trail and the parking lot.

MILES AND DIRECTIONS

0.0 Start at the trailhead at the parking lot. Start the Yellow Trail.

0.01 Machinery for the lower towline on your right in wooded area.

0.06 Intersection of the Blue Trail, which is not recommended. Stay on the Yellow Trail.

0.14 Intersection of the Red Trail on right. You have the option to take this for a gentler, more roundabout way up the slope. The shortest way to the summit machinery is to continue the Yellow Trail.

0.18 Intersection with the White Trail on right. This is another option to boot around some of the steepest sections of the Yellow Trail.

0.24 Intersection of the Yellow and White Trails. Turn right onto the White Trail for the summit machinery ahead.

0.25 Reach the summit ski tow machinery.

0.35 Continue on the White Trail past the gears and take a small, unmarked path on your left for a short distance. Explore.

0.40 Return to the Yellow Trail.

0.50 Arrive back at the trailhead and parking lot.

11 VALLEY FALLS PARK TRAILS

Valley Falls Park is a 7-acre property in Vernon, CT, that includes stone ruins associated with early textile mills, summer houses, and even an incipient trout hatchery.

Start: Valley Falls Park, 300 Valley Falls Rd., Vernon, CT
Distance: 2.74-mile loop, then out-and-back
Hiking time: About 1 hour
Difficulty: Easy
Trail surface: Dirt and stone
Seasons: Best in late fall/early spring
Other trail users: None
Canine compatibility: On leash

Land status: Town of Vernon, CT, Park
Nearest town: Vernon, CT
Fees and permits: None
Schedule: Year-round
Maps: USGS Rockville, CT, Quadrangle
Trail contact: Vernon Parks and Recreation, 120 South St., Vernon, CT 06066; (860) 870-3520; parkandrec@vernon-ct.gov

FINDING THE TRAILHEAD

Take exit 84 to exit 66. Eastbound: Turn right at the end of the exit onto CT 541 toward Tunnel Road. Westbound: Turn left off the exit onto CT 541 toward Tunnel Road. From both exits, turn left onto Tunnel Road. Within a half mile, turn left onto Valley Falls Road. The park entrance will be 1 mile on your right. **GPS:** 41.822327, -72.443402

THE HISTORY AND RUINS

Industrial operations at Valley Falls date back to at least 1740 when Thomas Johns dammed a shallow pond to create sufficient water reserves to run a sawmill. After the American Revolution, the property changed hands, turning to the manufacture of flax oil in 1809. The "oil mill" prospered and by the 1850s introduced wool carding and spinning to its operation, requiring additional buildings, including a barn, housing for workers, and a higher stone dam for more waterpower.

The cotton mills at Valley Falls increased manufacturing when the Hartford and Providence Railroad built lines through the area providing ready and efficient transportation to move products to market. While the mill and land were sold several times throughout the 19th century, land and tax records suggest that each operation was relatively profitable. An 1860 inventory shows that the expanded cotton operation included "4 acres, a factory, other buildings including a stone house, 4 spinning frames, 1 spreader, dressing frame, wafer, 1 spooler, 1 kneifer (pince-nez eyeglasses), 1 scratcher, 1 turning lathe." By the end of the Civil War, the property enlarged to 150 acres as part of the Anson Lyman Farm.

Trout breeding on Railroad Brook developed when Christian Sharps purchased the property in 1871. If the name sounds familiar, Christian was better known as the inventor of the "Sharps Rifle," the preferred firearm of Union soldiers during the Civil War. Sharps manufactured his rifles in nearby Hartford. After the war, when the demand for rifles decreased, Sharps decided to venture into the business of trout breeding.

Top: Stone ruins from Sharps Trout Hatchery.
Bottom: Waterfall over cotton mill stone dam.

Cotton mill stone ruins.

Purchasing two neighboring farms, Sharps proceeded to build a cottage and install pools, penstocks, and a hatchery facility along Railroad Brook south of the millpond. The enterprise had the capacity to hatch over 300,000 trout per year and Sharps expected to become the largest trout producer in the United States.

Unfortunately, his dreams were never fulfilled. Christian Sharps died suddenly on March 13, 1874, shortly after establishing his hatchery. Upon his death, the Sharps family left Vernon and abandoned the fish-breeding operation.

More misfortune was in store. On February 3, 1877, almost three years after Sharps passed, the cotton mill at Valley Falls was destroyed by fire, ending the history of manufacturing along Railroad Brook and Valley Falls.

In the 20th century, the property was retained by some rather eccentric and wealthy proprietors. First came Hans Munchow in 1910, a supposedly Hungarian aristocrat, whose lifestyle and demeanor must have seemed quite odd in rural Connecticut. Munchow planned to put up a villa but fell in love with his secretary, amassing debts that caused him to leave Valley Falls to travel west supposedly to produce movies in Hollywood.

American aristocracy, members of the Gilded Age, took up residence at Valley Falls when Mary Batterson Beach (her father, James Batterson, was founder of Traveler's Life Insurance Company), purchased the Sharps/Munchow farm in 1915 as a summer home. Mary and her husband, Dr. Charles Coffing Beach had their primary home in Hartford, a short stroll from Mark Twain's old residence. Dr. Beach had a medical practice and served as health officer for his father-in-law's life insurance company.

The Beach family made a few changes at Valley Falls, including the building of a large summer home with an arbor-covered rose garden, tennis court, and swimming pool. The pool was located below the sluice dam near the stone ruins of the old cotton mill. (Today it lies buried under the Braille Trail.) The Beach family expanded the property to include a total of 266 acres. When the doctor and his wife died (1948 and 1951,

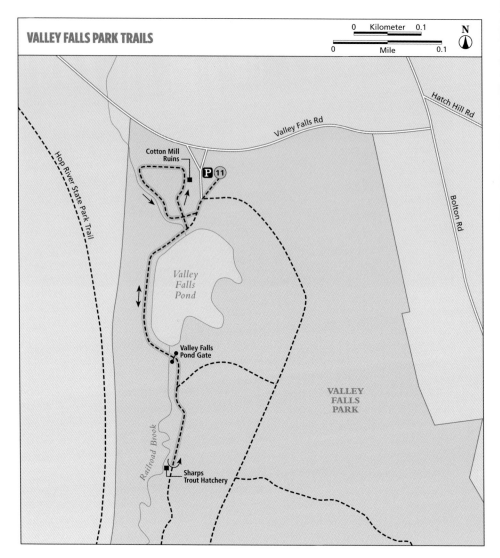

respectively), their son, Charles Jr., made Valley Falls his permanent home. Fortunately, most of the Beach family's property would become Valley Falls Park.

THE HIKE

From the parking lot, descend the slope toward the millpond and the trailhead. Take the time to review the kiosk maps and rules and regulations for the park. Proceed down along the fence line to the beginning of the Braille Trail on your right. This is a unique trail system that allows the vision-impaired the opportunity to walk among the stone ruins offering guide ropes and history boards in braille.

Take the Braille Trail switchbacking downslope. (Underneath your feet, now covered for safety purposes, are the remains of the Beach family's elegant swimming pool.) The trail will take you to a number of stone ruins associated with the cotton mill operation. Kiosks provide histories and descriptions.

The Braille Trail is a loop, so return to its starting point. Connect with the Yellow Trail and cross the dam. Be sure to take in the landscape from on top of the dam: millpond to waterfall to stone ruins. Envision how wooden sluices would have transported water from the dam to the cotton mill's wheel to drive the carding machinery. The entire operation is laid before you if you are observant.

After crossing the dam, wooden steps assist hiking the up-and-down terrain around the millpond. Cross a wooden bridge over Railroad Brook where gates were installed to control the waterflow into the pond. The well-marked Yellow Trail runs along the east side of Railroad Brook.

When you arrive at the first double-marked tree, the trail will veer upslope to the left and downslope on the right with a small path leading to the brook. Take a moment and look downslope to what looks like a low stone wall in the floodplain. This is one of the stone ruins associated with Christian Sharps's trout hatchery.

Carefully descend to the brook. You may have to negotiate over water depending on the time of year. Once down onto the floodplain of Railroad Brook, follow a narrow path that leads to the stone ruins. Small stone dams held back water creating trout breeding pools. Follow the path southward for remnants of the Sharps hatchery. There is not a lot of archaeological visibility here, but rather subtle changes in the landscape, some stone features, and meandering of the brook that are all clues to the fish breeding operation.

After viewing the fish hatchery ruins, you can retrace your route returning to the trailhead. Should you decide to trek farther, an unmarked path will reconnect to the Yellow Trail, which continues to the southern end of the park. Take the Loop Trail on your left, which will horseshoe northward, eventually intersecting with the Main Road Trail returning to the trailhead. There are no stone ruins along either the Loop or Main Road Trail, but the hike is enjoyable.

MILES AND DIRECTIONS

0.0   Start at the trailhead downslope from the parking lot.

0.02 Begin Braille Trail.

0.09 Turn right on the path toward the mill ruins.

0.12 Cotton mill stone foundation.

0.14 Mill tailrace and waterwheel pit.

0.17 Ruins of worker's house and well/cistern.

0.31 Return to Braille Trailhead. Turn right and hike over the dam.

0.37 Begin Yellow Trail across the dam.

0.49 Cross wooden bridge over control gates for millpond.

1.26 Turn onto small pathway downslope to Railroad Brook.

1.37 Stone ruins of Sharps Trout Hatchery.

2.74 Arrive back at the trailhead.

12 DIVIDEND POND TRAILS

Dividend Brook drains into the Connecticut River in the town of Rocky Hill, CT. Explore stone ruins associated with water-powered industrial mills dating back to the 17th century. The park contains ten archaeological sites, four dams, and two millponds along the trails and has been designated a Connecticut State Archaeological Preserve.

Start: Old Forge Road entrance
Distance: 1.98-mile loop
Hiking time: About 1.5 hours
Difficulty: Easy
Trail surface: Dirt—footpaths and old roads
Seasons: Best in Oct through May
Other trail users: Yellow Trail allows motorbikes
Canine compatibility: Dogs on leash

Land status: State of Connecticut/ Town of Rocky Hill Park
Nearest town: Rocky Hill, CT
Fees and permits: None
Schedule: Year-round
Maps: USGS Hartford South, CT
Trail contact: Town of Rocky Hill Parks and Recreation Department, 761 Old Main St., Rocky Hill, CT 06067; (860) 258-2772; www.rockyhillct.gov

FINDING THE TRAILHEAD

From I-91, take exit 23, West Street (CT 411). Drive eastward to Main Street, CT 99 (1.7 miles) turning right at the light. Proceed south for 0.6 miles to Old Forge Road on your left. Turn and follow for 0.7 miles. Parking lot and entrance is on your right. There is a kiosk providing information on the archaeological district and a map of the trails. **GPS:** 41.646080, -72.633789

THE HISTORY AND RUINS

Ten archaeological sites located along the Dividend Pond Trails are associated with water-powered industries beginning in 1677 and operating into the late 1800s. Landscapes associated with these early industrial complexes have been preserved and are clearly delineated along the trail.

Dividend Brook cuts through an area early town residents called "Pleasant Valley," extending between CT 99 to the west and the Connecticut River to the east. The brook has relatively fast-moving water with two natural waterfalls. The drop in elevation toward the river made this watershed ideal for water-powered industries.

Rev. Gershom Bulkeley was an eclectic force to be reckoned with and one of the exceptional personalities of 17th-century New England. Second minister of the Congregational Church in Wethersfield, Bulkeley also turned his attention to medicine, surgery, chemistry, philosophy, and alchemy. He mastered several languages including Greek, Latin, and Dutch, and served as a magistrate for the Colonial Government, was commissioned as Justice of the Peace, and was one of the few Puritan voices skeptical about evidence presented against those accused in the New England Witch Trials. On top of all these endeavors, Gershom Bulkeley began operating a gristmill at Dividend Brook in 1677, then part of Wethersfield in the Connecticut Colony.

Unfortunately, the site of Bulkeley's first "corne mill" located at the easternmost waterfall on Dividend Brook was adversely impacted by the development of the Connecticut

Waterfall over dam at Billings Manufacturing Company (1884).

Valley Railroad in 1868. The gristmill's stone dam created Lower Dividend Pond. In 1680, Gershom Bulkeley relocated his gristmill upstream to the base of the second natural waterfall. He created a new, longer, and higher dam that still withholds water (Upper Dividend Pond). The gristmill remained in the Bulkeley family for over 150 years.

Farther upstream near today's CT 99, Deacon Simon Butler built his own gristmill in 1775. Fifty years later his son, Captain William Butler, erected a sawmill farther downstream, forming a larger holding pond to run the operation. The sawmill was destroyed by fire in 1868.

Bulkeley's second gristmill evidently passed out of family ownership and was converted to a forge where a "Mr. Russell" took advantage of the powerful water flow manufacturing axes around 1830. In 1845, Wells and Wilcox manufactured edged tools like chisels, hoes, and saws at the same mill. Joseph Lory, emigrating from England as a blacksmith, produced the first ever "Never Slip" horseshoe there in 1866. The forge eventually passed to C. E. Billings, who founded a new building housing a drop forge, which can still be seen today.

Downstream from the Butler sawmill and upstream from Wells and Wilcox, in 1854, William Sage Butler and Robert Sugden Jr. established another foundry, creating a 3-acre

Millstone from Bulkeley's second gristmill.

pond whose dam was breached in 2001. Butler and Sugden manufactured shears and other hardware that were sold throughout the United States and Canada. Three years later, Butler invented a single-shot loading pistol, cast in one piece with a bored-out barrel and frame fitted with a trigger mechanism and started to manufacture weapons. Butler's foundry was destroyed by a fire believed to have been set by an arsonist. Afterward, the partners went into business with various entrepreneurs, rebuilt the foundry, and produced numerous consumer goods such as miniature toys, cast iron banks, and various chandeliers. This operation was also destroyed by fire and was never rebuilt. While the earthen dam ruptured in 2001 by floodwaters, the sluiceway providing waterpower, waterwheel pit, and slag piles from the foundry furnace are still visible.

The Friends of the Office of State Archaeology, Inc., conducted archaeological excavations at the site in 2002, recovering evidence of buildings and artifacts (e.g., scissors, tumblers, etc.) manufactured at the foundry.

Finally, in 1884, Charles Billings and George D. Edmunds erected a brick factory on the southern hill, expanding the second Bulkeley dam to a length of 150 feet. The pulleys rotating long belts from the mill to the hollow below are still visible. Billings and Edmunds continued their business at least until the 1890s, becoming the last factory operated by the rushing waters of Dividend Brook.

THE HIKE

The Old Forge Road entrance has a kiosk telling the history of Dividend Pond Trail. From the kiosk, there are differing routes to the archaeological ruins. We advise the White Trail to your left, downslope running parallel to Old Forge Road. The first archaeological site encountered will be stone ruins of the 1845 Wells and Wilcox Manufacturing Co. (No. 1). All that remains today of this large factory are stone steps and the standing wall of the foundation seen through a wooded area.

Continue the trail to a short standing, mortared stone pillar. This was the entrance to Gershom's son, Edward Bulkeley's Homestead (No. 2), which was built in the mid-18th century. The pillar made from river stones was constructed later in time, but the outline of the old house foundation can still be discerned in the wooded area behind the kiosk.

Opposite the Bulkeley Homestead, a V-path leads downslope toward the waterfall and the site of Bulkeley's second gristmill (No. 5), Russell's forge, Wells and Wilcox Manufacturing, and where Lory produced his "Never Slip" horseshoes. Plenty of industrial activity for over 200 years on this spot! Enjoy the waterfall descending from the top of the expanded dam holding back Upper Dividend Pond. Keep your eyes open for a metal pipe which transported the pond's flow to the waterwheel and later turbine. The waterwheel is gone, but you can still see the wheel pit. Look closely at the ground near the stream and you may see two stone grist wheels from Bulkeley's second "corne mill," which have been partially exposed by water erosion. Across the stream and waterfall, look up to the ruins of the Billings and Edmund's brick factory. You will come to this site again, later on the trail.

Return upslope to the White Trail and continue along with Lower Dividend Pond to your right. Another kiosk describing Rev. Bulkeley's original gristmill (No. 3) will appear. Follow the trail to your left and enter a dirt road, which lies on top of the original 1677 dam. Cross and search for cut stone that may have been part of Bulkeley's mill. Follow the road to your right and reconnect with the trail, traveling along the south side of the Lower Pond leading upslope toward (No. 4) Billings Manufacturing Complex (1884). From this site you will overlook the ruins previously visited at the base of the dam across the stream, providing a wonderful overview adjacent to the waterfall. This was the last and largest of the industrial factories built along Dividend Brook and whose ruins are best preserved.

Continue along the White Trail left of Upper Pond. The trail splits with either path merging again near the 1854 Butler & Sugden Shear Factory (No. 7).

Turn right and cross a wooden bridge to see the Shear Factory (No. 8). This is where archaeological excavations were conducted in 2002.

At this point you have two choices: First, you can walk down Pleasant Valley Road (to the southwest) and reconnect at June's Trail where the Butler grist and sawmills were located in 1775 and 1829, respectively (No. 9 and 10). Unfortunately, there are no ruins to see along this trail, but it is a pleasant walk, and historically significant. Or, second, turn right at the cul-de-sac back on the White Trail following along the north side of Upper Pond, returning to Bulkeley's second dam (No. 6).

As you approach the end of the pond, carefully take the stone steps on the right down to the top of the dam. Enjoy a pleasing view of the pond. Walk out to the end of the dam, but please, for your safety, do not attempt to cross the top where the water flows to the waterfall. From the top of the dam, you will have a good view of the Billings ruins across the brook.

Return to the stone steps, turn right, continuing down the dirt road to the trailhead and parking lot.

(Note that the town allows dirt bikes on the Yellow Trail, so hike there with caution, but if you do, there is a good view of the southern sandpits.)

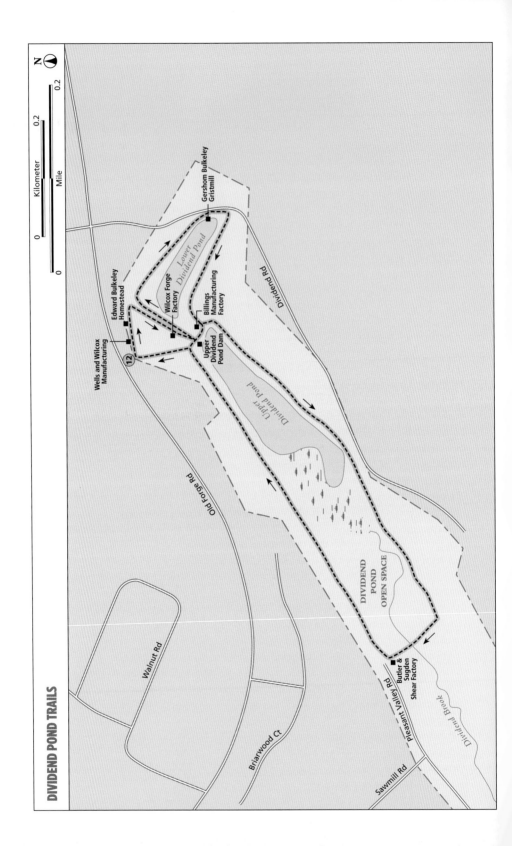

DIVIDEND POND TRAILS

N

Kilometer
0   0.2

Mile
0   0.2

Wells and Wilcox Manufacturing

Edward Bulkeley Homestead

Wilcox Forge Factory

Lower Dividend Pond

Gershom Bulkeley Gristmill

Billings Manufacturing Factory

Upper Dividend Pond Dam

Upper Dividend Pond

Dividend Rd

Old Forge Rd

Walnut Rd

Briarwood Ct

DIVIDEND POND OPEN SPACE

Butler & Sugden Shear Factory

Pleasant Valley Rd

Sawmill Rd

Dividend Brook

12

MILES AND DIRECTIONS

0.0   Start at the Old Forge Road Trailhead and take the White Trail on your left and follow downslope.

0.02 Reach the site of Wells and Wilcox Manufacturing.

0.05 Edward Bulkeley Homestead. Take the path on the right, making a V-turn toward the base of the second dam.

0.11 Site of multiple mills and base of waterfall. Explore. Return upslope back to White Trail.

0.17 White Trail; turn right downhill with Lower Pond on right.

0.42 Site of the original Gershom Bulkeley Gristmill. Continue to the left and onto a dirt road, and cross to observe the ruins and waterfall below the road. Reconnect with the White Trail along the south side of the Lower Dividend Pond.

0.59 Billings Manufacturing Factory, the second dam and waterfall. Continue White Trail left side of Upper Pond.

Stone mill foundation.

1.09 4-way intersection; turn right.

1.14 Cross the wooden bridge over Dividend Brook.

1.16 Butler & Sugden Shear Factory kiosk.

1.19 Turn right at the cul-de-sac and reenter the trail. Follow with Upper Pond on your right back to the second dam.

1.56 Take the stone steps on your right down to the top of Bulkeley's second dam. Walk to the end of the dam but please do not cross. Retrace back up the stone steps and bear to the right.

1.98 Arrive back at the trailhead and parking lot.

13 FARMINGTON CANAL HERITAGE TRAIL AND FARMINGTON RIVER TRAIL

The Farmington Canal operated from 1829 to 1848 extending for over 80 miles from New Haven, CT, to Northampton, MA. Other trails follow the canal towpath, but the Avon trails permit hiking within the canal bed, providing a unique perspective on the canal's operation.

Start: Old Farms Road, south boat launch parking lot
Distance: 4.26-mile loop
Hiking time: About 2.5 hours
Difficulty: Easy, with one steep hill
Trail surface: Dirt
Seasons: All seasons
Other trail users: Bikes
Canine compatibility: On leash

Land status: Town of Avon, CT
Nearest town: Avon, CT
Fees and permits: None
Schedule: Year-round
Maps: USGS Avon, CT, Quadrangle
Trail contact: Town of Avon, Parks and Recreation Department, 60 West Main St., Avon, CT 06001; (860) 409-4332; www.avonct.gov

FINDING THE TRAILHEAD

From I-84, take exit 38 (CT 4 Farmington). Follow CT 4, then turn right onto CT 10 north (Waterville Road) for about 3 miles. Turn left on Avon Old Farms Road crossing the bridge over the Farmington River. Fisher Meadows Recreation Area will be on your right, but take the first gravel driveway on your left, which will U-turn toward the river and the boat launch area. Parking is available on your left and the trailhead will be on the right. From US 44, turn onto CT 10 southbound, then turn right onto Avon Old Farms. **GPS:** 41.772261, -72.823567

THE HISTORY AND RUINS

The heyday of canal building in the northeastern United States emerged after the American Revolution. Previously, freight and passengers traveled along waterways (coastline and major rivers) and wagon roads. Overland journeys were beset with difficulties, including rough, potholed dirt lanes subject to erosion during rainstorms, continual slowdowns fording wetlands and rivers, and steep hills to climb through twisting, corrugated terrain. Wagons often broke down under heavy weight, horses were ornery, and oxen pulled slowly. Passengers experienced countless discomforts on rutted roadways. Water canals, where feasible, transported freight and passengers faster (around 4 mph), smoother, and more comfortably. The stumbling block was to find a canal path that was workable in terms of construction and maintenance costs.

In the early history of Connecticut, New Haven and Hartford competed as the state's capital. Hartford had the Connecticut River permitting transport of goods and passengers to the coast and interior New England, greatly enhancing its financial worth. While New Haven had access to coastal commercial shipping traffic, it was at a disadvantage having no easily accessible route to the northern interior. The Farmington Canal was conceived to solve this problem by presenting an alternative inland route for New Haven

Arched bridge over Thompson Brook.

to tap into the potential commerce of Massachusetts and upper New York, hence playing on a more level economic field with Hartford.

The four-year construction of the Farmington Canal began in 1825 with operation until 1848. The canal extended over 80 miles north from New Haven harbor, linking with the Hampshire and Hampden Canal, terminating in North Hampton, MA, on the Connecticut River. When completed it became the longest canal in New England.

The Avon, CT, portion of the Farmington Canal was finished in 1829 and was made possible by the construction of two stone works. First, a 280-foot-long aqueduct allowing a 14-foot-wide wooden sluice to cross 36 feet above the Farmington River. This required a high earthen embankment on the west shore to merge with the more elevated east bank allowing level water flow. Six stone piers supported the aqueduct, some stone ruins of which are still visible. Another less extensive undertaking was the Thompson Brook Culvert, requiring a 10-foot stone arch for water to flow underneath the canal.

While the canal trip was smooth and did good business most years, keeping the canal operating was a rough ride for the company and its investors. Maintenance costs, severe storms, droughts, and disputes with property owners brought constant setbacks, closures, and vandalism. In addition, the canal operated seasonally, unable to function during the cold, icy New England winters. The finale came as rail traffic advanced. Railroads were less expensive to construct and maintain, could operate yearlong, and carried more freight and passengers while offering more direct routes. Canals simply couldn't compete.

THE HIKE

Combining the Farmington River and Canal Trails through two municipalities (Farmington and Avon) affords an enjoyable trek through diverse environmental habitats, geological features, and historical stone structures.

Begin your hike at the south side boat launch by the Farmington River on Avon Old Farms Road. The trailhead will be on your right as you loop and drive toward the river and boat launch. Follow the Farmington River (Yellow) Trail throughout your walk.

The first part of the trail leads south through a wooded area. Cross Thompson Brook via a wooden bridge and turn left at the trail intersection. After a second wooden bridge the trail follows the river closely on your left.

At 1 mile, the Farmington/Avon town line is designated by a cement survey marker on your left between the trail and the river. Soon, the Farmington Canal Aqueduct, an impressive stone and earthen berm will loom in front of you like a lost Mayan pyramid.

When you reach the embankment, turn onto a small path to your left and get a wonderful view from underneath the 1828 aqueduct. Be sure to also focus your attention across the river for views of the stone bridge abutments that would have linked to the canal aqueduct. This is best seen during the winter when vegetation is at its lowest.

Return to the Yellow Trail, rising on your left to the top of the aqueduct and canal bed. Turn left and walk toward the river to see the ruins of the bridge abutments from above. To your right as you face the river is a depression of the abandoned Unionville Feeder Canal that transported water from a dam farther up on the Farmington River, where the town hall is today on CT 4.

Turn around and continue the trail bearing left and set out on the 10-foot-wide towpath.

As you approach Town Farm Road, the trail will veer to the left, crossing the canal bed and rising upslope. At Town Farm Road, look to your right; the canal would have traversed the road at the end of the wooded area. This was also the site of a basin to "hold" barges waiting to be loaded and unloaded while unheeding canal traffic. Basins served as "ports" and were usually located near the center of towns. There are two canal basins along this trail.

Cross Town Farm Road and follow yellow blaze markers. You will be entering private property, so be respectful and stay on the trail. Climb a steep hill, trekking through wooded areas rejoining the canal bed up ahead when the Farmington River (Yellow) Trail joins the Farmington Canal Trail.

As you descend from the hilly section, the T-intersection of the two trails will appear. Turn left, and note another "holding basin" on your left. As you hike the Canal Trail, you will be walking within the canal bed for the next three-quarters of a mile—a unique experience.

Soon you will reach the stone Thompson Brook Culvert, a 10-foot arch bridge that was constructed to allow the canal to cross over the top of the waterway. There is a wooden bridge to cross the culvert protecting the fragile stone arch from being climbed upon.

Stone abutment for the Farmington Canal.

After the wooden bridge, turn right, following the yellow blaze markers taking you off the Farmington Canal Trail. Thompson Brook will be on your right. Avon Old Farms Road will periodically peek through the vegetation on your left.

Emerging from the woods, cross Tillotson Road and turn right. Turn left into a trail-head parking area and continue through an open field.

At the end of the field, the trail will bend right and follow Thompson Brook on your left. Take the trail cutoff on your left to recross the wooden bridge. At this point, you will have completed a loop. Cross the wooden bridge back to the trailhead and parking lot.

Note: To view additional stone ruins of the Farmington Aqueduct, we recommend hiking the Canal Aqueduct and Henry Mason Trail (2.1 miles round-trip) on the east bank of the Farmington River found at the junction of CT 10 (Waterville Road) and Aqueduct Lane.

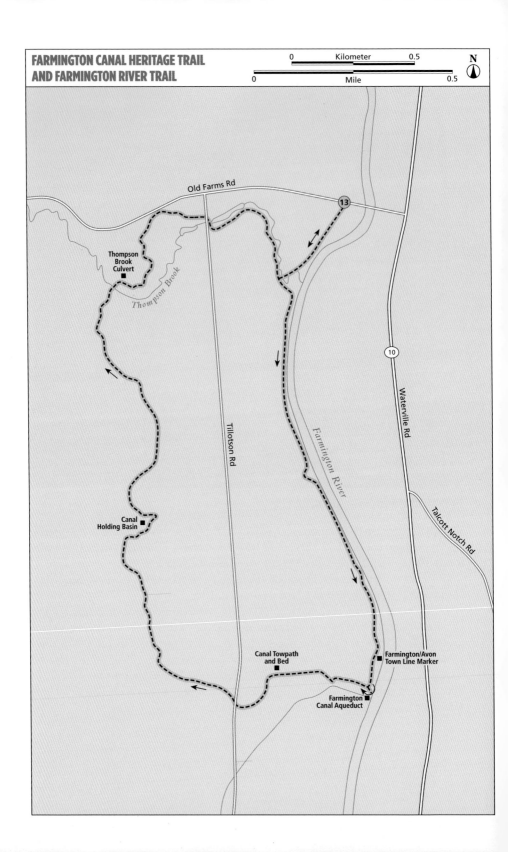

0   Kilometer   0.5

0   Mile   0.5

N

Old Farms Rd

13

Thompson
Brook
Culvert

Thompson Brook

10

Waterville Rd

Tillotson Rd

Farmington River

Talcott Notch Rd

Canal
Holding Basin

Canal Towpath
and Bed

Farmington/Avon
Town Line Marker

Farmington
Canal Aqueduct

MILES AND DIRECTIONS

0.0 Start at the trailhead off Avon Old Farms Road. Take the Yellow Trail south along Farmington River.

0.24 Cross wooden bridge over Thompson Brook.

0.26 Turn left at T-intersection.

0.75 Second wooden bridge.

1.16 Farmington/Avon town line.

1.34 Trail bends right by a high stone and earthen embankment—the western end of the Canal Aqueduct. Turn left, downhill toward the river. Look across the river for stone-built embankments supporting the Towpath Bridge. Views will be best when vegetation is less dense. Walk back to the trail and bear left along the embankment on your left.

1.49 With the canal above you on your left, the trail will rise to join it. Turn left along the top of the aqueduct back toward the river.

1.51 Note feeder canal to the right and what would have been the Towpath Bridge straight ahead toward the east. Turn around and continue trail hiking the old towpath with canal on your left.

1.69 Trail crosses the canal bed to the left and rises.

1.80 Reach Townline Road. Look to your right where the Farmington Canal would have crossed at the edge of the existing forest line. Cross the road and continue the trail uphill. This is a steep area and on private property, so please stay on the trail.

2.17 T-intersection. Turn left, uphill where the Yellow Trail intersects with the Farmington Canal Trail. You will be hiking within the canal bed. Note the wetlands on the left are the remains of the old holding basin.

3.06 Bear left.

3.16 Reach Thompson Brook Culvert and its 10-foot stone arch bridge. Cross wooden bridge not disturbing the stone ruins. On the far side of Thompson Brook, take Yellow Trail to your right, leaving the Farmington Canal Trail.

3.61 Cross Tillotson Road. (*Note:* Townline Road in Farmington becomes Tillotson Road in Avon.) Turn right toward a small parking lot and reconnect with the trail.

3.64 Reach parking lot. Water Supply Pond #2 appears on your left and the trail passes over open fields. After crossing the fields, the trail bends right and reenters the woodland with Thompson Brook on your left.

4.00 Turn left, downhill, crossing the first wooden bridge completing the trail loop.

4.26 Arrive at the trailhead and parking area.

14 GAY CITY STATE PARK TRAILS

Stone ruins at Gay City State Park are associated with a Methodist community established in 1796, whose members embraced industrialism, operating a series of mills along the Blackledge River. Sites include an old colonial roadbed, house foundations, water-powered mill ruins, sluiceways, and a cemetery.

Start: CT 85, Hebron, CT
Distance: 2.89-mile loop
Hiking time: About 44 minutes round-trip
Difficulty: Easy
Trail surface: Paved and dirt
Seasons: All seasons
Other trail users: Paved roads open to motorbikes and cars
Canine compatibility: On leash
Land status: State of Connecticut Park

Nearest town: Hebron, CT
Fees and permits: Fees for out of state vehicle parking and overnight camping may apply
Schedule: Year-round
Maps: USGS Marlborough, CT, Quadrangle
Trail contact: Department of Energy and Environmental Protection, State Parks Division, 79 Elm St., Hartford, CT 06106-5127; (860) 424-3000

FINDING THE TRAILHEAD

From CT 66 in Hebron Center, travel north on CT 85 for 7 miles. The park entrance will be on your left. From Hartford, take I-84 east and merge onto I-384 to exit 4 (Highland/Wyllys Streets). Turn left at the end of the exit; turn right onto Highland Street (CT 534), which becomes Camp Meeting Road merging onto CT 85 south. Stay on CT 85 for 3 miles; the park entrance will be on your right. **GPS:** 41.7199, -72.4365

THE HISTORY AND RUINS

The northwest corner of the town of Hebron, CT, was home to a small, dispersed rural community from approximately 1750 to 1900 and was known by numerous names, including Great Farm, Factory Hollow, and Gay City. Though the property exchanged hands multiple times, it was not until the mid–18th century that Reuben Sumner first settled the land and primarily devoted his time to subsistence agriculture, developing his "Great Farm."

At the start of the American Revolution, Great Farm's population grew to include several unrelated families with diversified economic activities harnessing waterpower from the Blackledge River, including three sawmills, a textile mill, a blacksmith shop, a cider press, several charcoal hearths, and a possible distillery, all concentrated along a 1-mile stretch of the river, hence earning the appellation, "Factory Hollow."

Rev. Henry Sumner built a woolen mill in 1812 operating until the factory burned in 1830, never to be rebuilt. His son, Charles, constructed a paper mill in 1870, which he managed until it, too, burned in 1879. Rev. Sumner was also the leader of a small Methodist community scrutinized closely by the town-controlled Congregationalists. Sunday services under Sumner's leadership were held in the schoolhouse and came under suspicion of the locals for conducting "dances," imbibing alcoholic spirits, and other frowned-upon activities.

Top: Stone foundation of Charles Sumner's paper mill site.
Bottom: The Theodore Porter House foundation.

There were other issues separating the Factory Hollow community from their neighbors. Allegedly two murders took place. A jewelry peddler was robbed and killed, supposedly by one of the village's charcoal colliers because his body was found burned in a charcoal hearth. There was also a blacksmith's apprentice, who evidently showed up late to work one morning and was found stabbed and beheaded, supposedly, by his boss! There is, by the way, no historical record of these crimes ever having been committed or anyone being arrested, but the tales do add to the legend of Gay City.

The Methodist community dispersed by 1830, probably the result of Sumner's woolen mill fire and the loss of jobs. Likewise, the destruction of the Charles Sumner paper mill marks the end of the industrial community in Factory Hollow. "Gay City" started to be applied to the area, though reasons are unclear. While John Gay was one of the founders of the community, town land deeds indicate that the Gays owned no land there after 1825.

Gay City was abandoned in the early 20th century when Emma and Alice Foster of West Hartford bought up property there as a summer retreat. In 1943, they bequeathed the property to the State of Connecticut for purposes of a park and protection of wildlife. The sisters also stipulated that the name of the state park would be "Gay City."

Archaeological excavations at Gay City began in 1973 under the direction of historical archaeologists Robert R. Gradie III (University of Connecticut) and Marion Meek, who excavated four structures: the Theodore and Jerusha Porter houses, the Charles Sumner paper mill, and the Henry Sumner House.

THE HIKE

Upon entering Gay City State Park on CT 85, a dirt drive is on your right (part of the original CT 85). Depending on the season of your hike, this drive may be blocked by a "No Parking" gate. If so, continue on the paved road, passing the ticket booth on your left. A short distance beyond the ticket booth, park in the lot on your right with a trail kiosk. Walk down the grassy hill toward the cemetery on your left across from the ticket booth. Continue to the park entrance walking up the short hill to an open grassy area and follow the hike instructions below.

If the main gate is blocked and the dirt road is open, we recommend driving to the end and swinging left uphill to a larger parking lot by the trailhead. We will start left at the kiosk by walking to a grassy knoll where the Henry Sumner house once stood.

The house was removed and rebuilt elsewhere in Hebron in 1965. The cellar hole was filled in, so no foundation is visible. However, look carefully at the ground to make out the original house dimensions by the settling of soils used to fill the cellar, resulting in a shallow depression.

Southward is a grassy plain across the park road and along CT 85. There stood the Stanford Stede House built opposite Rev. Sumner's residence at the road intersection. Farther out on the grassy area was a one-room schoolhouse where the Methodist community held services. Both structures were dismantled decades ago.

This intersection was a very important transportation lane. The north-to-south CT 85 connected the town centers of Hebron and Bolton, CT, while the east-to-west road (now the park entrance) connected the Factory Hollow community to the Connecticut River in Glastonbury and was called Eastbury Road, over which charcoal and lumber were transported to the Hartford area and shipping docks on the Connecticut River.

Fireplace and chimney ruins of Alice and Emma Foster's summer retreat house.

Follow the paved road west into the park to the Gay City Cemetery set back on your right. The low stone wall surrounding the cemetery is not original, but constructed by the state park. In addition, tombstones have been moved to create two neat rows. No one knows the extent of the burying ground or how many people are buried there, so please be respectful as the specific location of the graves is unknown.

Leaving the cemetery, continue westward farther into the park. When the paved road bends to the right, continue straight, entering the dirt road, which begins the Blue Trail. In a few steps, turn left onto the Red Trail for a tenth of a mile. A footpath on your left leads uphill to a large stone fireplace stack. This impressive fireplace is the sole remnant of an early 20th-century summer retreat house. Large flat cut stones seen on the ground were used for the sill and front door stoop. There is no cellar hole. The hunting lodge was built after the Gay City community abandoned the area.

Retrace your steps and return to the Blue Trail (old Eastbury Road); turn left hiking downhill to the heart of Factory Hollow. Near the base of the hill, a short path on your left will lead to the stone ruins of the Jerusha Porter House above the bank of the Blackledge River.

Continue downhill on the Blue Trail to a wooden bridge crossing the Blackledge River.

Note the dry-laid stone foundation of the original bridge on both banks of the river under the existing wooden bridge. You are now in the heart of Factory Hollow. Instead of crossing the bridge, we recommend turning to your left hiking along a small footpath beside the river heading south. This will lead to the ruins of Rev. Sumner's 1812 woolen mill. Bear right at the fork in the narrow footpath, staying close to the river. The collapsed stone dam straddles the river and stone pillars mark the mill. This represents all that is left of the woolen mill. Fire destroyed the building in 1830 and subsequent storms washed away much of the stone foundations. Retrace your steps and return to the wooden bridge crossing over the river.

Once across the river, note what looks like a large stone wall on your left as you advance upslope. This is the stone ruin of the Porter family barn. Right after, you will come to the intersection of the Yellow Trail, also on your left. Follow the Yellow Trail for about 40 feet and look right to see the foundation of the Theodore Porter House. The exact age of the house is unknown but the cellar has no chimney stack, which may indicate the house was built during the mid-19th century and used a wood-burning stove for heat. Also, observe the finely carved sill stones, some of which are still in place while others have collapsed into the cellar hole. This was a well-built, expensive house.

Return to the Blue Trail, turn left (upslope). Near the top of the hill, the trail veers to the right, but the series of double stone walls continues straight—the original roadbed. The Blue Trail bends left and crosses on top of an earthen dam. On the far side of the dam, look for stone slabs set up to allow passage over the drainage canal, which brings water flow to the millpond below. Carefully walk over the stones up the hill. This is a short divergence from the trail to cross the water overflow. You will quickly reunite with the Blue Trail.

The intersection with the Red Trail will soon be on your right. Immediately on your left across from an old wooden signpost, look for a dirt drive. Follow off the trail downslope looking to the right to see a stone foundation with a collapsed chimney stack. This house foundation dates to the 18th century and represents one of the oldest structures in the Gay City area.

Return to the Blue Trail and retrace your steps eastward back over the dam and the wooden bridge. Once re-crossing the bridge, turn left onto the White Trail leading to Charles Sumner's paper mill.

Cross a small wooden bridge over the paper mill's tailrace, which conveyed water away from the mill and back into the river. To the right is the stone-lined channel which housed the waterwheel. The long rectangular shape of the mill accommodated lengthy papermaking machines. The paper mill burned to the ground in 1879, marking the end to the industrial phase of Factory Hollow. Stone ruins are all that is left.

Continue on the White Trail along the sluice of the headrace, which brought water to the mill from the pond to the north. Follow the sluice to Gay City Pond, the paper mill's water source. On the right along the sluice trough would have been a gate to control the

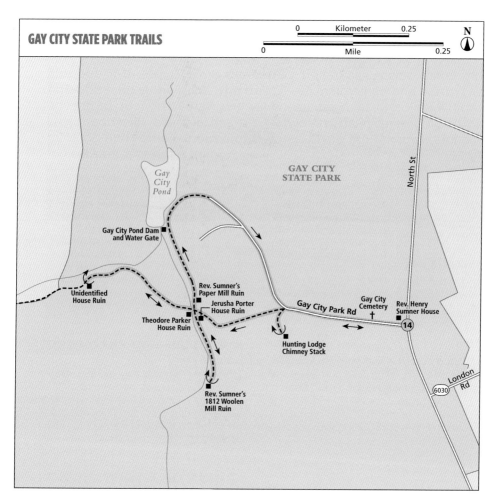

water's flow. On your left, under the grassy berm, is the old stone dam, which has been covered and stabilized.

Follow the trail to your right around the hill through the park's swimming and picnic areas. Walk the paved road back to the trailhead and parking lot.

MILES AND DIRECTIONS

0.0 Depending on where you can park, walk toward the high grassy knoll at the park entrance.

0.05 Rev. Henry Sumner House.

0.17 Gay City Cemetery. Continue down paved road until it bends to the right.

0.33 At the bend of the paved road, enter the dirt Blue Trail (old Eastbury Road) with the Youth Group Camping Area on right.

0.36 The Red Trail is on the left. Take it to the fireplace site.

0.46 Find the footpath on your left leading upslope to the fireplace.

Jerusha Porter House foundation.

0.49 The old hunting lodge. Walk back to the Red Trail and retrace your steps to the Blue Trail.

0.69 Reconnect with the Blue Trail turning left downslope along the old roadbed.

0.87 Arrive at the Jerusha Porter House foundation. Return to the Blue Trail and continue downhill.

0.91 Wooden bridge over the Blackledge River. Do not cross yet, but turn left on footpath along the river (south).

1.04 The 18th-century stone dam to the original woolen mill. Retrace your steps back to the wooden bridge.

1.21 Cross over the river bridge and continue upslope on the old roadbed.

1.23 Take the Yellow Trail on left for about 40 feet. As the trail bends to the right, look right for the stone foundation of the Theodore Porter House. Retrace your steps back to the Blue Trail.

1.25 Blue Trail; turn left and continue upslope.

1.40 The Blue Trail crosses over an earthen dam with the subsequent pond on your left.

1.55 Reach the pull-off for the Red Trail on your right. There is a kiosk with trail maps to help orient you.

1.56 Look for a clearing (dirt driveway) at the intersection of the Red Trail, on your left across from an old wooden signpost. Turn downslope toward the reservoir for an unidentified 18th-century stone house ruin. Explore and return to the Blue Trail, and turn right, retracing your steps back over the dam and downslope to the wooden bridge over the Blackledge River.

1.91 Cross the wooden bridge, and turn left onto the White Trail.

1.96 Arrive at the stone ruins of Charles Sumner's paper mill. Continue the White Trail northward.

2.16 Gay City Pond. Follow the dirt trail to your right around a small hill by the swimming and picnic areas. Hike along the paved road back to the park's entrance and trailhead.

2.89 Arrive back at the trailhead and parking lot.

15 THE PRESERVE TRAIL

Hike the "Back Highway," a Colonial era road linking Old Saybrook and Essex, CT, while visiting the historic Ingham family house foundation, sizeable stone dam, a unique narrow stone barway, a modern memorial, and the Whisper-In-The-Wind phone station.

Start: West Preserve parking lot, Ingham Hill Road
Distance: 2.88 miles out-and-back
Hiking time: About 1.5 hours
Difficulty: Easy to moderate
Trail surface: Dirt, rock ledge
Seasons: All seasons
Other trail users: Dirt bikes and horses

Canine compatibility: On leash
Land status: Essex Land Trust
Nearest town: Centerbrook, CT
Fees and permits: None
Schedule: Year-round
Maps: USGS Essex, CT, Quadrangle
Trail contact: Essex Land Trust, PO Box 373, Essex, CT 06426; www.essexlandtrust.org

FINDING THE TRAILHEAD

From I-95, take exit 65 (CT 153) northbound. Around the 4-mile mark, turn right onto Ingham Hill Road and follow to the end. The West Preserve parking area will be on your left. From CT 9 southbound take exit 3. Stay straight onto CT 621, then turn right onto CT 153 (Plains Road), and at 1.5 miles turn left onto Ingham Hill Road. Traveling northbound on CT 9, also take exit 3, turn left, and left again onto CT 153 (Plains Road), continuing to Ingham Hill Road on your left. **GPS:** 41.325748, -72.424865

THE HISTORY AND RUINS

The Pequot Nation sold the land that makes up much of The Preserve in Essex and Old Saybrook, CT, to the Ingham family in the 1600s. The area was known as Pequot Hill and Pequot Swamp. Archaeological sites testify to Native American use of the land for thousands of years. During historical times, the Western Nehantic and Hammonasset Tribes were known to hunt along its wetlands and hills.

Joseph Ingham managed the property in 1710, with his descendants remaining until 1904. Inghams farmed, pastured, and harvested wood and all the stone ruins seen on the trail are associated with the Ingham family. Parts of the Red Trail today follow "Back Highway," a colonial road laid out in 1736, connecting Pequot Swamp and the Ingham farm to today's Ingham Hill and Plains Roads.

In the early 21st century, "The Preserve" was proposed for economic development (homes, golf course). An archaeological survey was conducted and five Native American sites were identified, along with the historical ruins of the Ingham family farmstead. Public response led to preservation efforts. With financial assistance from the State of Connecticut, the Towns of Essex and Old Saybrook, the Essex Land Trust, and private donations from over 700 people, the Trust for Public Land was able to acquire the property for $9.9 million in 2015. This remarkable alliance of preservationists and local and state governments resulted in the establishment of "The Preserve," a 968-acre coastal forestland available for conservation and public enjoyment.

Top: Cellar hole and stone foundation of the Ingham House.
Bottom: Pequot swamp pond stone dam.

THE HIKE

The West Preserve parking and trailhead will begin your hike. From the trailhead kiosk, take the Barbara Edwards (Red) Trail in the northeast corner of the parking area. The trail will bring you uphill to a knoll and split. Stay straight, slightly bearing left.

After crossing the Essex–Old Saybrook town line, enjoy the Suellen Kozey McCuin Memorial, where you will find a welcoming bench over a cascading brook and a Whisper-In-The-Wind telephone attached to one of the trees. (Go ahead, pick up the phone and listen to the "wind.") The trail splits between the Red and Green Trails; be sure to continue the Red Trail.

The loop will join up ahead. Turn left past a resting bench and continue down the old "Back Highway." After passing under utility lines, two trails will break off on your right. First, the combined Yellow/Red Trail, then, the Yellow Trail. Stay straight, remaining on the Red Trail.

Stone walls will line the trail. At the top of a hill sits the ruins of the Ingham House, which is set back on the left. Take the small path to view the cellar hole, noting that what you see represents a partial cellar with the actual house dimensions much more sizeable. The house lies on elevated, well-drained soils over an inland wetland. Explore. Return to the Red Trail.

Across the trail, straight ahead from the Ingham House stone ruins, look for a large stone wall with three glacial erratic boulders along it. While there is no path leading to these stone ruins, carefully make your way toward the boulders and explore the stone enclosure for the Ingham family's domesticated animals. Note a very unusually narrow barway (a gateway closed by bars usually fitting into posts). Return to the Red Trail and turn right.

When you come to the Dam (Green) Trail on your left, take it to the barrier holding back waters from Pequot Swamp Pond. The large stone dam is situated in a gully between high hills. This is a loop trail, so continue as the trail bends to the left and it will bring you back to the portion you previously hiked when you entered the Dam Trail. Turning right will rejoin the Red Trail. Turn right again and retrace your steps back to the trailhead and parking area.

MILES AND DIRECTIONS

0.0 Start at the trailhead at the West Preserve parking lot, heading out on the Barbara Edwards (Red) Trail.

0.06 Trail forks; stay left.

0.14 Cross the town line into Old Saybrook, CT.

0.26 Reach the Suellen Kozey McCuin Memorial and the Whisper-In-The-Wind phone.

0.35 Bear right on the Red Trail.

0.45 Reach utility pole. Turn left on the old road ("Back Highway") staying on the Red Trail.

0.57 Cross under power lines.

0.76 Intersection of the Yellow/Red Trails. Bear left remaining on the Red Trail.

0.86 Look for a stone enclosure uphill on your right.

0.91 Intersection with the Yellow Trail. Stay on the Red Trail.

Top: Stone wall complex on Ingham Farm.
Bottom: Stone walls.

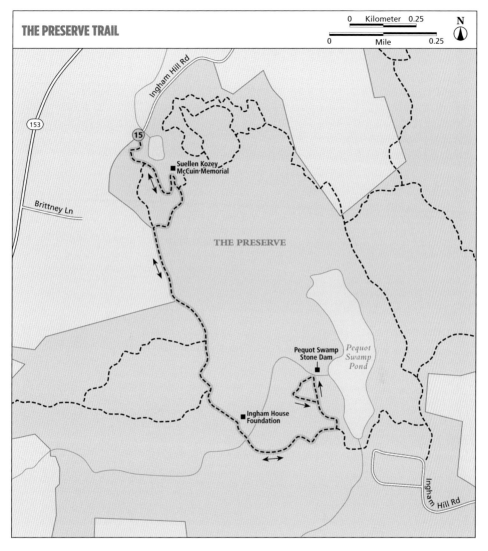

1.0   Ingham House foundation. Take the small path on the left to the stone ruins. Return to the trail.

1.06   Across the trail from the Ingham House there are a series of stone walls and enclosures. Though you can see the stone ruins from the trail, there is no path, so carefully hike into the wooded area beyond the stone wall. Explore. Return to the trail and continue to your right.

1.35   Reach intersection with the Dam (Green) Trail on your left. Take this loop trail, which will bring you back to the Red Trail.

1.43   Reach Pequot Swamp Pond stone dam. Continue the loop and rejoin the Green Trail. Turn right returning to the Red Trail. Turn right again and retrace your steps back to the trailhead.

2.88   Arrive back at the trailhead and parking lot.

16 CANFIELD-MEADOW WOODS TRAIL

Hike through a kaleidoscope of different-colored trail markers: Yellow, Red, Orange, Black, and Blue, all looping together and leading to interesting stone ruins, including a colonial farmhouse foundation, quarry, town-line boulder, and some of the highest stone walls you will see in New England. Geology fans will also find the trail a treat.

Start: Trailhead on CT 154, south of Deep River Center
Distance: 2.94 miles loop
Hiking time: About 2.5 hours
Difficulty: Easy to moderate
Trail surface: Dirt
Seasons: All seasons
Other trail users: None
Canine compatibility: On leash
Land status: Essex Land Trust
Nearest town: Deep River, CT
Fees and permits: None
Schedule: Year-round
Maps: USGS Deep River, CT, Quadrangle
Trail contact: The Essex Land Trust, PO Box 373, Essex, CT 06426; www.essexlandtrust.org

FINDING THE TRAILHEAD

There are four entrances into the Canfield-Meadow Woods Preserve, three in the two towns of Essex and Deep River, CT. To view stone ruins, we recommend the Deep River Trailhead (CT 154), located about 1 mile south of Deep River Center (on left) or by taking exit 4 off CT 9 heading north (on the right). **GPS:** 41.371758, -72.429046

THE HISTORY AND RUINS

The town of Deep River was originally the northern portion of "Saybrook Colony" settled on the west mouth of the Connecticut River in 1644. This district, also known as Eight Mile Meadows and Potapaug Quarter, incorporated as its own municipality in 1859, renaming itself "Saybrook." However, the name led to some confusion with the nearby town of "Old Saybrook." So, after World War II, the town changed its name yet again, this time to Deep River.

Primarily noted for its shipbuilding, quarrying, and ivory piano key manufacturing, Eight Mile Meadows/Potapaug Quarter/Saybrook/Deep River was also home to numerous historical farmsteads, whose vestiges are evident in the Canfield-Meadow Woods Preserve. The stone ruins of a classic 18th-century center-chimney farmhouse, a small quarry, and a matrix of stone walls testify to the long-term agrarian use of the land.

The stone walls are of particular interest. Many are relatively high and suggest sheep pasture boundaries. Elevated stone walls with perceivable gaps between fitted stones were usually built to discourage sheep from attempting to leap the fence.

THE HIKE

Begin your hike at the CT 154 trailhead in Deep River. There is little space for parking, so if the lot is full use your map to find another trailhead and work your way to the stone ruins. Be sure to stop at the trailhead kiosk to reorient yourself.

Top: Town line boulder with inscribed 1812 date.
Bottom: Essex-Deep River town line boulder.

Enter on the Main (Yellow) Trail, which begins by skirting adjacent private properties and crossing tracks of the Valley Railroad. This is an active rail line; use caution when crossing. On the far side of the tracks a white post (#6) marks your entrance to the trail beyond.

Walking along the remnants of an old dirt roadbed, you will encounter the first set of stone ruins, a stone bridge over a stream crossing. Be observant to your left and note the low stone retaining wall securing the roadbed from erosion. These stone features introduce you to the farm and quarry activities ahead. The old roadbed, built before the Valley Railroad, required structural support connecting the farm to CT 154 and access to Deep River and Essex.

Continue to intersections with the Easy (Purple) Trail and the Overlook (Blue) Trail. Stay straight on the Main (Yellow) Trail; you will be returning to this area at the end of the hike. Continue to Split Rock, an interesting geological feature. This glacial erratic was probably dropped by receding ice between 18,000 to 16,000 years ago.

Up ahead is "The Gap," where three trails converge. Take a sharp left turn and follow the Old Cellar (Red) Trail. As the name implies, there is an 18th-century cellar hole of a colonial saltbox house on this loop. There are also remains of a small quarry that the trail dissects. Look for cut stones on the ground. The dispersed distribution of block suggests a processing area operated by early settlers.

Looping Old Cellar Trail, a series of stone walls appears on your left. On your right side, somewhat hidden by vegetation and a slight rise is the cellar hole of a large 18th-century farmhouse, complete with the base of a chimney stack in the center. Walk off the trail via a small path and circle around the cellar hole. Note that much of the stone foundation has been covered with ground vegetation, so the granite blocks are difficult to see, especially during the summer. This was a sizeable house, occupied by a large farming family.

After viewing the cellar hole, continue on the trail skirting a wetland and connecting with the Loop (Orange) Trail. Notice the pattern of stone walls on both sides of the wetland and their size. These stone walls are some of the highest you will see in New England, suggesting that they separated pastures for sheep herding. As textile mills expanded in the mid-1800s throughout New England, the demand for wool increased. Local Connecticut sheep farmers supplied much of this need. The large pasture lands and the high stone walls testify to a successful wool industry.

Following the Main (Yellow) Trail, connect with the Loop (Orange) Trail, where you will turn left and continue to walk adjacent to additional stone walls until arriving at the "Town Line Boulder." The trail ascends a knoll along a stone wall, then takes a sharp bend to the right. The boulder will appear in front of you on the right. This is not only a marker for the Essex/Deep River boundary, but also the point where the town line changes direction, angling toward the east.

With the incorporation of the town of Saybrook (later Deep River) in 1859, the town's selectmen were required to walk municipal borders every decade to ensure proper survey and maintenance. The Town Line Boulder has recorded dates chiseled into the stone. Circumnavigate to the right around the rock and the dates will be visible. The Town Line Boulder is a truly unique survey marker and in and of itself is worth the hike for the history and archaeology buffs.

There will be two trail options up ahead: 1. a shortcut continuation on the Loop Trail (to your right) or 2. join up with the Long (Green) Trail (also on your right),

High stone wall to deter sheep from jumping.

then networking to the Link (Gray) Trail. Both options will connect with the Primitive (Black) Trail. We recommend staying on the Loop Trail linking to the Primitive (Black) Trail on your left.

Follow the Black Trail to the Overlook (Blue) Trail, turning left. This will circle a high elevation before descending back to the Main (Yellow) Trail.

The Overlook Trail will provide vistas to the north and some interesting geological features. Keep your eyes open for further areas of quarrying and old roadways as you descend the hill.

Reaching the intersection of the Main (Yellow) Trail will complete the interlacing loop. Turn left passing the stone bridge and retaining wall once again, continuing to the Valley Railroad tracks and trailhead.

MILES AND DIRECTIONS

0.0   Start at the trailhead on CT 154 south of Deep River Center. Follow Main (Yellow) Trail behind the trailhead kiosk.

0.11 Carefully cross the Valley Railroad tracks; look for white pole #6 to guide you onto the trail.

0.15 Cross a brook with a flat stone-lined bridge. Note the stone retaining wall on the left supporting the old roadbed.

0.27 Intersection with the Overlook (Blue) Trail on the right. Stay straight (Yellow Trail).

0.28 Intersection with the Easy (Purple) Trail. Once again, continue straight on the Yellow Trail.

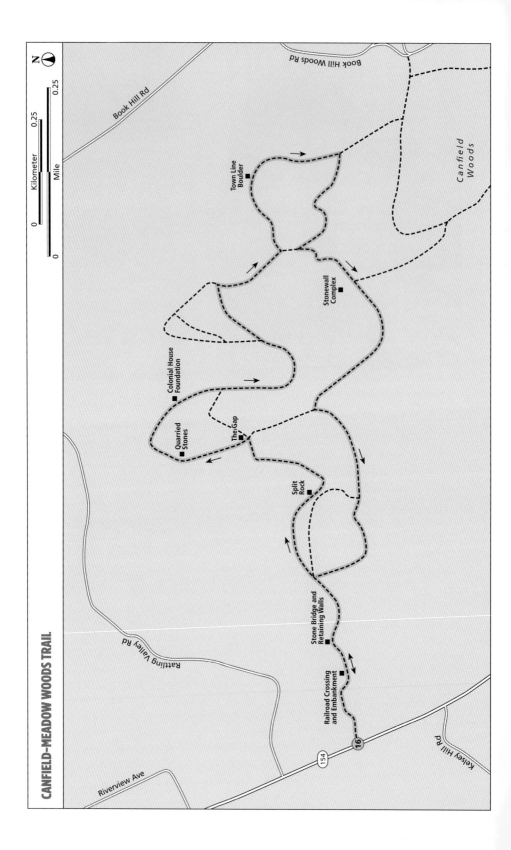

CANFIELD-MEADOW WOODS TRAIL

N

Kilometer
0   0.25   0.25

Mile
0   0.25

Book Hill Rd

Book Hill Woods Rd

Canfield Woods

Town Line Boulder

Stonewall Complex

Colonial House Foundation

Quarried Stones

The Gap

Split Rock

Rattling Valley Rd

Stone Bridge and Retaining Walls

Railroad Crossing and Embankment

154

16

Riverview Ave

Kelsey Hill Rd

0.40 Reach Split Rock. After inspecting this interesting natural fissure, bear left and continue the Yellow Trail as it runs adjacent to the Easy (Purple) Trail. Soon the Yellow Trail will turn to the left and cross a small wetland with a temporary wooden bridge. Make the V-turn and continue.

0.56 Another wooden bridge over wetland and another V-turn to left.

0.67 Reach The Gap, a three-way intersection where the Yellow, Blue, and Red Trails converge. There is a posted trail map to assist. Take a 90-degree turn to the left and hike the Old Cellar (Red) Trail.

0.80 Cut stones on both sides of the trail that may indicate a small quarry used to chisel fountain stones.

0.97 Stone walls appear on both sides of the trail. Take the small path on the right to the "old cellar" hole, the trail's namesake. Carefully walk around the depression for a view of foundation stones and the collapsed center stack of the chimney. Continue on the Red Trail.

1.06 Connect back to the Main (Yellow) Trail bearing left.

1.21 Cross the wooden bridge over the stream. Trail bears to the left.

1.29 Trail reaches an intersection with the Slope (also Yellow) Trail on the left. Either route will loop you to the same point ahead. However, we recommend staying on the Main (Yellow) Trail by bearing right and proceeding uphill.

1.32 Cross a stone wall, and turn right, hiking alongside the stone wall.

1.42 Reach the second intersection with the Slope (Yellow) Trail. Turn right, immediately crossing a stone wall barway.

1.56 Cross a high stone wall and come to the intersection with the Loop (Orange) Trail. Turn left with the stone walls on your left.

1.66 Cross a stone wall.

1.68 Cross a second stone wall.

1.75 Reach the Townline Boulder on right. Walk around the rock looking for carved dates "1812–1916." Continue the Loop (Orange) Trail, crossing into the town of Essex portion of the preserve.

1.94 Loop (Orange) Trail forks. Turn right and follow as the trail winds through additional stone walls.

2.01 Reach "Ancient Rocks" sign.

2.14 Reach the intersection with the Primitive (Black) Trail with kiosk. Turn left and follow Black Trail markers.

2.24 Reach the intersection with the Link (Gray) Trail on your left. Stay on the Primitive (Black) Trail.

2.28 Intersection with the Margaret Canfield Trail also on your left. Once again, continue straight following Black Trail markers.

2.40 Note stone mounds on your right, which may be associated with Native Americans.

2.54 Reach the end of the Primitive Trail and come to the intersection with the Overlook (Blue) Trail. Turn left and follow Blue Trail markers.

2.56 Stone bench on your right. As you continue, descending downslope, be sure to look for the geological "folds" of the bedrock caused by the collision of tectonic plates.

2.94 End of the Overlook (Blue) Trail as it intersects with the Main (Yellow) Trail. Turn left and you will recross the stone bridge, railroad tracks, and return to the parking area.

17 SALT MEADOW TRAIL, STEWART B. MCKINNEY NATIONAL WILDLIFE REFUGE

The Stewart B. McKinney Refuge's Salt Meadow Green Trail offers a glimpse into prominent 20th-century landladies and their celebrated guests, including First Lady Eleanor Roosevelt. Stone ruins along the trail invite the hiker to imagine celebrity luncheons along the Connecticut coast amid the beauty of the region's salt marshes.

Start: 733 Old Clinton Rd., Westbrook, CT
Distance: 1.25-mile loop
Hiking time: About 1 hour
Difficulty: Easy
Trail surface: Dirt and stone
Seasons: Best in late fall/early spring
Other trail users: None
Canine compatibility: No pets allowed

Land status: US Fish and Wildlife Service
Nearest town: Westbrook, CT
Fees and permits: None
Schedule: Closed to hiking June through mid-Sept
Maps: USGS Essex, CT, Quadrangle
Trail contact: Stewart B. McKinney National Wildlife Refuge, 733 Old Clinton Rd., Westbrook, CT 06498; (860) 399-2515; www.fws.gov

FINDING THE TRAILHEAD

Take exit 64 off I-95, and turn south on CT 145. At the stop sign, turn left on Old Clinton Road. The visitor parking area is about 1 mile up on the right. From Route 1 (north or south), drive to Westbrook Center and turn onto Old Clinton Road by the ancient burial ground. Proceed for about a mile and a half; the refuge entrance will be on your left. The trailhead starts at a kiosk after you pass the historical houses. **GPS:** 41.287010, -72.471458

THE HISTORY AND RUINS

Esther Everett Lape, a professor and journalist, and her partner, Elizabeth Fisher Read, a noted activist and lawyer, built a magnificent stone residence in 1927 on the historic farm site of Enoch Murdock in Westbrook, CT. The new Alpine-style fieldstone manor upon "Murdock Hill" was envisioned by Lape and Read as a summer retreat to escape the stifling heat and humidity at their principal home in New York City. The "Cascina" style of the building is unique for the area, suggesting the mountain retreats of Italy and Switzerland.

The Westbrook property borders salt marshes within the Menunketesuck River drainage. Esther and Elizabeth discovered the place while traveling by rail along the Connecticut coast in search of land with a view of Long Island Sound. While the old Murdock property did not offer a coastal view, both women immediately fell in love with the "perfect combination of woodland and meadows." They called their new summer retreat "Salt Meadow"—the same name that the US Fish and Wildlife Service maintains in their management of the property today.

Stone-mortared "box," an outdoor refrigerator.

Esther and Elizabeth spent many summers at Salt Meadow developing gardens with colorful flowerbeds, carving trails through the woodland, riding horses, and playing badminton, among other outdoor pastimes. The Lape-Read House includes a second floor where guests could be comfortably accommodated. One of their close friends who made frequent visits to Salt Meadow and stayed in one of the second-floor guest rooms was First Lady Eleanor Roosevelt.

New trails were specifically laid out to enjoy wonderful views of the salt marsh with its abundant wildlife. One low-lying terrace along the trail with a particularly advantageous viewpoint of the salt meadow was selected as a resting and luncheon location. There, Esther and Elizabeth designed a picnic area built with local stone and imported slate including a circular table with surrounding benches, a raised stone box serving as

Circular stone table at McKinney Wildlife Refuge.

an ice cooler, and possibly a small wading pool. This is where the women hosted friends and family, serving refreshments while looking at the splendor of their estate's natural resources.

When Eleanor Roosevelt visited Salt Meadow, she traveled by train. Railroad engineers would stop the locomotive at the bottom of Murdock Hill, even though no station existed there, and let the First Lady disembark in the countryside where Esther and Elizabeth escorted Eleanor up the trail to the stone lodge.

In 1972, Esther Lape donated the land to the U.S. Department of the Interior. Today, Salt Meadow is part of one of the most important wildlife refuges in North America with over 280 species of migratory birds descending on the properties during the spring

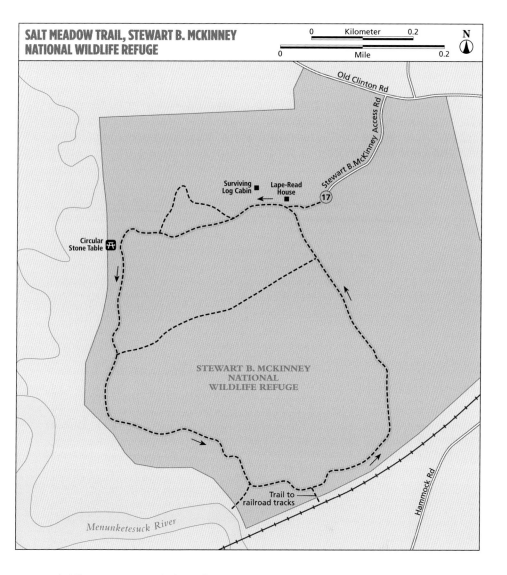

0   Kilometer   0.2

0   Mile   0.2

N

Old Clinton Rd

Stewart B. McKinney Access Rd

Surviving
Log Cabin

Lape-Read
House

17

Circular
Stone Table

STEWART B. MCKINNEY
NATIONAL
WILDLIFE REFUGE

Hammock Rd

Trail to
railroad tracks

Menunketesuck River

and fall seasons. In total, the refuge comprises 950 acres in 10 units across the state of Connecticut—including barrier beach, intertidal wetland, and island habitats.

THE HIKE

Park and take the walkway to your right passing the Enoch Murdock and Lape-Read houses. Be sure to read the kiosk signboards narrating the history of the stone structures and their owners.

As you proceed, a small log cabin on your right is the last survivor of four log structures built from timber on the property felled by the Hurricane of 1938. Elizabeth Read conceived that the toppled trees could be reused to create rustic log cabins and barns adding to the ambiance of the estate.

Enter the shaded trailhead kiosk containing maps and descriptions of the trail systems. Take the Green Trail downhill switching back along the slope. Near the bottom, by a terrace over the meadows, the trail swings to the left. There is a short segue to the right, with a lookout on the river and meadow below.

At this bend, look for a series of discrete stone ruins—the picnic area where Esther and Elizabeth entertained with luncheons and drinks overlooking the meadows. The most obvious feature is the slate circular table with its surrounding bench. Well-built with mortared stone, the table's design allows for several people to partake in refreshments while enjoying the natural setting.

On the left, look for an open stone-mortared "box" standing about 2 feet high constructed into the side of the slope, which most likely was used for holding ice keeping drinks and food cool—the early 20th-century equivalent of a portable cooler.

Behind the stone table on the right is a mysterious stone ruin. Unfortunately, there are no written records of its purpose, though it is a small feature of mortared stone constructed in a low rectangular outline. A wading pool or a fire pit?

Continue southward along the Green Trail encountering a number of stone wall intersections. Crossing the stone walls, note the stones on the trail. Stone walls were built with a foundation belowground to support the aboveground wall. For the trail crossings, aboveground stones were removed but not dug out, so you walk over the buried stone wall foundations.

The Blue Trail intersects with the Green Trail on your left; bear right remaining on the Green Trail. A little farther down when the trail bends to the left heading east, look for a small dirt path downhill toward the railroad tracks below. This is the path Eleanor Roosevelt used when the engineers stopped the train to let the First Lady disembark to visit her friends and spend some quiet summer days at Salt Meadow.

The Green Trail continues back uphill to the Lape-Read House. However, take time to enjoy the deciduous forest and scrub-shrub habitats on the way back. Remember, these habitats are associated with a human-made landscape and contribute to the cultural and natural resources of the refuge.

To observe more of the property, take the Blue Trail through the woodland. You will be greeted, depending on the time of the year, by colorful flowerbeds and plants. The deciduous woodland habitat in the refuge is some of the oldest remaining maritime forest left in the state.

MILES AND DIRECTIONS

0.0 Begin at the Salt Meadow trailhead kiosk (Green Trail).

0.33 The circular stone table surrounded by stone benches, the "ice cooler."

0.42 Cross stream with cement causeway.

0.51 Blue/Green Trail intersection. Stay right to continue on the Green Trail.

0.56 Wooden lookout.

0.85 Connecting path leading down to the railroad; the trail returns to the Lape-Read and Murdock Houses and parking lot.

1.25 Arrive back at the trailhead.

18 WESTWOODS TRAIL

Unusual stone carvings on this trail have inspired some rather extraordinary interpretations. Could they have been sculpted by Christian monks holding services at a 1,500-year-old Byzantine Church in Connecticut? Reality is a bit more mundane. The clues may involve an abandoned granite railroad quarry. A fun hike for the whole family that will necessitate ground exploration and theory-developing amid panoramic Lost Lake.

Start: Trailhead at 1 Sam Hill Rd., Guilford, CT
Distance: 1.38 miles out-and-back
Hiking time: About 1 hour
Difficulty: Easy
Trail surface: Dirt
Seasons: All seasons
Other trail users: Mountain bikers, snowshoers
Canine compatibility: On leash
Land status: Guilford Land Conservation Trust; Connecticut State Forest

Nearest town: Guilford, CT
Fees and permits: None
Schedule: Year-round
Maps: USGS Guilford, CT, Quadrangle
Trail contact: Guilford Land Conservation Trust, PO Box 200, Guilford, CT 06437; (203) 457-9253; www.info@guilfordlandtrust.org; Connecticut Department of Energy and Environmental Protection, 79 Elm St., Hartford, CT 06106-5127; (860) 424-3000; www.ct.gov/deep .cockaponset

FINDING THE TRAILHEAD

From I-95, take exit 58 (CT 77). Head south toward Guilford Center Green. Turn right onto Broad Street, and then left onto Whitfield Street. At the end of the Green, turn right onto Water Street (CT 146) and follow to Sam Hill Road on your right before Water Street takes a sharp bend to the left. Turning onto Sam Hill Road, the trailhead and parking lot are on your immediate left. **GPS:** 41.269480, -72.696098

THE HISTORY AND RUINS

In the early 1990s, before the advent of emails, we received a phone call from a Catholic priest in Chicago. He had read an article reporting the discovery of an Early Byzantine Church in Guilford, CT. The priest was an expert in Early Christianity and had studied Byzantine churches in north Africa. He read that stone ruins and carvings in Guilford represented a 1,500-year-old outdoor church complete with a throne, an overflowing fountain sculpture, altar, candelabra, and a baptismal font. He had never heard of anything comparable in North America and his interest was piqued.

We realized the site that the priest was interested in was the Guilford portion of Cockaponsett State Forest. Today, it is part of the Westwoods Preserve. We tried to explain that the Byzantine interpretation was inaccurate; the stones were carved by Italian masons working a nearby granite quarry for the railroad in the 1880s. The priest, however, was intrigued and asked if we would give him a tour of the ruins. He flew to Connecticut to study the site firsthand.

Top: Cut-granite boulder perched on ledge.
Bottom: Quarried blocks of granite.

In the early days, railroads employed stonemasons to quarry large blocks of granite for embankments, bridge abutments, and other infrastructural requirements. Italian masons were especially prized due to their noted stoneworking skills.

Setting out from Sam Hill Road Trailhead, we reached the historic quarry first and toured among the large-sized square blocks of granite chiseled from bedrock. Then, we hiked up the ridge to examine the stone carvings of the supposed Byzantine Church which, if true, would be the oldest of all Christian houses of worship in the Americas.

Once there, the priest carefully surveyed the landscape, including the ridge, sparse forest, and Lost Lake beyond. He silently examined the carved seat called the Bishop's Throne, which was less than a foot off the ground facing the lake. He studied the spewing stone fountain, which some have also interpreted as a flower with petals. Taking his time, the priest traced the pattern of the drill holes hammered into a rock outcropping, the stepped grooves, and a small flat shelf—the "altar." Finally, he inspected a carved rectangular water basin—the supposed baptismal font. A bit discouraged, the priest acknowledged that this was not the 1,500-year-old Byzantine Church he had hoped it would be.

The Italian masons were more likely expressing their artistic creativity. And the drill holes might well be the work of apprentices learning the craft of stone cutting. The stone was soft and easily sculptured, presenting the masons with the opportunity to express themselves artistically beyond the tiresome repetition of strictly cutting granite "blocks" at the quarry.

THE HIKE

Westwoods Trail is extensive. However, to view the old granite quarry and the stone carvings only requires an easy loop of less than a mile and a half on the White Trail.

Start behind the kiosk at the Sam Hill Road entrance (#3) and follow the White Circle Trail. Be sure to bear left, staying on the White Circle when it intersects with the Orange Trail that veers off to the right. There is a trail split when the Circle Trail joins up with the White Square Trail on the right—look for the circle and square symbols on the White Trail markers to distinguish. (The White Trail encompasses your entire hike, so this chapter will refer to the symbols without repeating "White.")

Move off the Circle Trail and onto the Square Trail and come immediately upon the old granite quarry. Explore as there is a lot to see here. Both sides of the trail will reveal stepped quarry levels and large blocks of granite dispersed around the former work areas. Follow around to the "Big Boulder" that sits like a Stonehenge monolith along the downward slope. Unfortunately, graffiti has been painted on much of the stone.

Retrace your steps back and bear left on the Circle Trail. You will be hiking with the quarry on your left. Notice more cut blocks around you. Look for drill marks that were mostly chiseled by hand using star drills. Continue the Circle Trail until you reach another intersection with the Square Trail. Turn left and climb a small hill to the top of the ridge.

This is where you can search for the carved stones believed by some to be associated with an Early Byzantine Church. As you come over the ridge, Lost Lake is below. As you start to descend the ridge toward the lake, take the small path on your right and be observant. On the ground will be scattered stones carved into images of flowers, a seat, and other unidentifiable patterns. Have fun exploring. Leaves on the ground might impede your view, so clear off the stones for better views of the carvings.

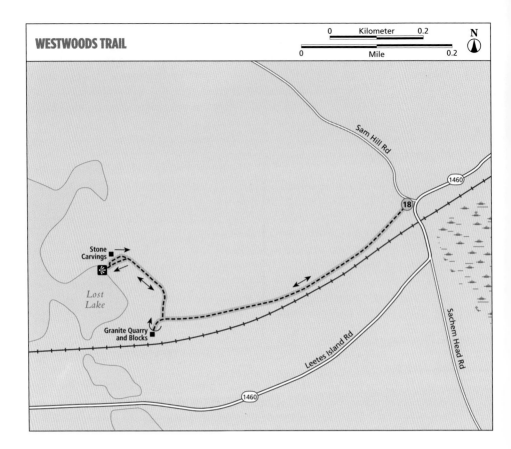

In your exploration around the top of the ridge, the area opens with sparse trees. Look to your left for an outcropping of bedrock with drill holes on the side wall—this was the supposed altar and candelabra. Up ahead, a little downslope, and on your left is the rectangular stone carved water basin—the supposed baptismal font.

Lunch and picnic at the bedrock ledge overlook of Lost Lake, which was historically harvested for salt hay and provides a wonderful vista toward the west.

After exploring, you will have two options. First, from the water trough, follow a small path to your right, which will reconnect you to the Circle Trail. Or, from the Lost Lake overlook, continue the Square Trail south which skirts the edge of the lake and returns you to the Big Boulder at the granite quarry. Note that the Square Trail will go through some low-lying areas and can be muddy, especially in the wetter seasons. Either option will return you to the Circle Trail, where you can turn left to the trailhead.

MILES AND DIRECTIONS

0.0 Begin at Trailhead #3 on Sam Hill Road. Follow White Circle Trail along railroad tracks.

0.29 Intersection with Orange Trail. Stay straight (left) on White Circle Trail.

0.31 Remain on White Circle as the path intersects with White Square Trail.

Carved flower motif from the supposed Byzantine Church.

0.35 Reach the granite quarry. Explore the cut blocks of stone used to support embankments for the railroad. Note the bedrock "steps" of the quarry on both sides and the high "Big Boulder" as the trail leads down the slope. We recommend that you do not proceed down the slope on the White Circle Trail but return and follow the White Square Trail bearing left.

0.59 Take the White Square Trail.

0.64 Climb to the top of the ridge overlooking Lost Lake. Take the little path on your right and explore.

0.65 Search the ground and stone carvings will begin to appear at this point: a flower, sitting area, and others. Rock outcropping on the left with drill holes.

0.74 Rectangular water trough cut out of stone on your left. Look for the path on your right and follow downslope to the White Square Trail.

0.85 Intersection with the White Circle Trail. Turn right to return to the trailhead and parking area.

1.38 Arrive back at the trailhead.

19 IRONWOODS PRESERVE TRAIL

This loop trail offers several environmental settings for the hiker to enjoy, including open meadows, woodlands, rocky ridges, streams, and ponds. The main cultural feature of the trail are stone foundations associated with late 18th- and early 19th-century bog ironworks. This is a great place to learn about the early water-powered iron industry while enjoying a pleasant hike through varied ecological zones.

Start: 227 Race Hill Rd., Madison, CT 06443
Distance: 2.34-mile loop
Hiking time: 1.5-2 hours
Difficulty: Easy
Trail surface: Dirt and stone
Seasons: All
Other trail users: Hiking only
Canine compatibility: On leash/pickup

Land status: Madison Land Conservation Trust
Nearest town: North Madison, CT
Fees and permits: None
Schedule: Year-round
Maps: USGS Guilford, CT, Quadrangle
Trail contact: Madison Land Conservation Trust, www.madisonlandtrust.org

FINDING THE TRAILHEAD

From I-95 take exit 61, CT 79 northbound. Turn left at the roundabout at the CT 80 intersection, heading west for about 1.5 miles. Turn right on Race Hill Road. One-half mile in, the road will take S-shape bends. The trailhead will be on your left just after the second bend. Turn into the gravel driveway to the lower parking area and trailhead. **GPS:** 41.356003, -72.664565

THE HISTORY AND RUINS

As the American Revolution wound to a close at the end of the 18th century, economic opportunities prevailed. Three industrial entrepreneurs—Henry Hill, Joseph Pyncheon, and Redad Stone—purchased 4 acres of land along a steady stream from Joshua Blatchley, a Madison farmer. Originally, they dammed the stream to set up a sawmill, but within a few years they recognized the potential of locally available bog iron ore. With plentiful wood for charcoal-making, they converted the sawmill into an ironworks.

Hill, Pyncheon, and Stone's ironworks was a relatively small operation, but it yielded a product of great strength, resistant to rusting. Due to specific work skills involved in maintaining the forge and balancing the appropriate heat for processing bog iron, they hired Noah Hotchkin to manage the operation. Hotchkin, and later, Abel Snow, ran the charcoal-fired forge reaching temperatures of 2,600 to 2,700 degrees F. The small forge was able to maintain these extremely hot temperatures due to a waterwheel-powered bellows.

The industrial process involved a delicate balance that required an exact and consistent temperature. Pieces of bog iron, the size ranging as small as a ping-pong ball to as large as a man's closed fist, were fed into the fire. The hearth's heat melted silicon-based impurities and produced a liquid slag, which was raked off. (As a result, the remains of slag can still be found littering the ground around the ironworks.) After cooling, small lumps of ore became malleable and were molded into bar shapes by a heavy trip hammer.

Top: Breached stone dam at ironworks.
Bottom: Stone dam at the millpond.

Ironworks memorial stone and mounted iron slag.

The ironworks ran successfully until 1820 when local bog iron and wood became depleted. Abandoned ever since, the stone ruins have great archaeological integrity, providing a wonderful means of rediscovering an early and rare local industrial process.

THE HIKE

Ironwoods Preserve contains a series of trail loops with varying hiking patterns to enjoy diverse environmental settings. However, we provide the most direct loop route to the ironworks ruins.

Starting at the parking area on Race Hill Road, the trail elevates gently and then drops to the first map kiosk (#13A). Bear right, making a U-turn, and continuing to an intersection at Sylvan Lake.

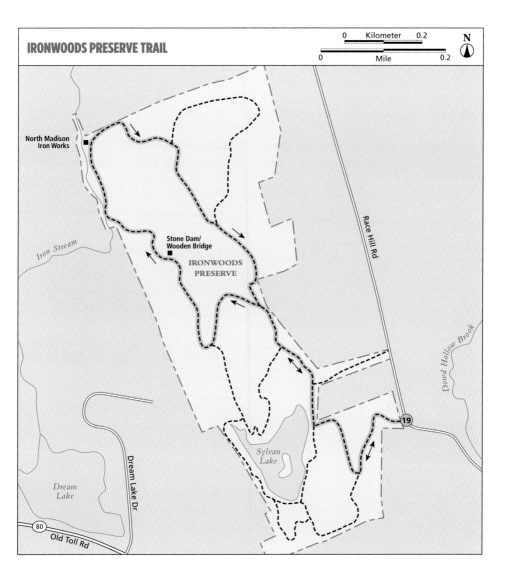

0   Kilometer   0.2

0   Mile   0.2

N

North Madison
Iron Works

Iron Stream

Stone Dam/
Wooden Bridge

IRONWOODS
PRESERVE

Race Hill Rd

Dowd Hollow Brook

19

Dream Lake Dr

Sylvan
Lake

Dream
Lake

80

Old Toll Rd

At Sylvan Like, turn right following the trail to the next kiosk (#13C). Look for an arrow directing to the ironworks. Turn right and at the next trail intersection bear left; you will come back to this point once you have completed the loop trail to the ironworks.

At the kiosk (#13E) intersection, stay straight, swinging north with a stream and wetlands on your left. A narrow pond appears on your right. The trail crosses a small dam at the southern end of the pond, with a wooden bridge. Continue for just over a quarter of a mile and you will come to the ironworks.

When you arrive, take the path down the slope to a granite monument erected by the Madison Historical Society commemorating the site of the historic ironworks. Note two stone foundations upslope from the monument and farther downslope toward the stream. Explore. Reconstruct in your mind's eye the overshot waterwheel operating the bellows, trip hammer, and anvil. Look for iron slag on the ground. (Remember not to take any slag pieces or remove them from their setting as that would be disturbing the integrity of the archaeological site.)

Return upslope to the trail, and turn left. Another small path on your left will lead to the top of the stone dam where you will be able to view the ironworks on your left from above and imagine the millpond impounded on your right. Return to the trail and continue straight through to the northern extent of the loop.

Eventually, you will encounter two kiosks (#13G and #13F) at both ends of another loop trail. Simply stay straight and you will return to the trail intersection you traveled coming out. Turn left and hike to kiosk #13D. With Sylvan Lake on your right, take the trail on your left leading uphill and eventually to kiosk #13A. Turn left and uphill to return to the trailhead and parking area.

MILES AND DIRECTIONS

"Iron Works" sign on trail.

- 0.0 Begin at the trailhead on Race Hill Road.
- 0.14 Map kiosk #13A. Bear to the right making a U-turn.
- 0.30 Intersection approaching Sylvan Lake. Turn right heading north.
- 0.45 Note stone mounds.
- 0.47 Reach kiosk #13C. Turn right at trail intersection.
- 0.55 Bear left at trail intersection.
- 0.68 Kiosk #13E. Stay straight.
- 0.72 Trail intersection. Bear right. Trail makes a U-turn at this point. Stream and wetlands should be on your left.
- 0.89 Reach small dam with pond. Cross wooden bridge.
- 1.17 Reach the ironworks. Take small path on your left leading down to stream and stone ruins.
- 1.18 Granite monument erected by the Madison Historical Society commemorating the ironworks. Explore. Return upslope to trail, and turn left to continue.
- 1.25 Take path on your left and walk to the top of dam. Observe the ironworks site from above. Go back to trail and continue straight ahead.
- 1.46 Kiosk #13G. Stay straight and cross wooden bridge.
- 1.62 Kiosk #13F. Stay straight on the trail.
- 1.66 Note stone wall on rock ledge to your left.
- 1.69 Cross stone wall.
- 1.73 Trail intersection. Turn right.
- 1.88 Kiosk #13D. Turn left to complete trail loop.
- 2.05 Trail intersection. Turn left, uphill.
- 2.20 Return to kiosk #13A. Turn left uphill to trailhead.
- 2.34 Arrive back at the trailhead and parking lot.

20 PAPERMILL TRAIL

The Hammonasset Paper Mill is located directly behind the trailhead. The stone ruins represent a significant industrial archaeological site listed on the National Register of Historic Places. We recommend taking the Papermill Trail to appreciate the extent of the millpond and Hammonasset River's role in this early industrialization process.

Start: Intersection of Green Hill Road and Fawn Brook Circle, Madison, CT
Distance: 1.78 miles out-and-back
Hiking time: About 10 minutes
Difficulty: Easy
Trail surface: Dirt
Seasons: All seasons
Other trail users: None
Canine compatibility: On leash
Land status: Madison Land Conservation Trust
Nearest town: North Madison, CT
Fees and permits: None
Schedule: Year-round
Maps: USGS Clinton, CT, Quadrangle
Trail contact: Madison Land Conservation Trust, www.madisonlandtrust.org

FINDING THE TRAILHEAD

From I-95, take exit 61 (Durham Road/CT 179) and travel northbound for about 1 mile. Turn right onto Green Hill Road and go 1.5 miles to Fawn Brook Circle on your left just before the bridge over the Hammonasset River. Turn onto Fawn Brook Circle and Trailhead #1 will be on your immediate right. Park on the grass in front of the posted trail signs. **GPS:** 41.3239013, -72.5934043

THE HISTORY AND RUINS

The Hammonasset Paper Mill was built soon after the conclusion of the American Civil War in 1865. The mill's main commercial production was manufacturing straw board used for fabricating boxes at that time. Earlier paper mills used rags and later mills worked wood pulp to make boxes, making this venture part of a changing technology throughout the 19th century. The Hammonasset Paper Mill closed in 1890, though the site continued to be used by a lumber company into the 20th century.

With the introduction of electricity and fuel-powered machinery, factory locations were no longer restricted to water sources. Hence, by World War II, the Hammonasset mill site was abandoned and the stone dam breached. In 1996, the stone ruins of the mill were listed on the National Register of Historic Places.

THE HIKE

There are four trailheads for the Papermill Trail. The mill ruins are located directly behind Trailhead #1 at the intersection of Green Hill Road and Fawn Brook Circle.

After exploring the paper mill ruins, follow the trail skirting the southern bank of the Hammonasset River. Note the wide floodplain that was the paper mill's pond, impounding water behind the downriver stone dam. This will give you an appreciation of the size of the millpond and the power source of the mill's operation.

The paper mill foundation ruins exhibit a complex set of various work activities, including stone-lined head- and tailraces, and several buildings. Look for iron rods into

Top: Hammonasset Paper Mill dam and rock ledge.
Bottom: Hammonasset Paper Mill stone ruins.

Paper mill furnace brick and stone ruins.

the stone as footings for large machinery. Can't find the waterwheel pit? That's because there isn't one! Operating power was achieved using a water-driven turbine, which came into use during the mid-19th century. Exactly where the turbine(s) were located within the paper mill ruins is unclear. However, they most likely were in one of the stone-lined depressions within the mill structure. These depressions could also have housed large vats required in the straw board-making process.

Be sure to inspect the remnants of the old stone dam, whose ruins can be seen on both sides of the river. The far, or eastern side, of the dam is in the town of Killingworth; the mill and western portion is in the town of Madison. The original dam would have been 20 feet long, 6 feet wide, and 14 feet high, restricting the Hammonasset River creating the millpond. The dam was most likely breached by the Hurricane of 1936 and the Hurricane of 1938.

After exploring the stone ruins, continue the trail in a counterclockwise direction toward Trailhead #2. The trail will follow the Hammonasset River and then advance inland. When the trail splits to the left, continue straight.

The trail zigzags left, then right and crosses a stream. When you reach a T-intersection with a kiosk, turn right, staying on the main trail crossing another stream. Hike a steep rise between private houses to Trailhead #2 at the Wickford Place cul-de-sac.

Retrace your steps back to Trailhead #1 and the paper mill. Should you wish to take a longer hike, do the Loop Trail, and follow the kiosk map for Trailheads #3 and #4. You can return to the parking area via the routes taken. Do not walk along Green Hill Road due to vehicle traffic and safety concerns.

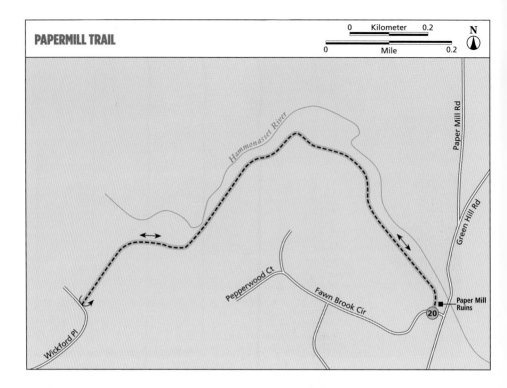

PAPERMILL TRAIL

MILES AND DIRECTIONS

0.0 Begin the hike at Trailhead #1, at the intersection of Green Hill Road and Fawn Brook Circle.

0.04 Hammonasset Paper Mill ruins on the right by river. Explore. Continue the trail following the river in a counterclockwise direction around the hill on your left.

0.56 Trail splits to the left. This is a short loop that will return you back to the main trail, but we recommend simply continuing straight ahead.

0.69 T-intersection with loop trail and kiosk (10c). Turn right and follow to Trailhead #2.

0.82 Cross stream. Trail will narrow between private houses.

0.89 Reach Trailhead #2 at the Wickford Place cul-de-sac. Retrace your steps returning to Trailhead #1 and the parking area, turning left at kiosk (10c).

1.78 Arrive back at Trailhead #1 and the parking area.

21 HARTMAN PARK TRAILS

This out-of-the-way gem is the perfect trail to see scenic vistas and one-of-a-kind stone ruins. The trail is well maintained and worth the adventure. Along the way you will encounter ruins of colonial farmsteads and mills, charcoal hearths, Native American ceremonial stone mounds, and some curious stone works. There are 11 known archeological sites along the trail.

Start: Hartman Park entrance, 122 Gungy Rd., Lyme
Distance: 3.14-mile loop
Hiking time: About 2 hours
Difficulty: Moderate
Trail surface: Dirt
Seasons: Best Mar through Nov
Other trail users: Cross-country skiers, mountain bikers, equestrian
Canine compatibility: Dogs on leash
Land status: Town of Lyme Park
Nearest town: Lyme, CT
Fees and permits: None
Schedule: Year-round
Maps: USGS Hartford South, CT
Trail contact: Town of Lyme, CT, 480 Hamburg Rd., Lyme, CT 06371; (860) 434-7733; Lyme Land Trust, Macintosh Road, Lyme, CT 06371; www.lymelandtrust.org/

FINDING THE TRAILHEAD

From CT 82 turn south onto Darling Road, across from the CT 11 southbound ramp (right and immediate left). At the intersection bear right onto White Birch Road, then left back onto Darling Road. Turn right onto Gungy Road and travel 1 mile. The park entrance will be on your left. From CT 156 in Lyme, turn right onto Beaver Brook Road and travel 2.7 miles to Gungy Road. Turn left and travel 1.5 miles to the park entrance on your right. There is a small parking area, and dirt road turnabout. **GPS:** 41.426842, -72.286704

THE HISTORY AND RUINS

Stone ruins at Hartman Park represent some of the earliest examples of colonial subsistence farming and settlement in the area. Remarkably, this land, which today makes up four continuous preserves and is bounded by Nehantic State Forest, has remained intact since the last of the historical farms were abandoned in the mid-1800s. No modern development has taken place and due to the efforts of the town of Lyme and The Lyme Land Trust, the preserves are open to the public for wildlife viewing, hiking, cross-country skiing, and the visiting of archaeological stone ruins.

When the English established Saybrook Colony in 1635, they set aside this land as a place for the local Nehantic Tribe to hunt and gather, while colonists maintained timber rights. In the 18th century, farmsteads were developed, and sheep and dairy cattle roamed the hills. Colliers maintained hearths throughout the warming months felling trees and creating large blocks of charcoal for the iron industry. Before long, the entire landscape was deforested, only to return when let fallow in the 20th century.

A sawmill and dam were built where valuable timber was cut into planks, staves, and boards for use by the colony as well as to be transported to England where wood was scarce. The sawmill operated from the founding of the Saybrook Colony until 1683, when the area was "overcut" and few trees were left standing.

Three Chimneys at Hartman Park.

By the 1850s, with the land damaged by overuse and the soils unproductive, farmers moved away to other parts of town, leaving the area to freed African and Native Americans settlers. A multi-racial community developed where occupants eked out a living on this rugged landscape.

THE HIKE

Numerous trails will take you to various archaeological features. We recommend a combination of Park Road (Purple) and the Heritage (Orange) Trails to see the most within a limited timeframe. Start at the Hartman Park entrance on Gungy Road. Follow Park Road downslope to the stone bridge and the water-powered sawmill site (No. 2).

Continuing Park Road upslope, pass the "School Room" (No. 1) on your left. This is not a historical site, but a contemporary outdoor education center offering picnic tables and a picturesque view of the millpond. You will return here at the end of the trail loop, but for now, continue northward on Park Road until you reach the intersection for the Heritage (Orange) Trail on your left.

Turn onto the Orange Trail, which transitions from a broad roadbed (Park Road) to a single-lane path. Continue across a wetland and under electrical power lines. Once across, you will come to a stone-paved road; turn left and look for the orange marker. Turn right and you will be back on the Heritage Trail.

In a short distance find the "Stone-End House" (No. 11). This stone ruin represents a small homestead where the fireplace and chimney were placed at one end of the structure. This is an early 1700s "Rhode Island" style farmhouse. Look for the fireplace and hearthstone.

Just to the north on your left is a charcoal hearth (No. 8). Charcoal production was a massive industry throughout Connecticut and large blocks of roasted charcoal were sent to the northwest corner of the state where it fired the iron furnaces for over 200 years. The hearth/kiln is represented by a circular low-lying mound (30 feet in diameter) surrounded by a trough allowing air to get into the hearth to increase heat and control the fire.

From here, the Heritage (Orange) Trail winds through forest and wetlands until you get to the junction of the Yellow Trail and a stone structure (No. 10) built against a large glacial erratic. One interpretation is that the enclosure was used for ceremonies by Native Americans or as a covered barn/shed to temporarily house sheep, swine, and/or cattle.

A short distance from the stone structure comes the most remarkable and unusual site on the hike, "Three Chimneys" (No. 9). Walk off the main trail uphill to a large open space walled by stone on your right. Here a collection of stone structures are unlike any we have seen throughout southern New England. The back northern wall has two stone chimneys constructed at its base resembling house foundations built at Plymouth Plantation in the 1620s. There is a third chimney at the far southern end of the enclosure. One theory is that the complex represents one of a series of forts built by Lion Gardiner to protect the Saybrook Colony in 1635. However, archaeological testing suggests 19th-century use of the enclosure. Explore for you are unlikely to see another stone complex comparable to it.

Leaving the Three Chimneys area, take a loop hike skirting wetlands to the next site, the historic Clark Farm (Nos. 7 and 8). Today the Clark house ruins are a pile of rocks, but you can make out the dimensions of the house by subtle contours on the ground. Also, there is charcoal kiln located behind the house and the remnants of a barn across the road.

Heritage (Orange) Trail reconnects with Park (Purple) Road. Turn right and continue on Park Road when Heritage Trail diverts to the left. If you wish, take a short walk on Heritage Trail to see a stone fireplace, which is all that remains of a collier's hut, home for the men cutting trees for the charcoal industry. Come back to Park Road and continue south toward the Lee Farm.

You will again cross under the power lines. Once back into the wooded area, look to your right downslope and you will see several stone cairns and walls, two of which run parallel and represent sides of an old colonial road. The cairns are said to have been built by Native Americans occupying the area before European settlement.

The Henry Lee family house (No. 4) appears next on your right. Unlike the Clark house, the stone foundation, cellar, and center-chimney stack are clearly visible. The Lee House was built in 1735 by Dan Clark and burned to the ground about 1890.

Park Road again intersects with Heritage Trail on the left in two places after the Lee House. Take the second turnoff to see the Lee Barn site (No. 3). This was a multi-story barn built sometime after 1840 and it is based on the wedge-and-feather technology used to split the stones for the foundation. It is a wonderful example of a large New England barn ruin.

Stay on the Heritage Trail to the "School Room." Pass a series of large stone walls and come upon two magnificent oak trees that have grown through the rocks of a stone wall! Once completing the loop, turn left back on Park Road to the parking lot, or continue straight through the School Room overlook to see the stone dam of the sawmill up close. If you choose the latter trail, you will reconnect to Park Road near the trailhead.

Close-up of chimney at Hartman Park.

MILES AND DIRECTIONS

0.0 Start at the Hartman Park entrance on Gungy Road.

0.14 Stone bridge. The sawmill is to your left. Only the stone dam is visible.

0.18 The School Room on the left can serve as an excellent picnic area when your hike is completed. Continue Park Road northbound.

0.37 Enter the Heritage (Orange) Trail and follow through a wetland and under power lines. When the trail meets a stone-paved road, turn left, and reconnect with the Heritage Trail.

0.62 Stone-End House.

0.67 The charcoal hearth on the left.

0.73 Intersection of the Yellow Trail (northbound) on your left but continue the Orange Trail.

0.98 Intersection of Yellow Trail (southbound) on your right. Once again remain on the Orange Trail.

1.14 On your left, a stone enclosure near another intersection with a Yellow Trail. Remain on the Heritage Trail.

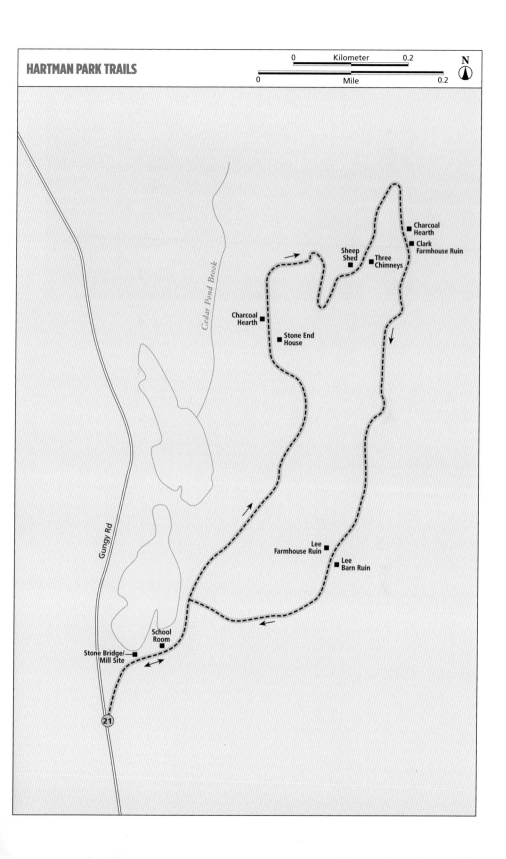

0　　Kilometer　　0.2

0　　Mile　　0.2

N

Cedar Pond Brook

Charcoal
Hearth

Sheep
Shed

Three
Chimneys

Charcoal
Hearth

Clark
Farmhouse Ruin

Charcoal
Hearth

Stone End
House

Gungy Rd

Lee
Farmhouse Ruin

Lee
Barn Ruin

School
Room

Stone Bridge/
Mill Site

21

Three Chimneys stone foundation.

1.24 Three Chimneys site will be on your right. Explore stone enclosure. Continue Yellow Trail.

1.65 The Clark Farm on the right and a charcoal hearth on your left. Heritage Road reconnects with Park (Purple) Road. Turn right (southbound) on Park Road. Clark Barn on the left.

2.05 After you cross under the power lines, look downslope on the right. There are ancient stone cairns and an old colonial roadway between double parallel stone walls.

2.41 The Henry Lee farmhouse on your right. Take the second cutoff for the Heritage (Orange) Trail on your left to view the Lee Barn.

2.69 Return back to Park Road and the School Room.

3.14 Arrive back at the trailhead.

22 MOUNT ARCHER WOODS TRAIL

A relatively easy hike along the top of Mount Archer with well-defined trails. Stone ruins date to the early 18th-century farming complex representing houses, barns, sheds, and penning areas, as well as pasture stone walls lining colonial road systems. Have fun identifying the various uses of past buildings by their stone ruins.

Start: Mount Archer Woods Preserve, Mount Archer Road, Lyme, CT
Distance: 3.7 miles out-and-back
Hiking time: About 1.5 hours
Difficulty: Easy
Trail surface: Dirt, roots, boulders
Seasons: Best in late fall/early spring
Other trail users: Mountain bikes, equestrians
Canine compatibility: On leash
Land status: Lyme Land Conservation Trust
Nearest town: Hadlyme, CT

Fees and permits: None
Schedule: Closed during deer and turkey hunting seasons. Check with Lyme Hunting Program: www.lymelandtrust.org/stewardship/huntingprogram.
Maps: USGS Hamburg, CT, Quadrangle
Trail contact: Lyme Land Conservation, PO Box 1002, Lyme, CT 06371; (860) 434-5051; www.lymelandtrust.org

FINDING THE TRAILHEAD

From the north, take CT 2 eastbound to exit 19, bearing right onto CT 11, which ends at CT 82 in Salem. Turn right onto CT 82 (East Haddam Road) and continue for 4 miles, turning left onto CT 156 (Hamburg Road). Go past the Lyme Town Hall and turn right onto MacIntosh Road, which winds uphill and connects with Mount Archer Road. Turn right and the entrance to the Mount Archer Woods trailhead will be up the hill and on your left.

From the south, take CT 9 north to exit 7. There is a long exit ramp leading to CT 154. Turn left and then right onto CT 82 (Bridge Road). Cross the Connecticut River at Goodspeed Opera House and continue up the hill staying on CT 82. Turn left at Town Road, remaining on CT 82 south to Hadlyme. At the Hadlyme Center stop sign, proceed straight onto Brush Hill Road which will lead into Mount Archer Road bearing left at the intersection with Tantumorantum Road. The trail entrance will be on Mount Archer Road on your right. **GPS:** 41.40528, -72.35874

THE HISTORY AND RUINS

There are few historical documents on the family that operated this hilltop farm during the 18th century into the early 19th century. Still, the Mount Archer ruins are intriguing and were obviously part of a major farming enterprise.

Observing the stone ruins, imagine a farmer bringing his flock of sheep in for the night. Or when you see the house foundation stones—two levels?—you can imagine someone cooking over the hearth or reading a book by candlelight. It is easy for the imagination to run wild along the trail as there is plenty of stone evidence for a complex farm, but little historical information.

Historical house foundation at Mount Archer Woods.

THE HIKE

Hiking the White Trail across the summit of Mount Archer is a relatively easy, circular walk with stone-built landscaping throughout the journey. The trails cover relatively flat terrain over one of the highest points in Lyme. Despite the elevation, there are several wet spots and vernal pools.

The trail begins with a series of slight ups and downs leading to the central farm complex at the half-mile mark. Stone mounds of possible Native American origin are encountered near the start of the trail. Please be respectful of all these structures and do not touch or remove any stones.

During the hike, note a series of tubes running close to the trail. The tubes are used to gravity-feed maple sugar from trees to containers. Enjoy following their path throughout the hike but, again, please do not touch or disturb the tubing.

The White Trail crosses a series of stone walls during the hike. The historical farm's primary economy was focused on dairy cattle and sheep—hence the complex of stone walls delineating pasture boundaries. Some of these walls run up and down steep hillsides, some are very high, some low, but all testify to the labor and needs of colonial farmers creating a living on a rugged topographical countryside. The location of the main farming activities is appropriately situated on the top of Mount Archer, while pastures are spread throughout the area.

When you encounter the house site, spend some time exploring the entire compound of stone ruins. The house is unique in having its front at ground level and the rear cut

Stone mound on White Trail.

back into the hill slope. Note the large pile of stone in the center of the house cellar—the center chimney stack. Climb the stone stairs on the left side to get a better perspective of how the house stood.

Continuing upslope are another series of stone foundations. There are no cellar holes, but most likely auxiliary farm buildings for dairying and sheep herding. Five structures appear around the house. Archaeological investigations could shed light on the purposes of each structure: blacksmithing, milking, sheep shearing, and/or carpentry.

Leaving the main complex, the White Trail continues through some narrow, well-marked paths. The markers are especially helpful during the summer months when ground vegetation is high. A mile into the hike, you cross over to the adjacent Eno Preserve. Turn left onto the Yellow Trail for half a mile before turning right on the Red Trail. This will lead to another series of stone enclosures and a stone foundation. This final ruin can be difficult to locate during the summer but search the trail to your left. The ruin could have been a field barn for animals in the lower pastures.

Retrace your steps back to the trailhead and parking lot, or if you wish to extend your hike by continuing on the Red Trail, turning right onto the Morgan Trail and then left on the northern end of the White Trail, which will lead you to Mount Archer Road. Turn to your right following the road to the Mount Archer Woods trail entrance where you parked your vehicle. Should you choose the extended route, please be careful walking on Mount Archer Road as it is narrow.

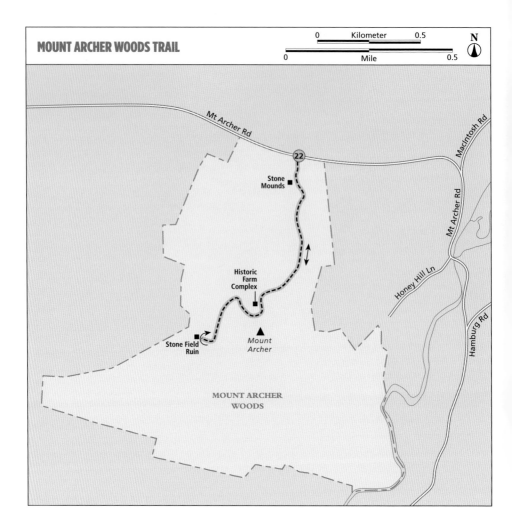

MILES AND DIRECTIONS

0.0 Begin at the trailhead at the parking lot on Mount Archer Road. Start the White Trail.

0.06 Appearance of stone mounds on the right side of trail.

0.28 Cross first in a series of stone walls.

0.38 Cross second stone wall.

0.46 Cross third stone wall to an open stone enclosure with ruins visible.

0.49 House ruin on your right side.

0.51 Take stone stairway on the right and climb to the top of the house ruins. Note possible ruins of a summer kitchen behind house and remnants of center chimney stack.

0.56 Walk upslope to terraced stone ruins of past farm buildings. After you are finished exploring the area, return to the White Trail. On your left, you will see a wide path that represents the old colonial road. Continue the White Trail across from the house ruins downslope crossing the fourth stone wall.

0.68 Cross fifth stone wall. Intersection with the Yellow Trail. Stay on the White Trail by turning right, upslope.

0.81 Cross sixth stone wall.

0.85 Cross seventh stone wall.

0.95 Cross the eighth stone wall and then walk parallel to the stone wall on your right.

1.00 Second intersection with the Yellow Trail. Turn left onto the Eno Preserve and Yellow Trail.

1.54 Pass through open stone enclosure.

1.67 Intersection with the Red Trail. Turn right, downslope.

1.85 Ruins of enclosure and stone foundation. Retrace trail back to the trailhead and parking lot.

3.70 Arrive back at the trailhead and parking lot.

23 MATTABESETT TRAIL, MICA LEDGES

The Mattabesett Trail extends for over 60 miles through Connecticut. This 4-mile-plus loop provides an array of interesting features, including challenging terrains, scenic views, natural ledges, and historical stone ruins: a late 18th-century smallpox Pest House, burying ground, and the "Selectmen's Stones."

Start: End of Cream Pot Road parking area
Distance: 3.51-mile loop
Hiking time: About 2 hours
Difficulty: Easy to moderate
Trail surface: Dirt and ledge
Seasons: All seasons
Other trail users: None
Canine compatibility: On leash

Land status: Trail easement
Nearest town: Durham, CT
Fees and permits: None
Schedule: Year-round
Maps: USGS Durham, CT, Quadrangle
Trail contact: Connecticut Forest and Park Association (CFPA), 16 Meriden Rd., Rockfall, CT 06481; (860) 346-8733; www.ctwoodlands.org

FINDING THE TRAILHEAD

From CT 17 southbound, go through Durham Center, turn left onto CT 77. Travel less than 1 mile, and turn left onto Cream Pot Road. Paved road ends but continue a short distance to the trail parking area. Northbound on CT 17, turn right onto CT 77 and follow above directions. **GPS:** 41.443142, -72.676097

THE HISTORY AND RUINS

The smallpox virus was brought to the Americas from Europe in the 16th century by explorers and traders interacting with Native Americans along the Atlantic seaboard. Native people had no previous exposure to the malady and tragically perished in great numbers after the disease was introduced. It is estimated that Native American populations in southern New England experienced three major smallpox epidemics before the Pilgrims landed in 1620.

Though having a degree of immunity from exposures to the variola virus, British settlers in the New World were also adversely affected by smallpox with the scourge running rampant into the 20th century. George Washington came close to losing his entire Revolutionary War Army due to smallpox infections before incorporating a controversial inoculation program that possibly saved his troops securing American independence.

In 1760, prior to the availability of a vaccine, the town of Durham was faced with an eruption of variola. Acting promptly, the town immediately approved the construction of a "House . . . for the reception of such persons as shall be taken with infectious disease."

The "Pest House" was not a hospital to treat those suffering from this dreaded infection since there was no cure for smallpox victims back then. Instead, this was a place to quarantine disease victims to control the contagion, and as a secluded place for them to die minimizing risks to their loved ones.

Top: Pinnacle Rock.
Bottom: Cellar hole and chimney stack at Durham Pest House.

Durham town fathers selected a remote area located northwest on Pisgah Mountain, a basalt ridge in the southern portion of town away from Durham Center, as the site for the Pest House. The wooden structure measured 30 feet long and 20 feet wide, having a partial cellar with two chimney stacks. The Pest House site has a burying ground so those unfortunate souls who died of the "pox" could be buried immediately preventing further contagion. There is only one engraved tombstone:

Mr. TIMOTHY
HALL
Died with the
Small Pox July
1771
in the 50th Year
of his Age

Tombstone of Timothy Hall (1777).

While Mr. Hall's tombstone is the only engraved marker, seven small flat fieldstones set upright in rows, some only inches above ground and partially covered by vegetation and fallen leaves, denote additional burials. Records indicate that thirty-one people were buried at the Durham Pest House, though the great majority received no grave markers whatsoever. The Pest House served Durham until 1792 when inoculation became acceptable and available.

Farther along the Mattabesett (Blue) Trail is the "Selectmen's Stones" marking the tri-town boundary for Durham, Guilford, and Madison. Today official town and state boundaries are surveyed and marked by granite columns with Geodetic Survey plates. Historically, New England town boundaries were designated by natural or stone-built indicators, such as stone walls, glacial erratic, or an outcropping of bedrock. Dates and town initials were often carved to denote surveys.

In Connecticut, town selectmen were responsible for surveying and inspecting their respective municipal boundaries every ten years. When three towns shared a survey point, it was especially important to provide a stone field designation when no natural feature was available at the junction. Stone piles attested that the selectmen did their job, but also that the survey results were accurate and agreed upon by the other towns. "Selectmen's Stones" on the Mattabesett Trail are relatively small, irregular, and rising about knee high. The last placed stone dates to 1904.

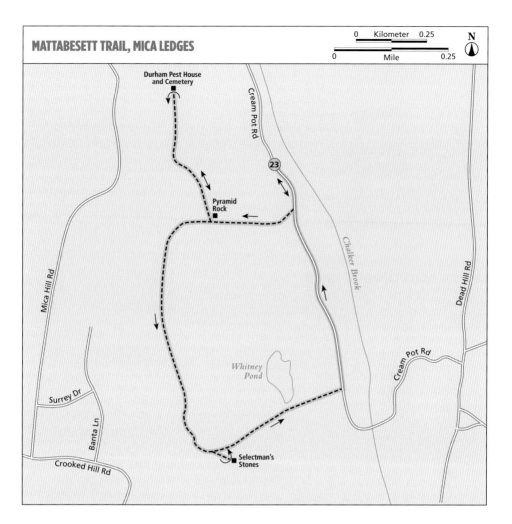

0   Kilometer   0.25

0   Mile   0.25

N

Durham Pest House
and Cemetery

Cream Pot Rd

23

Pyramid
Rock

Chalker Brook

Mica Hill Rd

Dead Hill Rd

Cream Pot Rd

Whitney
Pond

Surrey Dr

Banta Ln

Selectman's
Stones

Crooked Hill Rd

THE HIKE

Start on the Blue-Yellow Trail, a continuation of Cream Pot Road, sometimes called "Selectmen's Path," as it was used by the town's first selectman to mark boundaries between Durham, Guilford, and Madison farther to the south.

Merge onto the Mattabesett (Blue) Trail and follow signs leading to "Pyramid Rock." There you will find the intersection with the Mica Ledge (Red) Trail and an interactive map to get your bearings. Pyramid Rock is not a human-made stone ruin, but a deposit from the last glaciation (c. 18,000–15,000 years ago) having a pyramid shape.

After exploring the vicinity of Pyramid Rock, look for an unmarked path across from the "Rock." This leads north to the Pest House Ruins one-third of a mile to the north. The path, which at times is hard to follow, bears to the left along a ridge, down a swale and old logging road. The Pest House is in a lightly wooded area between a basalt ridge and wetland (GPS: 41.4454608, -72.6806076).

A partial cellar hole with surrounding foundation and the well are downslope by the wetland. Two chimneys straddle both sides of the cellar hole. Continue northward to the burying ground (GPS: 41.44599406, -72.6808128). The tombstone of Timothy Hall is the only engraved stone, but close ground inspection will locate upright fieldstones (only inches above the surface) that mark burials of unrecorded smallpox victims. Retrace your steps back to the Blue Trail.

Back at Pyramid Rock, continue right on the Blue Trail. This portion of the trail becomes hilly, stony, and at times moderate in difficulty leading south to the Selectmen's Stones. Along the way you will be rewarded with scenic views of the valley.

As you approach the Selectmen's Stones ruin, pass the intersection of the Yellow Trail on your left. Stay on the Blue Trail for a short distance to reach the Selectmen's Stones. Retrace your steps back to the Yellow Trail intersection, and turn right.

The Yellow Trail will loop you back to the Blue–Yellow Trail and your trailhead, passing the Mica Ledge (Red) Trail intersection and Whitney Pond.

MILES AND DIRECTIONS

0.0 Park at the end of Cream Pot Road (Blue-Yellow Trail). No trailhead kiosk.

0.28 Intersection with Mattabesett New England (Blue) Trail. Merge right onto Blue Trail toward Pyramid Rock.

0.38 Intersection with Mica Ledges (Red) Trail (J1). Stay straight on Blue Trail.

0.56 Reach Pyramid Rock with interactive map. Explore this large glacial erratic. Take unmarked trail on right for Pest House Ruins.

0.89 Reach Pest House and burying ground. Explore.

1.22 Return to Pyramid Rock. Turn right onto Blue Trail.

1.88 Reach scenic overview.

2.14 Intersection with Yellow Trail (J4). Stay on Blue Trail for a short distance to the Selectmen's Stones. There is an interactive map at this intersection.

2.18 Reach Selectmen's Stones. Retrace your steps back to Yellow Trail intersection (J4).

2.22 Return to Yellow Trail intersection; turn right.

2.41 Intersection with Red Trail (J3) with interpretive map. Continue straight on Yellow Trail.

2.49 Cross brook with Whitney Pond on your left.

2.93 Staying on Yellow Trail, path turns left onto a dirt access road (Whitney Road) north.

3.13 Reach the intersection of Cream Pot Road, which diverts to your right and Whitney Road (J2). Continue through vehicle gates northbound (Cream Pot Road) on Yellow Trail.

3.23 Intersection with Blue Trail, completing loop. Stay straight on the Blue-Yellow Trail to the parking area.

3.51 Arrive back at the parking area.

24 MATTABESETT TRAIL, MOUNT HIGBY

There are not only wonderful west-facing vistas on Mount Higby's traprock ridges, but the chance to discover a 1954 airplane crash site and a cave once occupied by the legendary Old Leatherman. We will guide you off trail to see these historical features, but they are well worth the excursion.

Start: John J. Tynan Trailhead, Higby Road, Middlefield, CT
Distance: 5.20 miles out-and-back
Hiking time: About 3 hours
Difficulty: Moderate
Trail surface: Dirt, stone
Seasons: Best in late fall/early spring
Other trail users: None
Canine compatibility: Under control
Land status: Connecticut Forest and Park Association

Nearest town: Middlefield, CT
Fees and permits: None required.
Schedule: Year-round
Maps: USGS Middletown, CT, Quadrangle
Trail contact: Connecticut Forest and Park Association, 16 Meriden Rd., Rockfall, CT 06481; (860) 346-8733; www.ctwoodlands.org

FINDING THE TRAILHEAD

There are three trailheads from which to enter Mount Higby: CT 66, Country Club Road, and the John J. Tyan entrance at 199 Higby Road. We recommend the latter trailhead for a full experience on Mount Higby. From I-91 northbound, take exit 18 to CT 66 East for approximately 3 miles. Turn left on Higby Road for 0.6 miles. The entrance to the Tynan Park Trailhead is on your left. Southbound on I-91, take exit 20, Country Club Road. Turn left onto Middle Street, then left again onto Country Club Road and proceed uphill. Turn right on Higby Road and Tynan Park will be on your right. **GPS:** 41.554236, -72.713175

THE HISTORY AND RUINS

The hiker will encounter one stone ruin along this trail, but what makes this a unique experience is the opportunity to see an intact aviation archaeological site and, within a short distance from the plane crash site, an encampment of the legendary Old Leatherman.

In 1954, over 60 airplanes, including Coast Guard and Civil Air Patrol fliers, searched for the missing twin-engine silver Beechcraft that was 36 hours overdue at Bradley Field, Windsor Locks, CT. The Beechcraft had begun its flight at LaGuardia Field two days earlier.

Onboard were the pilot, Donald Goodridge, of Hamburg, NY, and a married couple, Mr. and Mrs. William W. Campbell of Lockport, NY, who were planning to visit friends in Chester, CT, that weekend. The Connecticut State Police set 6:10 pm, Friday, October 31, 1954, as the crash time based on a watch found near the wreckage.

The airplane was flying in hard-driving rain with poor visibility, heading west, several miles off course, when it struck Mount Higby in Middlefield, CT. The plane almost made the ascent over the basalt ridge, clipping the tops of three oak trees before bursting into flames, burning the three bodies beyond recognition (*Hartford Courant*, 1954).

Then, it happened again. A single-engine Cessna Skylark 172, flying low in fog crashed into the same ledge 40 feet from the summit of Mount Higby, in August 1966. Slamming into the mountainside, the plane landed nose down against a tree. There were two fatalities: the pilot, Richard C. Grimaldi, and John T. Emmanuel, both in their 30s, returning from a weekend with friends on Martha's Vineyard and Block Island (*Hartford Courant*, 1966).

The hiker will pass remnants of the earlier Beechcraft 1954 disaster. The distribution of the metal debris laying on the ground surface includes gears, wheel supports, engine parts, and aluminum sheeting. The distribution of wreckage debris provides the aviation archaeologist with a means to reconstruct the flight's direction, impact, and speed of the crash. It is important not to touch, move, or take any of the plane's remnants. Please be respectful as this is a memorial site to the three people who lost their lives.

To the immediate north of the aviation site is a basalt overhang that legend has it was occupied by the Old Leatherman, one of the celebrated personalities in eastern New York and western Connecticut history. No one knows his identity. What we do know is that he started trekking through the northeast beginning in 1858, continuing until his death in 1889. He walked country roads and railroad tracks and, commencing in 1883, settled into a "clockwise circuit" inland from the Hudson River to the Connecticut River, down to the coast and back to the Hudson. It was a 365-mile loop that the Old Leatherman completed punctually every 34-or-so days like clockwork, averaging 10 miles per day. So precise was the Old Leatherman that people kept diaries of his appearances, predicting exactly when he would return to their town a month later. The Old Leatherman never spoke to anyone, avoided all contact with people, and never hurt or bothered anyone; he just kept walking.

Probably the most distinguishing characteristic of this unusual man was his "uniform," which gave rise to his name. He dressed himself entirely with patches made from the tops of discarded leather shoes. He wore a long, leather coat with pockets inside and out, a leather cap with visor, and carried a leather backpack slung over his shoulder on a stick. He was the "Leatherman." A wooden staff and a crudely made copper smoking pipe completed his outfit.

The Old Leatherman slept under lean-to rock shelters, toppled boulders, and constructed makeshift huts. He usually spaced his encampments 10 miles apart and always near freshwater sources. Where he had one shelter, another was never far away in case there was an unexpected problem.

On Mount Higby, very close to the 1954 Beechcraft plane crash, is a small overhang of bedrock that was occupied by the Old Leatherman on his circuit through the Meriden area. In a way, there is not much to see, no ruins or built stone structure, but what a great place to tell the Old Leatherman story and imagine the lean-to of wooden branches against the stone wall crafting living space underneath and visualizing the garden he tended on the slope below the "cave."

THE HIKE

The hike from Tynan Park (Blue-Red Trail) starts off relatively easy at the southwest corner of an open field behind the trailhead. Hike downhill from the parking lot through flat wetlands associated with Cross Fall Brook. A little after a quarter of a mile into your hike, you will cross a stream and on the far side to the left look for a small stone

Top: Natural basalt "bridge" at Mount Higby.
Bottom: Old Leatherman Cave on Mount Higby.

Wreckage of 1954 Beechcraft plane crash.

foundation. This unidentified stone ruin is most likely the remnant of a farm structure built into the side of the terrace hill. Note that it has a cellar hole and may have been a temporary dwelling.

Just shy of a mile, you will come to the intersection of the Blue Trail. Turn left onto the Blue Trail and start a moderate hike up to Mount Higby. Follow the Blue Trail to the summit. Since you will be approaching from the east, the terrain is not as steep as the south- and west-facing cliffs. However, do watch out for broken up traprock and loose stones on the ground. Also, don't be confused by yellow markings; they designate private property boundaries close to the trail. Be sure to remain on the trail and following the blue markers to the peak.

When you reach the top of the basalt ridge, stay alert as the trail at times comes close to the cliff edge. Enjoy the wonderful vistas you will see along the way.

Along the ridge, you will come to an outcropping of basalt on your right (cliffside) that forms an arch through the rock—sometimes referred to as the "Natural Bridge" (GPS: 41.551822, -72.739103). This is your gauge for turning left off the trail downslope to the plane crash site. There is no marked trail to guide you, but hike downhill along a swale between small basalt exposures. The grass is relatively short but there are a lot of fallen tree branches, so be careful and loop toward the northeast. When you reach a lower terrace, the area opens to another swale on your left. Follow and it will lead directly to the crash site (GPS: 41.5510335, -72.7389067).

Spend some time searching for the various airplane parts and notice their distribution across the landscape. Can you reconstruct the path of the plane into the mountainside? And remember, please do not touch, take, or move any of the plane parts. We have noticed from earlier hikes that people have taken pieces of wreckage. This is very unfortunate and disrespectful. Please don't be one of them.

After exploring the crash site, continue downslope following a basalt outcropping on your left. At the end of the exposure, find a small stone campfire circle, then turn left and hike downslope to the face of the outcropping. Again, there is no trail or path; make a U-turn below the rock face, go uphill a slight distance, and the Old Leatherman Cave will be on your left (GPS: 41.5518223, -72.7391029). The "cave" is really a basalt outcropping where the rock has eroded at the base of the exposure.

Retrace your steps back to the plane crash site and up the swale toward the arched stone "Natural Bridge" on the Blue Trail. Turn right and retrace your steps back to Tynan Park and the trailhead.

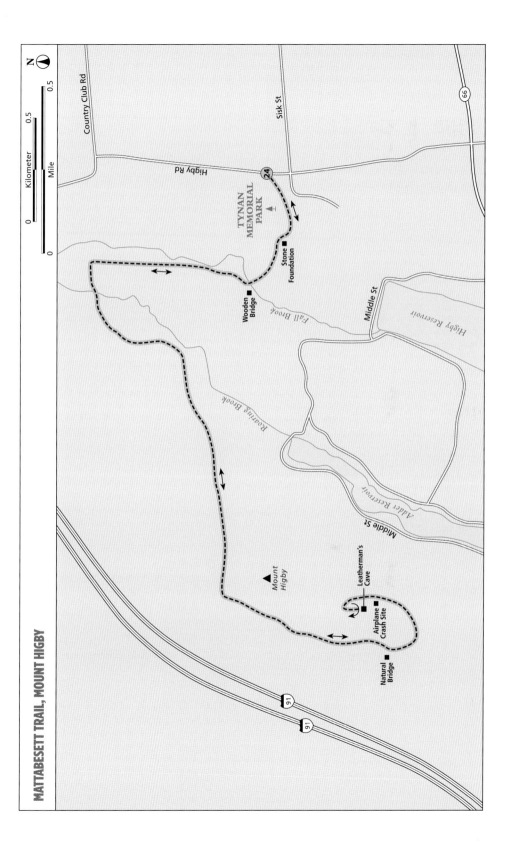

MATTABESETT TRAIL, MOUNT HIGBY

MILES AND DIRECTIONS

0.0 Begin at the Tynan Park Trailhead. Hike through the grassy open area diagonally toward the southwest (your left) and follow the Blue-Red Trail.

0.25 Cross over wooden planks through muddy area.

0.30 Cross small brook.

0.32 Stone foundation on left built into the slope.

0.48 Cross wooden bridge at Fall Brook.

0.62 Bear right at intersection, continuing the Blue-Red Trail. Barbwire fencing will appear along the right side of the trail.

0.84 Intersection of the Blue Trail. Turn left and follow west to the summit of Mount Higby. Yellow markers designate bordering private property, so please stay on the trail.

1.10 Bear right, staying on the Blue Trail.

1.85 Bear left going uphill, again staying on the Blue Trail.

1.93 Basalt stone pile on your right.

2.05 Bear left along the edge of the basalt ridge. Be careful as the trail comes close to the cliff edge in some spots.

2.33 Basalt archway—"Natural Bridge"—on your right (GPS: 41.551822, -72.739103). Turn left, off the trail, and continue downslope through a narrow swale between outcroppings in a northeasterly direction.

2.43 Turn left (north) on a lower terrace through another swale and the airplane crash site will be in front of you.

2.47 Arrive at the crash site. Explore for pieces of wreckage, part of the debris field (GPS: 41.5510335, -72.7389067). After exploring the crash site, continue downslope in the same direction. Note the outcropping of basalt on your left and follow the ridge until it ends. Turn left at a small stone campfire circle and proceed downslope to view the rock outcropping from below. Remember, there is no trail here, so be careful with your footing as you proceed down the short hill. Turn left again, making a U-turn upslope.

2.54 Old Leatherman's Cave will be on your left (GPS: 41.5518223, -72.7391029). Retrace your steps back to the plane crash site, then upslope back to the basalt arch bridge and the Blue Trail. Turn right on the Blue Trail returning to Tynan Park.

3.35 Be sure to turn left, uphill continuing on the Blue Trail.

5.20 Arrive back at the Tynan Park Trailhead and parking lot.

25 BLUFF POINT STATE PARK TRAILS

Bluff Point State Park offers hiking, bicycling, horseback riding, and beaches. However, few recreationalists are familiar with a significant part of the park's history that includes Native American settlement, the 1712 Winthrop House, a 19th-century railroad depot, and an early 20th-century cottage community swept away in the 1938 hurricane.

Start: Trailhead at the southern end of parking lot
Distance: 3.45-mile loop
Hiking time: About 2.5 hours
Difficulty: Easy
Trail surface: Dirt roadbed
Seasons: All seasons
Other trail users: Bikes, horses
Canine compatibility: On leash
Land status: State of Connecticut Park

Nearest town: Groton, CT
Fees and permits: None
Schedule: Year-round
Maps: USGS New London, CT, Quadrangle
Trail contact: Department of Energy and Environmental Protection, Parks Division, 79 Elm St., Hartford, CT 06106; (860) 424-3000

FINDING THE TRAILHEAD

Take exit 88 off I-95. Southbound turn left; northbound turn right and travel 1 mile to the Route 1 intersection. Turn right on Route 1, then at 0.2 miles turn left on Depot Road. At 0.3 miles bear right and pass under a bridge into the state park. Roadbed turns to dirt/gravel with the Poquonnock River on your right. Trailhead is at the southern end of parking lot. **GPS:** 41.335452, -72.033081

THE HISTORY AND RUINS

They referred to him as "the Younger," the eldest son and namesake of his father Jonathan Winthrop, Governor of the Massachusetts Bay Colony, who inspired the concept of a "City on a Hill" providing Puritans with their providential vision of New England. The eclectic Winthrop the Younger became governor of the Connecticut Colony, establishing a family dynasty that defined Puritan convention.

Following the Pequot War (1636–37), tribal land was colonized by the English and claimed by Right of Conquest. John Winthrop the Younger was provided with land grants to Fishers Island and the mouth of the Thames River ("Nameaug"), which would become the city of New London. He was also granted permission by colonial authorities to develop a farming plantation on former Pequot homeland. The colonists called it "Winthrop's Neck," and it consisted of coastal regions including today's Bluff Point, Mumford Cove, and Groton Long Point.

Tribal oral traditions and archaeological sites at Bluff Point testify to the utilization of coastal resources by Native Americans for thousands of years. The countryside of Winthrop's Neck provided subsistence needs as well as valuable shellfish beds for the manufacturing of wampum, which was transformed from its spiritual role into articles of trade between Europeans and other Native American tribes.

Jonathan Winthrop House foundation.

The Winthrop family never lived on Bluff Point but leased the property to tenant farmers, including Edward Yeomans, who in c. 1712 constructed a large colonial saltbox house on the summit of the hill. The Winthrop family continued to own the land until 1818. The 18th-century residence built by Yeomans would stand until 1962 when it was destroyed by fire, leaving only its stone foundation.

Transportation advances during the Industrial Revolution by the mid-19th century included the transition from water canals to railroads as the most effective means of carrying freight and passengers. The economic necessity of connecting New York City and Boston via rail became readily apparent to businessmen and travelers. As railroad lines flourished into the late 1800s, consolidation of independent railroad companies rendered Groton's Bluff Point an important "midway" locale between the two major metropolises.

In its heyday, Midway Railroad Depot contained over 20 miles of track providing space for seventy complete forty-car freight trains and a large roundhouse with twenty stalls to reconnect locomotives to differing train routes. This essential railroad intersection survived into the 1920s. Today the roundhouse and other facilities are to the east of the Bluff Point State Park parking area and, unfortunately, overgrown with vegetation and inaccessible to the public. Nonetheless, the historical significance of the Midway Depot was acknowledged by its entry into the National Register of Historical Places and as a Connecticut State Archaeological Preserve.

Bluff Point passed in ownership to Henry Gardiner in 1858 and was known as "Gardiner's Point." The Gardiners rented the farm to John Ackley in 1907, who made his living pasturing livestock and planting potatoes. Recognizing the potential of the land beyond farming, Ackley subleased parcels along the high coastal bluff to summer campers, who flocked to the beautiful seaside. By the 1930s, over one hundred summer cottages lined the bluff. This campers' paradise was, unfortunately, short-lived. In one catastrophic storm, the Hurricane of 1938, the cottages were leveled, never to be rebuilt. All that remains are stone footings and walkways where the cottages once stood. The well-built colonial Winthrop House was the only surviving structure on the "Point."

During this cottage period, the name "Bluff Point" came into usage. In 1963, the state of Connecticut acquired 246.6 acres of this coastal peninsula, followed a decade later by federal matching funds for another 530 acres. Today, Bluff Point is preserved not only for year-round recreation, but also as a "Coastal Reserve and Natural Area Preserve," where ecologists and biologists can study marine resources within this fragile ecosystem.

THE HIKE

From the trailhead kiosk at the southern end of the parking area, follow the treelined roadbed which runs along the east side of the Poquonnock River. There are numbered trails with alphabetic markers that provide specific locations in case of an emergency. The trail system is well thought-out, maintained, and accessible.

The first fork in the road is marked signpost #1. Bear left, uphill into the interior of the Point to the Jonathan Winthrop House foundation a mile up the trail. Keep a look out for stone walls as you approach the old farmhouse ruins.

The Jonathan Winthrop House is clearly marked with kiosks providing the history of the families and occupants of the structure. Historical photographs aid in your mind's-eye

Stone enclosure at low tide.

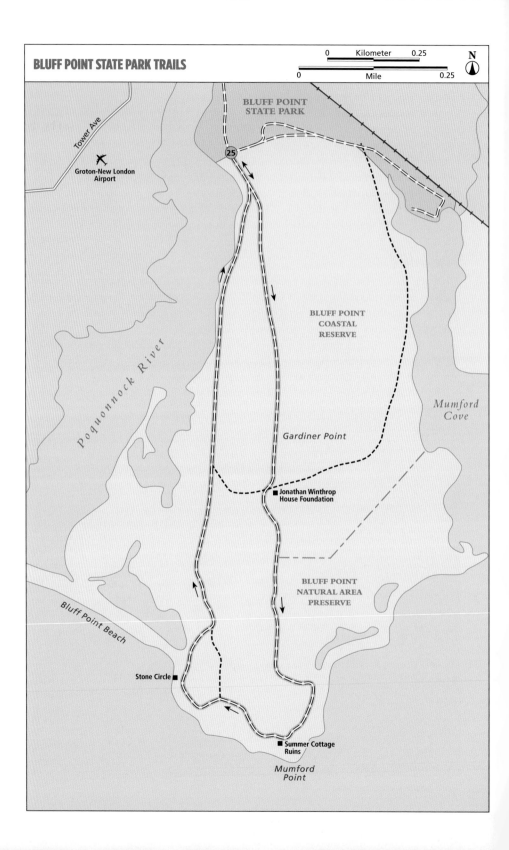

BLUFF POINT STATE PARK TRAILS

0   Kilometer   0.25

0   Mile   0.25

N

BLUFF POINT
STATE PARK

Tower Ave

Groton-New London
Airport

25

BLUFF POINT
COASTAL
RESERVE

Poquonnock River

Gardiner Point

Mumford
Cove

Jonathan Winthrop
House Foundation

BLUFF POINT
NATURAL AREA
PRESERVE

Bluff Point Beach

Stone Circle

Summer Cottage
Ruins

Mumford
Point

reconstruction of the 18th-century house. Walk around the stone foundation, noting the chimney stack, stairway into the cellar, and later extensions to the original residence. Based on the stone ruins, can you determine where the front door was located? Kitchen? The evidence lies on the ground.

Continue down the trail to your right as you face the house ruin then merge left around a bend. The glacial erratic set back in the woods, Sunset Rock, was used by the cottagers to view beautiful sunset vistas and hold Sunday services.

The trail bends to the left and then circles around to the right nearing the coastline. Take a small, nondescript path on your left and walk to the bluff overlooking Long Island Sound. The vegetation will not be helpful in your search, but this is where the seasonal cottages were located. Carefully inspect the ground for stone walkways and footings—all that is left of the cottages destroyed in the Hurricane of 1938.

Continue around the point to a kiosk with trail map providing orientation. Downslope from the kiosk is a walkway to the beach on your left. Feel free to spread a blanket and enjoy. Notice the "stone corral" in the water. We are unsure of its origin but have fun speculating.

Return to the trail and turn left. As you hike with the river to your left, look for kiosks providing information on coastal resources and Native American adaptations.

Continue and return to the trailhead and parking area.

MILES AND DIRECTIONS

0.0 Begin at the trailhead at the southern end of the parking lot.

0.10 Trail forks (Signpost #1). Take the left, inland trail uphill.

0.53 Wooden bench on left marked "E." (Alphabetic markers on trails are for emergency purposes.)

0.54 Stone walls on your left.

0.63 Cut stone on right of the trail.

0.94 Reach the Jonathan Winthrop House foundation. Explore. Continue as trail bends to the right.

0.97 Be sure to bear left staying on main trail.

1.18 Wooden bench "D."

1.45 Sunset Rock.

1.68 Wooden bench "C."

1.82 Take small path on left toward the water overlook. This is where the cottages were before being destroyed by the hurricane.

1.90 Return to main trail, turn left and continue.

1.97 Arrive at signboard and map. Take path to the water overview, returning to main trail.

2.00 Take pathway to the beach area (#10). Note the "stone corral" on the water. Return to main trail turning left.

2.92 Coastal Resources kiosk. Blue Heritage Trail.

3.35 Reach #1 signpost, completing loop from the 0.1-mile mark.

3.45 Arrive back at the trailhead and parking lot.

26 COOGAN FARM TRAIL

This short trek is a must-see stone ruin. While you can visit standing Gilded Age mansions, most famously in Newport, RI, you will rarely have opportunity to view the stone and brick foundation and cellar shells of what would have been a grand forty-nine-room stately mansion overlooking the Mystic River.

Start: Coogan Farm, CT 27, Mystic, Connecticut
Distance: 0.94 miles out-and-back
Hiking time: About 30 minutes round-trip
Difficulty: Easy
Trail surface: Dirt, farm road
Seasons: All seasons
Other trail users: Hikers
Canine compatibility: On leash

Land status: Denison Pequotsepos/ Coogan Farm Nature and Heritage Center
Nearest town: Mystic, CT
Fees and permits: None
Schedule: Year-round
Maps: USGS Mystic, CT, Quadrangle
Trail contact: Denison Pequotsepos/ Coogan Farm Nature and Heritage Center, 109 Pequotsepos Rd., Mystic, CT 06355; (860) 536-1216

FINDING THE TRAILHEAD

From I-95, take exit 90 and proceed south on CT 27 (Germanville Avenue) toward Mystic Seaport. Coogan Farm entrance will be less than 1 mile on your left, opposite Elm Grove Cemetery. **GPS:** 41.367192, -71.961511

THE HISTORY AND RUINS

Human occupation of the Coogan Farm site extends back into the Pre-Contact Period, evidenced by Native American stone projectile points recovered from the farm's cultivated fields. Coogan represents the first Colonial Era farm on the east side of the Mystic River, dating to the 17th century when Captain John Gallup received a 500-acre land grant from Governor Jonathan Winthrop Jr. as payment for Gallup's participation in the Pequot War. For more than 350 years, many farming families worked the stony hillside cultivating crops, tending orchards, and pasturing domestic cattle.

Clara Avery Morgan inherited the farm from her father and when she married Clarence A. Coogan in 1918, the property became known as the "Village Farm," which remained in the family until 2013. Coogan maintained a butcher shop selling meat and dairy products to the local community. The farmhouse still stands and is an educational welcoming center. All that remains of the barn is the stone foundation.

Prior to the Morgan/Coogan ownership, Elizabeth (called Charlotte) Greenman Stillman purchased the land in 1888 to build a summer home for her and her husband, Thomas Edgar Stillman, a New York City lawyer. This transpired in the era Mark Twain would describe as "The Gilded Age," where wealthy business elites (sometimes derogatorily referred to as "Robber Barons") built large coastal mansions to escape New York City's stifling summer heat waves.

Architect William B. Bigelow was hired to design a forty-nine-room mansion commanding views overlooking the town of Mystic, its waterfront and river. Construction started by digging the cellar and laying foundation stones. However, due to financial

Barn foundation at Coogan Farm.

constraints, construction ceased in 1894 before the superstructure was in place. The tragic deaths of both Elizabeth in 1901 and Thomas five years later left the mansion unfinished with only the foundation ruins at the top of the hill left standing.

Stillman's daughter, Mary Emma, married Edward Harkness and together they built their own summer mansion Eolia, which visitors can tour at Harkness Memorial State Park in Waterford, CT. In honor of her parents, Mary funded the construction of the Greenman Chapel at Elm Grove Cemetery across from her parents' mansion ruins.

THE HIKE

The trail starts at the farmhouse and ruins of the stone barn foundation. Behind the trailhead kiosk, descend stone steps to the barn foundation. The barn superstructure was dismantled in the 1930s but the ruins remain as the centerpiece of the historic farm complex.

There were two entrances: the lower open side of the foundation leads into the lower-level area where farm animals could enter. The second floor, above the foundation, is where hay and wagons were stored.

Leave the barn foundation to your right and continue along a dirt farm road on the Blue Trail toward the back of the property. At the T-intersection, turn left on the Red Trail and follow until the road bends sharply to the right. As it does, you will be facing a high stone wall animal enclosure.

The Connecticut Natural Resources Conservation Service (NRCS), Department of Agriculture, conducted ground-penetrating radar surveys to determine if any structures were built within the large stone enclosure. The radar study proved negative suggesting the enclosure was primarily used to pen animals.

Immediately upslope from the stone enclosure is the Hamm Pavilion. Though not historic, it is a pleasant area to relax and have lunch.

Take the time to pass through the open barway uphill on the right entering an enclosed field where picnic tables are also available and offers a wonderful view of the Mystic River. A kiosk tells of the "Peace Sanctuary" on Great Hill in Groton, which can be seen

Top: Stone stairway into the lower level of Coogan Barn.
Bottom: Brick and stone cellar of the Stillman Mansion.

COOGAN FARM TRAIL

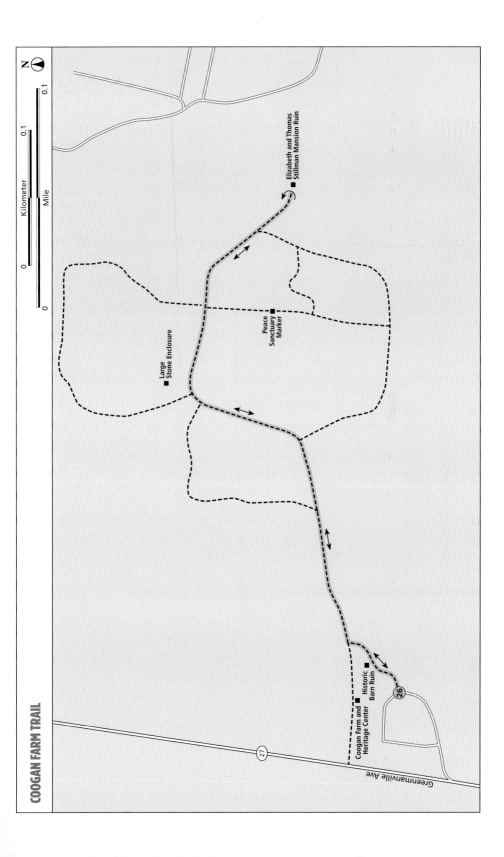

Kilometer
0   0.1   0.1

Mile
0   0.1

N

Large
Stone Enclosure ■

Peace
Sanctuary
Marker ■

Elizabeth and Thomas
Stillman Mansion Ruin ■

Coogan Farm and
Heritage Center ■

Historic
Barn Ruin ■

26

27

Greenmanville Ave

Elizabeth and Thomas Stillman Mansion stone foundation.

across the river to the west, where abolitionists, reformers, and suffragettes from all over the world attended peace gatherings in the wake of the turbulent years of the Civil War.

Continue uphill on the Red Trail for a short distance. The trail bends left leading to an open clearing and the stone and brick ruins of the Stillman mansion.

Learn more about the Stillman family and their unfinished mansion at the kiosk. Walk along the right (south) side to the back of the ruins where stone stairs descend into the cellar. Enter and view the well-built foundation from the interior. Brick archways would have held Stillman's wine collection. Notice the beautifully carved and mortared granite used to support the intended mansion and the fancy stone arches for the cellar windows. Take pictures, as you will never see the stone ruins of a Gilded Age mansion open to the public. Enjoy.

For a longer hike, continue the Red Trail reconnecting with the Blue Trail to the Denison Homestead. Otherwise, retrace your steps back to the trailhead.

MILES AND DIRECTIONS

0.0 Begin at the trailhead on the east side of the parking lot. Start on the Blue Trail.

0.1 Ruins of historical barn structure immediately behind the trailhead.

0.18 Trail splits. Turn left and join the Red Stillman Trail.

0.21 Stone enclosure. Road bends to the right; proceed uphill.

0.27 Enter through barway opening on the right, leading into stone-wall enclosed pasture.

0.31 Signage for the "Peace Sanctuary"—return to barway and continue to your right uphill.

0.43 Stillman Mansion ruins.

0.94 Arrive back at the trailhead and parking lot.

27 NATCHAUG STATE FOREST TRAIL, NATHANIEL LYON

This hike encompasses farm and mill stone ruins of the Lyon family homestead. Amasa Lyon operated a sawmill on Beaverdam Brook and his son, Nathaniel Lyon, was the first Union officer killed during the Civil War. A truly historical hike through the lens of stone ruins.

Start: Nathaniel Lyon Memorial State Park, Kingsbury Road, Eastford, CT
Distance: 2.13 miles out-and-back
Hiking time: About 1.5 hours
Difficulty: Easy
Trail surface: Dirt
Seasons: All seasons
Other trail users: None
Canine compatibility: On leash
Land status: State of Connecticut

Nearest town: Eastford, CT
Fees and permits: None
Schedule: Year-round
Maps: USGS Hampton, CT, Quadrangle
Trail contact: Department of Energy and Environmental Protection, 79 Elm St., Hartford, CT 06106-5127; (860) 424-3000

FINDING THE TRAILHEAD

From US 44 in Eastford, travel south on CT 198. Take your first left onto General Lyon Road. After passing General Lyon Cemetery on your right, turn left on Pilfershire Road (0.3 miles) and proceed into Natchaug State Forest. Turn right on Kingsbury Road and within a quarter of a mile, turn right again into Nathaniel Lyon Memorial State Park. Pick up the Natchaug (Blue) Trail starting by the Lyon House chimney ruin. **GPS:** 41.847521, -72.082291

THE HISTORY AND RUINS

Nathaniel Lyon was born in the family home on July 14, 1819, when Phoenixville was still a part of Ashford, CT. The Lyon family farmed the land, but Amasa Lyon, Nathaniel's father, mainly ran a sawmill on Beaverdam Brook a mile south of the homestead. Young Nathaniel grew up tending to farm chores and attending local schools. A serious, studious, yet short-tempered lad, he impressed many in the local community, who recommended him to US Representative Orrin Holt for appointment to the United States Military Academy at West Point, New York, in 1837.

Nathaniel Lyon graduated from West Point, fought in the Mexican American and Seminole Wars, and served during "Bleeding Kansas" as that state agonized over the issue of slavery. Lyon also seized and secured the federal arsenal in St. Louis, Missouri, before armaments could be commandeered by Southern sympathizers, hence, keeping Missouri in the Union when the Civil War commenced. This latter achievement earned him the rank of general.

He was one of the best officers in the Union Army. Mounted atop his steed on August 10, 1861, during the Battle of Wilson's Creek (Missouri), rallying his Iowa troops forward into the overwhelming force of the Confederate Army, General Nathaniel Lyon received a mortal rifle wound to the chest. He was the first Union general to die in battle in the American Civil War. The entire nation mourned.

Chimney ruin at the Lyon homestead.

The special train carrying Nathaniel Lyon's mortal remains made ceremonial stops in St. Louis, Cincinnati, Pittsburgh, Philadelphia, Baltimore, and New York City before reaching Connecticut's capitol where the general laid overnight in the Senate Chamber. The next day, a 300-wagon procession brought the nation's hero home to his final resting place in the family plot at Old Phoenixville Burying Ground, less than a mile from his birthplace. There 20,000 people attended the funeral and solemn military burial.

The Lyon homestead was abandoned by the early 20th century falling into disrepair enough for the house to collapse within the cellar hole. The State of Connecticut acquired the land that included the Lyon farm and sawmill in 1917, calling it "Eastford Forest."

From 1933 to 1941, the forest served as the home of Camp Fernow, a Civilian Conservation Corps (CCC) post. One of the many improvements the CCC workers made within the forest was filling in the cellar hole of the Lyon farmhouse, restoring the fireplace/chimney stack, and creating the memorial park in honor of Nathaniel Lyon's birthplace.

THE HIKE

The Natchaug (Blue) Trail is a 17-mile stretch through three Connecticut towns and two state forests. This portion of the trail begins at General Lyon Memorial Park, and goes south to Beaverdam Brook and the stone ruins of the water-powered sawmill that was operated by Amasa Lyon.

Start at the fireplace ruins of the historic Lyon family house, which was a classic 18th-century New England saltbox. As you face the open hearth of the fireplace, hike to your left, past wooden fences and into the open field. On the far side of the field, pick up the Blue Trail marker into the woodlands. After crossing a brook, a stone wall will be in front of you and the trail bends left crossing Kingsbury Road.

The trail winds through forest running along the west side of the Beaverdam Marsh Area on your left and Kingsbury Road (unseen over the hill) on your right. A scatter of stone walls appears upslope on the right. Within a mile, the trail comes to an earthen dam, parking lot, and the outlet for Beaverdam Brook. While you can walk down the length of the dam to see the stone-lined sluice, you will want to enter the parking area and hike up the dirt drive connecting with Kingsbury Road, which at this point is a graded gravel bed.

Top: Stone complex at the Lyon homestead.
Bottom: Amasa Lyon's sawmill and trail bridge.

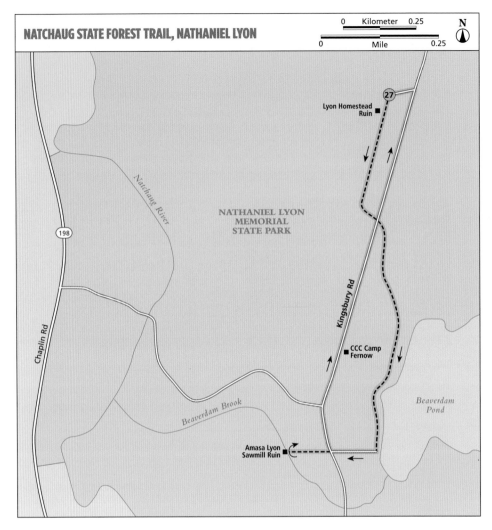

Cross Kingsbury Road following the Blue Trail marker. With another set of stone walls on the right, the trail descends to Beaverdam Brook and dissects the stone ruins of the Amasa Lyon sawmill via a wooden bridge offering an excellent view of the mill ruins. Be sure to cross the bridge and view the waterwheel well.

Retrace your steps back up the hill and return to Kingsbury Road. Instead of crossing over to the parking area, turn left on Kingsbury Road and follow it back to General Lyon Memorial Park.

On the way, you will pass the Natchaug Forest Ranger's Headquarters and former CCC Camp Fernow. There are standing CCC camp structures as well as foundation ruins on the ground. Signposts have historical information about Camp Fernow. Continue Kingsbury Road northbound back to General Lyon Memorial Park.

Amasa Lyon's sawmill along Beaverdam Brook.

MILES AND DIRECTIONS

0.0 Start at the General Lyon stone chimney memorial. Facing the open hearth, hike the open field on your left to the Blue Trail marker entering woodland.

0.17 Cross small brook.

0.29 Trail bends left.

0.31 Cross Kingsbury Road and pick up Blue Trail on far side.

0.55 Bench. Stone walls on the right; Beaverdam Marsh Area on the left.

0.86 Earthen dam and parking lot. Turn right and hike up dirt drive.

1.0 Reach Kingsbury Road (gravel). Cross picking up Blue Trail.

1.03 Stone walls appear on your right. Trail slopes downhill.

1.14 Reach stone sawmill ruin on Beaverdam Brook. Cross bridge and explore. Retrace your steps back uphill.

1.28 Return to Kingsbury Road; turn left.

1.49 CCC Camp Fernow.

2.13 Arrive back at the trailhead.

28 NATCHAUG STATE FOREST, ASHFORD WOODS

This out-and-back hike is not associated with a formal trail system but takes you along a historical gravel road in the state forest. There are a variety of stone ruins, including house foundations, a quarry, and burying grounds. What makes these stone features distinctive is that they represent a 19th-century African and Native American community, providing a rare glimpse of disenfranchised peoples often underrepresented in the historical record.

Start: Intersection of Pilfershire and Fayette Wright Roads, Natchaug State Forest, Eastford, CT
Distance: 3.01 miles out-and-back
Hiking time: About 2 hours
Difficulty: Easy
Trail surface: Dirt and gravel road
Seasons: All seasons
Other trail users: Motor vehicles
Canine compatibility: On leash

Land status: State of Connecticut Forest
Nearest town: Eastford, CT
Fees and permits: None
Schedule: Year-round
Maps: USGS Hampton, CT, Quadrangle
Trail contact: Department of Energy and Environmental Protection, 79 Elm St., Hartford, CT 06106-5127; (860) 424-3000

FINDING THE TRAILHEAD

From US 44 in Eastford, travel south on CT 198. Take your first left onto General Lyon Road. After passing General Lyon Cemetery on your right, turn left on Pilfershire Road and follow to the end. Park at the intersection of Pilfershire and Fayette Wright Road. Hike uphill to your left along Fayette Wright Road. **GPS:** 41.843767, -72.055311

THE HISTORY AND RUINS

The northeastern portion of Natchaug State Forest supported a diverse 19th-century community of related families sharing African American and Nipmuc Indian descent. The series of stone ruins along and off Fayette Wright Road have primarily been associated with the Lambert, Weeks, and Webster families in a settlement known as "Ashford Woods" (the area was formerly part of the town of Ashford) before being absorbed within today's state forest. This once active community, occupied by at least five families, has long been abandoned but stone ruins and historical research keep alive the compelling story of its inhabitants.

Extensive research into these families by local historian Donna Dufresne has demonstrated that the Websters and Lamberts were descendants of enslaved people on the Jonathan Randall farm in Pomfret, CT, originating through the marriage of Waity Brooks (Nipmuc/Narragansett) and Rueben Randall, born enslaved on the Randall estate in 1777. Family genealogy states that Websters were also members of the Nipmuc Tribe, an identity sustained in their daily lifestyles.

Left: Weeks family burying ground.
Right: Webster family house foundation.

Since people of color are usually underrepresented in New England historical accounts, Ms. Dufresne and other researchers have relied on existing genealogical records and descendant oral traditions, mending scantly available sources on the community. Local folklore suggests that Ashford Woods may have started as a Nipmuc settlement.

The Lambert and Webster families intermarried and eked out a hard living by farming, charcoal burning and quarrying. Based on its size and depth, the Cat Den Quarry was a notable economic enterprise situated across from the Weeks Cemetery and south of the Webster/Weeks family house, whose stone ruins are visible today.

Census, land records, and maps show that Chester Webster and William Bates purchased 16 acres of land in Ashford Woods in 1839. An 1868 census map places the William Bates house on the northeast side of the property with Chester Webster's house just to the southwest where cellar holes are visible. By 1880, Bates was still living at Ashford Woods, but the Webster family had moved to Pomfret.

The Weeks Family Burying Ground in Ashford Woods with its stone wall enclosure lies across the road from Cats Den Quarry. Joseph Weeks bought the quarry and surrounding land from John Griggs in 1809. Sylvester Weeks, who fought in the Civil War is buried here.

Although called the Lambert Cemetery, an unbounded burying ground on the northeast portion of the state forest is located on land that belonged to the Webster family. Here Websters and Lamberts are buried behind a stone wall. The graves remain

Tombstone of Charles Webster.

unmarked, though there are stone mounds in this area that may incorporate both African American and Native American burial traditions.

Today, the most prominent feature of Lambert Cemetery is the commemorative military tombstone for Civil War veteran Charles Webster, which reads:

Charles Webster
Co. H. 29th Regt.
Conn Vols.
Died June 17, 1864
AE 22

Charles volunteered for the Union Army in late 1863, mustering in Company H, 29th "Colored" Regiment on March 8, 1864. Sadly, Charles contracted typhus and pneumonia while bivouacking in New Haven awaiting orders to ship out. He was one of 152 soldiers from the 29th Regiment to die of health disorders. Records show that Charles was to be stationed in Hilton Head, South Carolina, with his regiment, but was too sick to travel. He was transferred to Knight Hospital in New Haven and given a military discharge on May 14, 1864. Ailing, Charles returned to his Eastford home, dying on June 17th.

The U.S. Army delivered Charles Webster's gravestone to Eastford after the war. Members of the Eastford Historical Society place an American flag by Charles Webster's grave in Natchaug Forest every Memorial Day.

THE HIKE

This is an easy out-and-back hike that will take you to several stone ruins associated with the Ashford Woods community. There is no formal trail system other than a gravel road currently maintained by state forest rangers and available to the public. However, you will be out in the far northeastern portion of the state forest, which experiences little foot or vehicular traffic.

Park along the side of the dirt road at the T-intersection of Pilfershire and Fayette Wright Roads and hike uphill traveling north. Within less than a quarter of a mile, observe a deep depression on your left, Cats Den Quarry, and the stone wall-lined Weeks family burying ground set back off the road on your right.

Explore the quarry and notice the stepped-back pattern to the granite bedrock. A series of drill holes chiseled for splitting the stone are evident in many places. For a small, family-run quarrying operation, a lot of granite was blocked and removed.

The Weeks Family Cemetery can be seen through the trees on your right, directly across from the quarry. Find a small path and follow to the graveyard. Note its bordering stone wall encircling the cemetery.

As you continue down this historical road, pay attention on the left immediately behind the quarry. Look for a ground depression that has been partially filled in with vegetation—the cellar hole to a large house site. Stonework behind was part of the farming complex.

There is an aboveground stone well on your right that was constructed by the Civilian Conservation Corps (CCC) in its improvement of the state forest in the 1930s. Stay on the main gravel road and continue northward.

After about a mile hike, you will be near a wetland below on the right. Directly opposite (on your left) before the roadway descends, will be a vehicle pull-off with a closed gate. Take the trail behind the gate and hike into the lightly wooded area with stone walls on the right.

Within a quarter mile, come to another trail (roadway) and turn right. At this junction you will see a stone-lined cellar hole. This house feature is associated with William Bates and Chester Webster who together purchased 16 acres of land there in 1839. The stone wall behind the house foundation nowadays serves as a property boundary, the other side of which is privately owned. However, walk to the stone wall and observe the military memorial marker to Charles Webster, Civil War African American/Nipmuc veteran.

Please appreciate that the memorial is on private property and remain on state land. While paying your respects to Charles Webster, take time to notice small stone mounds.

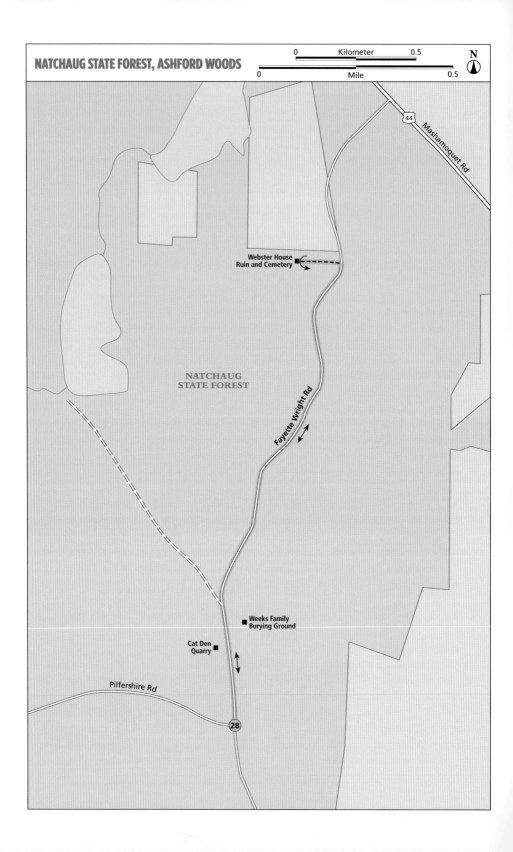

0   Kilometer   0.5

0   Mile   0.5

N

44   Mashamoquet Rd

Webster House
Ruin and Cemetery

NATCHAUG
STATE FOREST

Fayette Wright Rd

Weeks Family
Burying Ground

Cat Den
Quarry

Pilfershire Rd

28

Cat Den Quarry.

These may indicate the presence of a larger burying ground, incorporating Native American and African American traditions.

After exploring the stone ruins, retrace your steps to the gravel road, turn right, and return to the parking area at the road intersection.

MILES AND DIRECTIONS

0.0   Start at the T-intersection of Pilfershire and Fayette Wright Roads, hiking north.

0.2   Stepped-granite quarry on your left. Weeks Burying Ground will be on your right set back from road.

1.20   Take dirt trail on your left at pull-off with gate barring vehicle entrance.

1.27   Take trail bearing right leading to the house cellar hole.

1.31   Turn right onto small path along stone wall. Charles Webster's memorial tombstone is visible over stone wall. Beyond the stone wall is private property, so be respectful and remain on state property. Retrace your steps back to Fayette Wright Road.

1.54   Arrive at Fayette Wright Road. Turn right retracing your steps.

2.75   Return to quarry/burying ground.

3.01   Arrive back at the parking area.

29 TRI-STATE TRAIL

Two out-and-back hikes along the rails-to-trails Air Line Railroad. One trail leads to the site of the "Great Train Wreck of 1891"; the other to the Tri-State Marker where Connecticut, Rhode Island, and Massachusetts unite. And you get to visit the ruins of a high, arched stone culvert under the railroad causeway and a rare stone-buttressed cattle bridge—a lot of history in a 3-mile trek.

Start: Trailhead parking lot at 662 East Thompson Rd.
Distance: 3.20 miles out-and-back, then loop
Hiking time: About 2.5 hours
Difficulty: Easy with one steep climb
Trail surface: Dirt, stone
Seasons: All seasons
Other trail users: Horses, bikes
Canine compatibility: On leash

Land status: State of Connecticut
Nearest town: East Thompson, CT
Fees and permits: None
Schedule: Year-round
Maps: USGS Oxford, MA, Quadrangle
Trail contact: Connecticut Department of Energy and Environmental Protection, 79 Elm St., Hartford, CT 06106-5127; (860) 424-3000; www.portal.ct.gov

FINDING THE TRAILHEAD

From I-385 take exit 50 in Thompson, CT. Turn right onto CT 200 then left on Thompson Road (CT 193). Bear right at East Thompson Road past the Thompson Speedway Motorsports Park. Be sure to bear right once again when East Thompson Road veers from Sand Dam Road. Trailhead will be on your left at the intersection with New Road. **GPS:** 42.008736, -71.808880

THE HISTORY AND RUINS

Spur-of-the-moment decisions and rescheduling created a "perfect storm" for a four-train railroad disaster on the cold and foggy morning of December 4, 1891.

Engineer Joe Page on the Local Southbridge Freight train (Engine #31) was attaching cars that had previously been dropped off at the East Thompson, CT, depot for his scheduled route to Webster and Southbridge, MA. There were no westbound trains due that morning, so Page put the cars on the main track for fastening to the locomotive.

Meanwhile, the Long Island & Eastern States Express, a passenger train, pulled into the Putnam, CT, train station, requesting a different engine (#105) due to some mechanical problems. That morning the Putnam station had three trains scheduled heading for Boston and needed to get them out of the station quickly. The dispatcher developed a plan: Two of the trains would head out to Boston via Track #1 westbound and the third on Track #2 eastbound. The L.I. Express would go out over the eastbound track, while the heavier and slower Boston Freight (Engine #175) train would set out ahead of the faster passenger train on the westbound track.

In addition, the Norwich boat train (Engine #62) carrying seventy-five passengers was given clearance to leave for Boston by the Putnam dispatcher—who forgot that the Local Southbridge Freight train was still sitting on the westbound track in East Thompson, where all three trains were scheduled to pass.

Tri-state granite marker. CAROL AND LEE WEST

The Boston Freight reached East Thompson first, plunging head-on with the Local Southbridge Freight train, derailing cars on both sides of the track. Minutes later, the Long Island Express, trying to make up for lost time, came barreling into the station, running too fast to stop when the engineer discovered the pile-up ahead, plowing into the initial wreckage, derailing even more cars onto the tracks. Three minutes behind the L.I. train came the Norwich boat train, traveling 50 miles per hour and unable to stop in time, crashing into the rear of the third train, bursting into flames.

Cattle crossing on Tri-State Trail. CAROL AND LEE WEST

Remarkably, only three individuals died: Engineer Harry Taber, fireman Gerry Fitzgerald, both on the Long Island & Eastern States Express, and one of their passengers, R.H. Rath of New York, whose body was never found.

An interesting side story to the multiple train wreck concerns a fireman named Mike Flynn, who was supposed to be on the Long Island train. Supposedly, Flynn did not go to work that day, claiming he had a premonition of the disaster. He was replaced by the unfortunate Gerry Fitzgerald.

The scene of the "Great Wreck" is on the Air Line Railroad route, which was conceived as a more direct course between New York City and Boston. Opening in 1873, the Air Line diverged at the New Haven station and followed an interior, diagonal direction to Boston, cutting 25 miles off the trip, saving considerable time.

However, rivalries with other railroads led to bankruptcy, closing the Air Line in the 1970s. Today, the portion of the line from Portland, CT, to Franklin, MA, is a rails-to-trails path. The Connecticut section is known as the "Air Line Trail" and the Massachusetts portion as the "Southern New England Truckline Trail."

The Tri-State Marker also has an interesting history. Land surveyors from the three New England states long disagreed on where the three-state boundary point

Stone culvert under railroad tracks. CAROL AND LEE WEST

was located. But in 1883, Massachusetts and Rhode Island came to an agreement and erected a 4-foot-high granite pillar, pyramid-topped Tri-State Marker at their designated position.

When you hike to the Tri-State Marker, note that the Massachusetts and Rhode Island sides, north and south respectively, have an "1883" date etched on their faces, but the Connecticut (west-facing) side has no date. Evidently, Connecticut did not agree with the placement, and probably still doesn't!

THE HIKE

This trail is a two-part, out-and-back hike: 1) to the Great Train Wreck of 1891 and 2) to the Tri-State Marker.

Starting from the trailhead parking lot at the intersection of East Thompson and Day Roads, enter the Air Line Trail heading west, behind the kiosk. Within a quarter of a mile, the stone ruins of the train depot will appear on your right behind the "East Thompson" sign. The train crash site is just a few steps farther. It is well marked with a kiosk explaining where and how the disaster occurred.

While there is little evidence of the train crash today, kiosks along the trail assist you in reconstructing the events of that fateful December 1891 morning. There is evidence of a small roundhouse (turntable) on the right as you pass the intersection. Though the turntable is on private property, associated stone ruins are discernible from the trail.

After visiting the crash site, reverse your steps back to the trailhead. Continue eastward across East Thompson Road and upslope to a closed vehicle gate. Take a moment before you pass around the gate and look back toward the trailhead parking lot and imagine the trestle bridge that spanned the roads below. At the gate resume your hike eastward on the Air Line Trail for the second out-and-back loop.

The first stone ruin on this portion of the trail will be the abutments of a cattle bridge—a rare safety feature built by the railroad to provide local dairy farmers an egress transporting their herds safely over the tracks. Take a path on the right far side of the abutment and climb to the top to get a better view on how the cattle moved over the bridge. Do not, by any means, attempt to cross the bridge. It is fragile and would be dangerous and illegal to do so.

Once back down on the Airline Trail, turn right and continue. Note the changed topography, where the tracks are set high above a wetland system. This is a human-made causeway that was constructed to keep the grade of the railroad level. A lot of manpower and effort went into developing the mound you are hiking on.

The wetland below extends on both sides of the tracks. As a result, the railroad built a stone-arched culvert so water could pass unimpeded. You will see remnants of the culvert from below when you take the Culvert (White) Trail up ahead on the right.

Once on the Culvert Trail, be sure to bear to your right circling back downslope toward the culvert. As you hike, a large stone retaining wall is on the right supporting the causeway and railroad tracks. Divert off the White Trail to a small path on the right taking you to the edge of the wetland where you will have a wonderful view of the keystone arched stone culvert.

Return to the White Trail and bear right. This will take you on a loop and connect with the Blue Trail. Notice stone structures along the way. One appears to be a fireplace and may have been part of a small collier's hut where workers lived during the tree-cutting and charcoal burning seasons.

The terrain is relatively flat through this area but will become steeper as you approach the Blue Trail. Turn right on the Blue Trail, and then left upslope on a side path ascending the hill. The path is not listed as a color-marked trail. It is primarily stone covered and steep, but it takes you directly to the Tri-State Marker.

(Should you wish a less strenuous path to the Tri-State Marker, keep on the Airline Trail going past the Culvert Trail cutoff and take Tri-State Marker Loop Trail farther ahead.)

Catch your breath and enjoy the historic boundary, a 4-foot-high granite post with a pyramid-shaped top. The north aspect of the marker reads, "MASS 1883"; the south side, "R.I. 1883"; and the west face "CONN," without a date.

Take the trail to the left (north) of the state boundary marker heading back to the Airline Trail and hike parallel to the Massachusetts/Connecticut border. Before reaching the Airline Trail, stop at the Bi-State Marker, where Connecticut and Massachusetts share another boundary.

Turn left and head back to the trailhead and parking lot.

TRI-STATE TRAIL

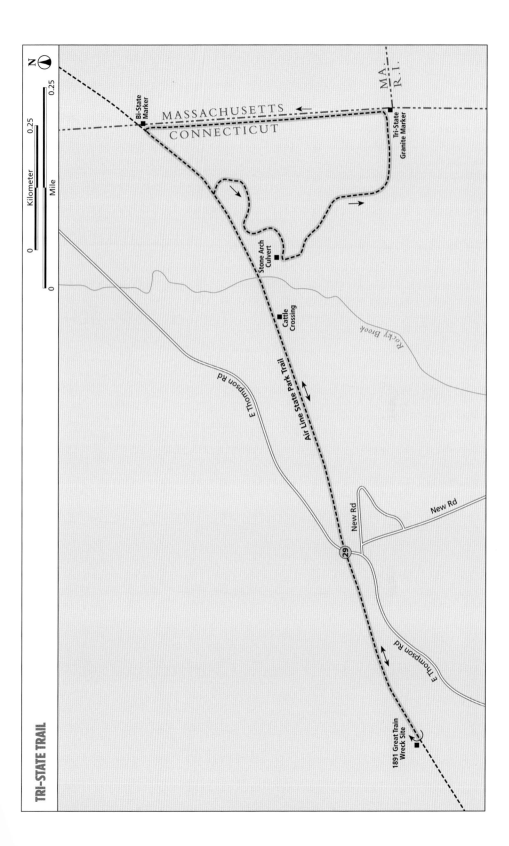

N

Kilometer
0   0.25   0.25

Mile
0   0.25

MASSACHUSETTS
CONNECTICUT

M.A.
R.I.

Bi-State Marker

Tri-State Granite Marker

Stone Arch Culvert

Cattle Crossing

Rocky Brook

E Thompson Rd

Air Line State Park Trail

New Rd

New Rd

29

E Thompson Rd

1891 Great Train Wreck Site

MILES AND DIRECTIONS

0.0 Start at the trailhead on East Thompson Road and head west.

0.22 Ruins of the East Thompson Train Depot on right behind "East Thompson" sign.

0.33 Ruins of roundhouse on right. See kiosk. You are standing at the site of the 1891 train wreck. Explore. Retrace your steps back to the trailhead.

0.66 Return to the trailhead. Cross East Thompson Road uphill to the vehicle barrier.

0.91 Reach cattle bridge with stone embankment supports.

0.96 Climb path on the right to observe the bridge from above. Do not go onto the bridge as it is very fragile.

1.11 Causeway leveling tracks over the valley below. You are walking on a human-made terrace.

1.28 Culvert (White) Trail on right. Take this trail loop.

1.32 Turn right again following "Culvert Trail."

1.45 Bear right on path to culvert and the "Great Wall," a retaining wall supporting the railroad causeway above.

1.48 Take small path on your right to view stone culvert from across the wetland. Return to Culvert Trail, bearing right.

1.57 Small fireplace on the right that may have been a collier's hut.

1.64 Intersection with Blue Trail. Turn right and follow downhill.

1.67 Cross the stone wall.

1.71 Trail bends. Turn left off the Blue Trail on a stony path uphill leading to the Tri-State Marker. Path is steep and not color marked.

1.83 Reach the Tri-State Marker. Turn to your left onto the blue-blazed Tri-State Trail starting downslope.

2.19 Reach the Bi-State Marker.

2.20 Reconnect with the railroad trail. Turn left toward the trailhead and parking lot.

3.20 Arrive back at the trailhead and parking lot.

MASSACHUSETTS

Becket Quarry, grout pile with "eyes" painted on granite blocks.

30 BECKET QUARRY TRAIL

One of the most fascinating historical/industrial archaeological hikes in New England. This abandoned quarry is a walk through a mining ghost town with stone and metal ruins still in their operational positions as if the quarrymen simply left at the end of the workday and never returned. You will love the woodland landscape and learn about quarry engineering by observing original and reconstructed machinery. Well-marked with excellent signboards.

Start: Trailhead on 456 Quarry Rd., Becket, MA
Distance: 1.96 miles out-and-back
Hiking time: About 1.5 hours
Difficulty: Easy
Trail surface: Dirt/gravel roadbed
Seasons: All
Other trail users: Hikers only
Canine compatibility: On leash
Land status: Becket Land Trust
Nearest town: Becket and Chester, MA

Fees and permits: $10 parking fee between Memorial Day and Labor Day
Schedule: Year-round
Maps: USGS Becket, MA, Quadrangle
Trail contact: Becket Land Trust, 4546 Quarry Rd., PO Box 44, Becket, MA 01223; www.landtrust@ BecketLandTrust.org; Historic Quarry Office, 12 Brooker Hill Rd., Becket, MA 01223; historicquarry@ BecketLandTrust.org

FINDING THE TRAILHEAD

From US 20 in Becket, MA, turn south onto Bonny Rigg Hill Road where MA 8 intersects. Follow to a four-way intersection turning left onto Quarry Road. The trailhead and parking area will be about a mile down the road on the right. Be sure to keep an eye out for posted signs as the entrance is around a bend in the road. **GPS:** 42.25119, -73.020249

THE HISTORY AND RUINS

Fine-grained, blue/gray-colored granite formed hundreds of millions of years ago in New England, hardening into bedrock. Due to its relatively light density, the granite materializes near land surface, then was scraped, scoured, and exposed by glacial ice advancing and receding tens of thousands of years ago. Bedrock in the township of Becket has exceptional quality granite, easily shaped and useful for various economic activities. To mine this valuable geological resource, the Chester-Hudson Quarry was launched in the 1850s. The quarry was responsible for an economic boom in the township of Becket.

The granite from Becket, famous throughout the region, was primarily used to make monuments, especially tombstones, into the mid-20th century. Carvers could chisel and sand the granite into various shapes and sizes, as well as engrave names, epitaphs, and commemoration of historic events. In the era when large family tombs and individual stone monuments were erected in New England cemeteries, the Chester-Hudson Quarry was a busy and profitable operation.

The quarry closed after World War II. Operational equipment, including derricks, winches, trucks, rail ties, cables, and pipes were abandoned in place with few attempts to

Top: Rusted (1940s) flat-bed quarry truck.
Bottom: Becket Quarry.

salvage equipment. Perhaps the owners anticipated reopening at a future date or planned to sell the apparatus lying about the site. Regardless, today the quarry serves as an outdoor museum of granite mining history.

Though officially closed in 1947, there were periodic attempts to reopen granite mining through the years. This led citizens of Becket to form the first Land Trust in Massachusetts (1991) with the goal of preserving forestland and the quarry's history. "Becket Quarry Trail" opened to the public in 2005 much to everyone's delight.

THE HIKE

The various trail systems of the Becket Land Trust property are separated into two areas: the Forest Preserve and the Historic Quarry. There are plenty of parking spaces, brochures, maps, and a self-guided historic quarry walk available at the trailhead kiosk. Historical features are clearly delineated by signposts and descriptions of equipment and technology.

Your exploration of the quarry starts at the parking area, where the remains of a Sullivan Drill (used to bore holes through granite for explosives to be planted) and a Downhaul Ball (used to take the slack out of the lift line) are located. The hike leading to the quarry begins behind the trailhead kiosk.

Journey upslope on the old quarry roadbed for about a half a mile. Grout piles of cut pieces of granite from the quarrying process line the trail. A large pile will appear on your right, then two smaller piles on your left as you approach the quarry.

Reaching the quarry finds a four-trail intersection with two rusted 1930–1940s trucks (#5) on your right and the Electrical Generator Shed (#7) on your left. Take the time to read the excellent signposts.

Make a V-turn at the trucks and walk a short distance to the Guy Derrick site (#6). Go to the end of the trail for a dramatic view of the water-filled quarry pit. Of course, when the quarry was in operation, the pit would have been dry with numerous workers cutting and shaping granite blocks for removal by the derricks, which lifted the stone out of the quarry pit for shaping and transport to markets. Step carefully as there are still cables and old pipes on the ground. Return to the four-trail intersection and the abandoned trucks.

Take the trail to your right circling the southern end of the quarry. You are hiking on an old rail grade. Granite blocks that were lifted from the quarry by the derricks were then loaded onto rail carts down to the main roadbed where the blocks would be further piled onto the trucks for transport out of the quarry.

At Signpost #12, you will see a Switch and Portable Compressor and have the option to take a path on your left down to the Motion, a prospecting pit dug to determine the depth of granite veins. If you choose this route, be sure to return to #12 and continue to the next station.

Continue the trail until you come to a kiosk with a trail map and intersection on the left. Turn left and take the path immediately on your immediate left, completing a V-turn. Proceed uphill to a concrete-block shed. While the shed may not be of particular interest, there are iron rails visible on the ground. Follow them to your right, up a slight incline to a tunnel carved out of the bedrock to transport small blocks via rail cart. Return to the kiosk. Turn left uphill.

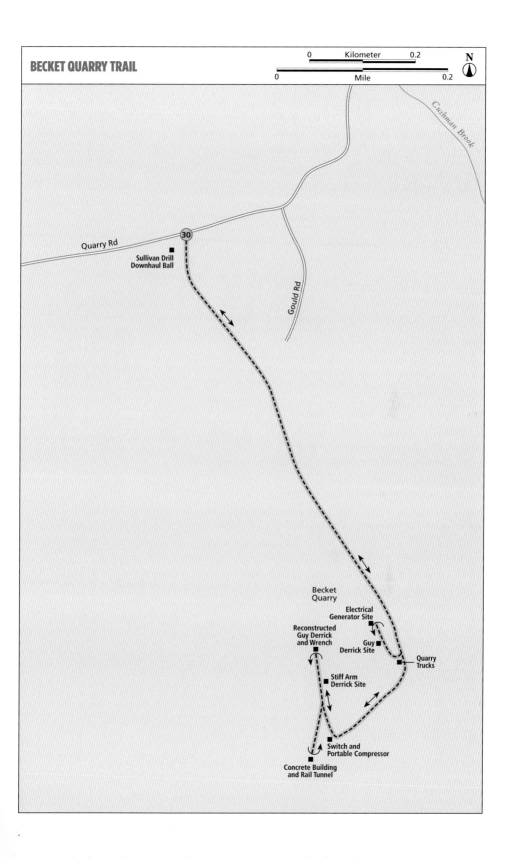

BECKET QUARRY TRAIL

0   Kilometer   0.2

0   Mile   0.2

N

Cushman Brook

Quarry Rd

30

Sullivan Drill
Downhaul Ball

Gould Rd

Becket
Quarry

Electrical
Generator Site

Reconstructed
Guy Derrick
and Wrench

Guy
Derrick Site

Quarry
Trucks

Stiff Arm
Derrick Site

Switch and
Portable Compressor

Concrete Building
and Rail Tunnel

Signpost #13 will appear on your right, the location of a Stiff-Arm Derrick used to lift the heavy blocks out of the quarry and pile them. Explore, but do not climb on the cut blocks or disturb any old equipment on the ground.

Continue to Signpost #14, a reconstructed Guy Derrick and Wench.

This marks the end of the historic quarry trail, so return downhill and around to the four-point intersection (#5). You can either return downhill to the trailhead and parking area or take additional trails through the Forest Preserve. Trail maps will assist you.

MILES AND DIRECTIONS

0.0 Start at the trailhead at parking area. On the right as you enter the parking area, look for an old metal drill projecting at a diagonal. This is the site of the Sullivan Drill and Downhaul Ball (#1).

0.50 Approaching the quarry notice grout areas on both sides of the trail. A large grout pile will appear on your right (#2) and just up the trail on your left, a smaller pile (#3 and #4). Look for the painted "eye" on your left.

0.56 Intersection of four trails with two rusted 1930–40s trucks on your right (#5) and ruins of the Electric Generator Shed (#7) on your left. There are interpretive signs associated with each historic landmark. Take the trail on your immediate right, making a V-turn.

0.60 Guy Derrick site (#6). Hike to the end of the trail for a great view of the quarry. Be careful as cables and pipes are lying on bedrock. View the quarry, then return to the intersection with the rusted trucks (#5).

0.72 Return to Signpost #5. Take the trail upslope to your right, which is an old rail grade around the southern portion of the quarry.

0.85 Switch and Portable Compressor on your left (#12). At this point, there is an option to take the rail grade to the left (#11) to the Motion. If you choose this route, be sure to return to the Signpost #12 and continue along the trail.

0.94 Trail intersection and kiosk map information on left. Take trail (path) on left making another V-turn and proceed upslope.

0.99 Arrive at concrete block shed. Inspect the ground for rail tracks; turn to your right following tracks to a carved-out tunnel constructed to carry quarry stones by rail cart. Return to main trail.

1.08 Map kiosk. Turn left, continuing upslope.

1.12 Signpost #13, a "still arm" Derrick with granite blocks cut and piled. Explore piled granite blocks. Note the rusted wheels of a rail cart opposite the signpost.

1.16 Reconstructed Derrick and Winch overlooking the quarry from above (#14). The trail ends at the quarry overlook. Return on the path you traveled to the four-trail intersection where the rusted trucks are located. Turn left for the old roadbed returning to the trailhead and parking area.

1.96 Arrive back at the trailhead.

31 KEYSTONE ARCH BRIDGES TRAIL

Talk about trails with unique stone ruins! How about a walk amid the longest and highest railroad in the world in 1841 supported by majestic stone arch bridges? Include the unfinished and abandoned stone structures of a 1960s-era artist colony replete with a tale of murder, an 18th-century colonial pioneer farmstead, scenic views along the West Branch of the Westfield River, and a waterfall in the Berkshires. All seen on the only-one-of-its-kind Keystone Arch Bridges Trail.

Start: Middlefield Road Trailhead, Chester, MA
Distance: 1.44 miles out-and-back
Hiking time: About 1 hour
Difficulty: Easy
Trail surface: Dirt and gravel
Seasons: All
Other trail users: Hikers only
Canine compatibility: On leash
Land status: Walnut Hill Wildlife Management Area
Nearest town: Chester, MA
Fees and permits: None

Schedule: Year-round
Maps: USGS Chester, MA, Quadrangle
Trail contact: Friends of the Keystone Arches, www.keystonearches.com; Keystone Arches, Inc., PO Box 276, Huntington, MA 01050; MassWildlife, Division of Fisheries and Wildlife, Walnut Hill Wildlife Management Area (WMA), Headquarters, 1 Rabbit Hill Rd., Westborough, MA 01581; (508) 389-6300

FINDING THE TRAILHEAD

Take US 20 to Chester, MA. Eastbound, turn left onto Middlefield Road (north). Travel 2.5 miles from the town center and the trailhead will be on your left. There are two parking areas: an upper paved lot just off the road and a lower dirt/gravel lot by the river. The upper parking area has a kiosk with maps and historical information, and will serve as our trailhead. **GPS:** 42.311416, -72.992697

THE HISTORY AND RUINS

Native Americans were the original inhabitants of the Berkshires, using the rugged terrain and waterways as places for hunting and fishing spanning thousands of years of occupation. Stone features along the Keystone Arch Bridges Trail span three centuries of American history. It was in the 18th century that the first Euro-Americans settled in these mountains. By 1762, the first property divisions were established in the Chester township by nineteen settlers acquiring and developing incipient farms and businesses. Three years later, Chester was home to 409 residents, primarily of Irish and Scottish descent, who had trekked from communities along the Connecticut River Valley taking advantage of available land opportunities in the hinterland.

One of these farming families purchased acreage north of the town center on the road to Middlefield. The land was rugged and mostly managed for pasturing of domestic animals, though a parcel on the eastern terrace of the Westfield River was flat and fertile enough to plant crops. There the family built a classic New England saltbox house with a center chimney. The success of these early farmers can be seen today in

Double Arch Keystone Bridge.

the series of stone ruins, such as a corn crib for crop storage and a barn for the housing of domestic animals.

In the early 19th century, the city of Boston found itself confronted with a commercial obstruction. The opening of the Erie Canal in 1823 brought prosperity to New York as goods from the Northwest Territory were easily transported to Albany and then siphoned to New York City via the Hudson River. The Big Apple experienced a rebirth of economic traffic while Beantown was in danger of being passed over as a significant trading partner. Boston's obstacle was that no canal routes could feasibly be constructed over the Berkshire Mountains to the Massachusetts coast.

A possible solution came in the form of the newly invented steam railroad system. Where tracks could be laid, railroads were providing expedited transport of goods overland through hill and dale (if the hills were not too steep). Could the new railroad technology navigate the mountains of western Massachusetts and save Boston's economy? By the early 19th century, no railroad in the world had ever attempted to cross such formidable mountains and steep slopes, and many engineers at that time thought it was an obstacle impossible to surmount.

Yet, to Boston investors, doing nothing was unacceptable. Surveying and developing a practical route through the Berkshires were assigned to Major George Washington Whistler, noted military engineer and father to painter James Whistler of *Whistler's Mother* fame. Major Whistler selected the West Branch of the Westfield River as the most reasonable railroad path through the mountains as it represented the lowest altitude in crossing

Unfinished artist colony building stone foundation.

the Berkshires. The many issues with choosing this route included steep narrow gorges and an exceptionally serpentine river. To build railroad passage would require a series of bridges, culverts, and retaining walls to continually cross and recross the watercourse.

In total, twenty-seven railroad overpasses would be constructed. The most remarkable were ten arch bridges of dry laid stone held in place by keystones supporting the entire edifice. The double-arch bridge on your hike rises 70 feet high—truly an engineering marvel in its day and inspiring awe today.

Incredibly, the once-thought-impossible 150-mile Western Massachusetts Railroad was completed within two and a half years, opening for service in 1841. In its day, it was the first gradient rail line to cross a mountain range; the highest and longest railway ever built; the first major infrastructure project to employ large numbers of immigrant workers (primarily Irish Catholic); and it established the railroad as the major long-distance transportation mechanism for the new country. Before long, water canals would give way for iron tracks and barges would give way to the trains.

Today, G. W. Whistler's genius and determination can be appreciated in the surviving stone arch bridges. While some of the bridges have been destroyed by floods, those that still stand are testaments to American ingenuity and human labor. In 2021, the Keystone Arches were designated as a National Historical Landmark by the U.S. Department of the Interior.

The stone and cement ruins of the unfinished 1960s Berkshire Cultural Center, a proposed artist colony, offers a tale of intrigue and desire. Charles Farmer, born in Hungary, was an established engineer owning and operating a major firm out of his mansion, Merriwold Castle, in New Jersey. He married Barbara Novaky, another native Hungarian, who was a patron of the arts and socialite.

Primarily through Barbara's urging and Charles's funding, they purchased property in the Berkshires on a terrace over the West Branch of the Westfield River, with hopes of developing a cultural center for artists to commune and be inspired by the natural scenic beauty of the mountains. The couple invested over $150,000 into the project when Charles started to suspect that Barbara really envisioned the cultural center as a tryst with her alleged lover, prominent sculptor Waylande C. Gregory.

The Farmers' marriage was already on the rocks with accusations of physical and verbal abuse. The suspicion of the affair with Gregory was evidently the last straw. The Farmers soon separated, with Barbara moving in with her brother. Charles withdrew his support of the artist colony and construction ceased in August 1963.

A month later, when Barbara returned to the mansion with her lawyer to collect some of her clothing, the distraught husband entered her bedroom from one of many secret passages in the "castle." Charles confronted Barbara, shot her three times with a pistol he had purchased days before, and turned the gun on himself, firing a bullet into his chest. Barbara was mortally wounded; Charles survived.

The courts judged Charles Farmer mentally unfit and sentenced him to the state hospital for the insane. After three trials, Charles was acquitted of murder in 1967, when the jury ruled that he was insane at the time of the shooting. He died eight years later.

The stone and mortar ruins of the unfinished and abandoned Berkshire Cultural Center stand like a "ghost town" and can be seen along the Keystone Arch Bridges Trail.

THE HIKE

The hike is an easy walk along an old roadbed converted to trails. There is an option after exploring the stone ruins to continue the KAB Trail leading to further arch bridges.

The trailhead has two parking areas: an upper paved lot containing a kiosk with maps and site histories, and a lower dirt/gravel lot closer to the river. Either parking area provides proximate access to the most impressive of the ruins—Whistler's double arch stone bridge. From the upper lot, hike downslope to the lower parking area, follow the sign on the left, and take the path leading down to the Westfield River. A magnificent view from below the 70-foot-high, dry-laid double arch stone bridge awaits. An amazing engineering feat, especially considering it was built in 1839 and keystones have sustained the structure for almost 200 years.

Return to the lower parking area, and turn left onto the trail. Cross an iron-grated bridge over a stream flowing down to the river. View the waterfall cascading toward you. Take a short path for a closer look at the waterfall. Return to the main trail and continue to your right.

The trail follows the fast-moving West Branch of the Westfield River on your left, bending in that same direction farther ahead. After the river bend, be alert for cement block barriers off the trail on your right. These mark the 1960s artist colony. The ruins of the clock tower can be seen rising above the tree line as well as some of the uncompleted building foundations, including a swimming pool. The artist colony ruins are off the trail and on private property so be respectful and view from a distance.

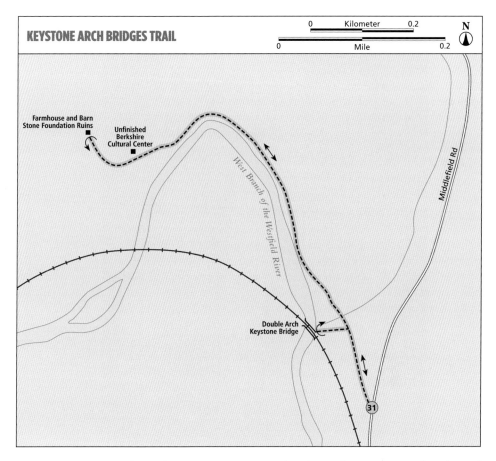

Farmhouse and Barn
Stone Foundation Ruins

Unfinished
Berkshire
Cultural Center

West Branch of the Westfield River

Middlefield Rd

Double Arch
Keystone Bridge

31

Continue on the trail to a gate restricting vehicular traffic. Bypass it and at the trail intersection, turn right linking to the KAB Blue Trail.

Slightly beyond the intersection, look to your left for a large rectangular depression in the ground. Walk off the trail and explore. The crater represents an 18th-century cellar hole of a farmstead dwelling house. The front door faces the trail. Carefully circle around the foundation to find the stairwell entering the cellar and the central chimney stack. The kitchen would have been behind the house as indicated by a stone-lined circular well beyond the cellar stairway.

Return to the trail, turning left to the next stone feature—the farm's barn. This is more apparent than the house since the barn was built into the side of a small knoll and the backwall of the foundation is prominent. The knoll allowed animals and wagons to enter from two levels. Walk beyond the barn along the trail and, on your left, you will see a set of standing stones in a rectangular formation. The stones supported the corn crib above the damp ground to avoid spoilage.

At this point, you have the option of retracing your steps back to the trailhead or continuing along the Blue Trail. Choosing the latter, follow signs for the KAB Trail and another kiosk upslope will provide a map to the pedestrian bridge and the other features.

Unfinished clock tower ruin of the Berkshire Cultural Center.

MILES AND DIRECTIONS

0.0 Start at the upper parking area trailhead on Middlefield Road, Chester, MA.

0.10 Reach the lower parking area by Westfield River. Take small path on left to the double-arched bridge.

0.13 Reach the east bank of the Westfield River viewing the double-arch bridge from below. Reverse steps returning to lower parking area.

0.16 Turn left and continue trail. Cross grate bridge. Note waterfall on your right.

0.58 After a left bend of the trail following the Westfield River, arrive at the abandoned artist colony on your right. Look up and see the clock tower.

0.66 Road gate. Proceed on the trail.

0.68 Trail intersection. Bear right onto KAB (Blue) Trail.

0.70 House cellar hole on left. Explore. Locate well behind the foundation.

0.72 Barn foundation built into the hillside and stone footings of a corn crib. Reverse hike back to upper parking area or continue the KAB Trail using map provided.

1.44 Arrive back at the trailhead.

32 OLD MILL TRAIL

Old Mill Trail is an out-and-back, handicap-accessible footpath. Textile mill ruins along the east branch of the Housatonic River during the 19th century are visible in stone foundations and landscape features. The trail is well-maintained with maps, brochures, and interpretive markers.

Start: Old Dalton Road and MA 8 intersection
Distance: 1.52 miles out-and-back
Hiking time: About 1 hour
Difficulty: Easy
Trail surface: Accessible trail
Seasons: Year-round
Other trail users: None
Canine compatibility: On leash
Land status: Berkshire Natural Resources Council

Nearest town: Dalton, MA
Fees and permits: None
Schedule: Year-round
Maps: USGS Pittsfield East, MA, Quadrangle
Trail contact: Housatonic Valley Association, (413) 298-7024; www.hvatoday.org; Berkshire Natural Resources Council, 20 Bank Row, Pittsfield, MA 01201; (413) 449-0596; www.bnrc.org

FINDING THE TRAILHEAD

Take MA 8 south from Dalton Center or north from Hinsdale. Turn onto Old Dalton Road, cross the river, and take your immediate left for parking and the trailhead. **GPS:** 42.447958, -73.130524

THE HISTORY AND RUINS

Charles H. Plunkett, a young entrepreneur from nearby Lenox, MA, desired to build a water-powered woolen mill in the Berkshires during the early 19th century. He found a suitable site along the surging waters of the east branch of the Housatonic River in Dalton, MA. However, another entrepreneur, Zenas Crane, had been using the river since 1801 for his paper-making company and he controlled most of the waterway. (Crane's factory has produced paper for the U.S. Treasury since 1879.)

Undeterred, Plunkett went farther upstream to Hinsdale, MA, where several sawmills had been operating since 1772. As the river drops 257 feet from Hinsdale to Dalton, this stretch presented an excellent conduit for water-powered industries. Plunkett purchased one of the sawmills and began producing his textile products under the name "Lower Valley Mill."

As business opportunities expanded, Charles partnered with his brother-in-law, Charles Kittredge, enabling them to build a second, even larger textile factory in the 1850s. Success continued into the 1880s, when the Lower Valley Mill employed 250 laborers, each putting in 60-hour workweeks. Long before child labor laws, children were used as "runners," replacing bobbins between the fast-moving and tight machinery, very dangerous work. This was sadly evident when Charles's younger brother Thomas had his arm crushed by the machines. In total, there were six textile mills operating in Hinsdale until 1930.

By 1905, Renfrew Mill developed a penstock system to transport water from Plunkett's original millpond down to factories in Dalton Center, feeding the turbines that created electricity for their business.

The wind-up came when the powerful storm of 1936 destroyed the old stone dam, ending 150 years of water-powered mills along the river. Abandoned, the stone and earthen ruins are all that remains of a once vibrant early industrial enterprise.

THE HIKE

Old Mill Trail is well marked and organized. Plenty of available parking with maps and history brochures are on hand at the trailhead. The trail itself is an easy ramble with the first 0.7 miles designed for handicap accessibility that encompasses all the stone features associated with the old mills. (As of this publication, the trail is not wheelchair accessible. Trail developers are hoping to rectify this situation soon, so check the website for updates before heading out if you need assistance: www.bnrc.org.)

The first portion of the trail crosses three wooden bridges that pass over the east branch of the Housatonic River and streams. Once across, look on your left for an abandoned, rusted 1938 Oldsmobile (Sign #5). (Not an archaeological ruin, but you don't get to see many of these classic cars anymore, especially in this condition.)

On the opposite side (right) of the trail from the discarded car is a large depression, the millpond formed by the impounding of water behind the 1851 stone dam that powered Plunkett's Lower Valley Mill. Once the dam was breached, the pond drained and was filled in by local and invasive plants.

Reaching Sign #7, turn right, taking a short dead-end path, reaching the concrete foundation and trench leading downriver that starts the penstock (a large pipe) built in 1905. The penstock, 4 feet in diameter, fed water to the turbines of Renfrew Mill in Dalton, about 1 mile downriver. The penstock was removed for scrap metal during World War II.

Continue the path to its end to view the stone remains of the original mill dam constructed in 1831 (Sign #8). Look across the river for stone ruins of the dam on the opposite side. The dam burst in 1936, flooding Dalton below.

Return to the trail and turn right, continuing to Sign #9. This area is dedicated to all the workers and their families who lived in walking distance from the mills. In many cases, whole families, including children, labored in the textile mills, and shopped at the mill store.

Sign #10 fronts the foundation of the Lower Valley Mill. Standing stones denote a corner of the building, and the overall rectangular outline of the mill. Due to the configuration of the textile machinery in the 19th century, woolen mills were typically long and narrow. Also, before electricity, light was generated naturally by a series of tall windows along the length of the structure. Additional stone ruins are visible at Sign #11 where Plunkett developed a second woolen mill.

Continuing the trail (#12) leads to a unique feature—an open penstock tunnel! It will seem like you are walking through a small gorge that has been dug out for a road, but this was once a tunnel in which the penstock passed through channeling water to the mills below.

When you reach the end of the accessible trail, you have the option to continue under MA 8 to the trail's terminus or reverse your steps and return to the trailhead. Should you continue, you will have the opportunity to see the metal penstock leading to the Renfrew Mill.

Top: Rusted 1938 Oldsmobile on Old Mill Trail.
Bottom: Stone and cement gate with penstock trench.

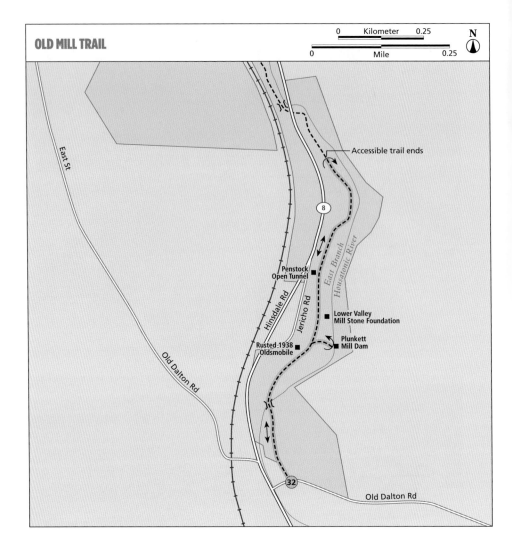

MILES AND DIRECTIONS

0.0 Start at the trailhead with kiosk.

0.08 Cross first of three wooden bridges over the East Branch Housatonic River.

0.22 Rusted 1938 Oldsmobile on your left (Sign #5). Look across to your right for the millpond.

0.27 Signpost #7. Turn right and reach the beginning of the 1905 penstock. Note the trench from the millpond.

0.30 Standing on the stone dam (#8), look across the river to see remains of the stone dam on the other side. Storms have dispersed stones downriver. Reverse your steps returning to the trail; continue right.

0.37 Signpost #9.

0.40 Signpost #10; stone ruins represent the corner of the mill building.

Stone foundation of Plunkett's Lower Valley Mill.

0.42 Come to the stone foundation of the woolen mill (Signpost #11).

0.45 Take the path on your right down to the river. There you will see stone ruins associated with Plunkett's second woolen mill. Return to the trail, turn right, and continue.

0.52 Signpost #12 tells of the sluice leading to the penstock transporting water to the Renfrew Mills downriver. Note as you hike that the trail runs down the middle of the open tunnel that housed the penstock.

0.63 Trail veers sharply to the right and downslope, following switchback pattern.

0.69 Signpost #13; stone works uphill on your left and a waterfall cascading over the river on the right.

0.76 Reach the end of the accessible trail. You have the option to continue crossing MA 8 to hike the rest of the trail or return to the trailhead.

1.52 Arrive back at the trailhead and parking area.

33 HANCOCK SHAKER MOUNTAIN NORTH TRAIL

For this hike, we recommend two adventures. First, tour the Hancock Shaker Village to provide historical context. The standing structures in the Hancock Shaker Village will help you visualize and interpret the stone ruins. The second, a hike through the abandoned Shaker North Family complex with ruins of a dwelling house, two water-powered mills, and other landscape features—great history, great ruins.

Start: North side of US 20, opposite Hancock Shaker Village
Distance: 2.18 miles out-and-back
Hiking time: About 1.5 hours
Difficulty: Easy
Trail surface: Dirt
Seasons: All
Other trail users: None
Canine compatibility: On leash
Land status: Pittsfield State Forest; Hancock Shaker Village
Nearest town: Pittsfield, MA

Fees and permits: None for Shaker Mountain Trail; entrance fee for village
Schedule: Year-round
Maps: USGS Pittsfield West, MA, Quadrangle
Trail contact: Hancock Shaker Village, 34 Lebanon Mountain Rd., Hancock, MA 01237; (413) 443-0188; www.HancockShakerVillage.org; Pittsfield State Forest, Department of Conservation and Recreation, 1041 Cascade St., Pittsfield, MA 01201; (413) 442-8992; www.massgov/dcr

FINDING THE TRAILHEAD

Take US 20 West from the center of Pittsfield for 5 miles. When you pass the intersection for MA 41, the trail pull-off and parking will be less than a half mile on the right. Hancock Shaker Village will be on the left. The trail begins at a closed gate and follows a dirt farming road leading toward Shaker Mountain. **GPS:** 42.431535, -73.339859

THE HISTORY AND RUINS

Although they called themselves the "United Society of Believers in Christ's Second Appearing," the surrounding community, especially non-believers, referred to them as "Shaking Quakers" or "Shakers." The name was inspired by the believers' rapturous dancing and singing during religious ceremonies. The Second Appearance of Christ was personified in their leader Ann Lee, better known as Mother Ann, who was forced to flee England in 1774 for the British colonies in North America to escape persecution. Arriving just prior to the onset of the American Revolution, Mother Ann and her disciples organized a series of "religious communes" throughout New England and farther west.

The Hancock Shaker community officially "gathered" in 1790 and rapidly grew into a population of 300 settling on 3,000 acres of land. To work and worship more efficiently, Shakers divided themselves into smaller communes called "Families." The main commune, or Center Family, is where the Hancock Shaker Village Museum resides today. Surrounding villages were referred to by their compass points from this center. The Shaker Mountain Trail passes through the "North Family" settlement.

Stone ruins of the Shaker North Family sawmill.

Shakers believed that they could recreate "heaven on earth" by communal living, celibacy, pacifism, and public confessions. They strongly supported gender and racial equality. They developed successful farming complexes and embraced the Industrial Revolution, building large barns, dwelling houses, workshops, and various mill operations. Their dairy products were sold throughout the region. Shaker industries included wood- and metal-working crafts. They were skilled in furniture-making, basketry, broom-making, and a host of other prized trades that have been well-recognized for their quality and are considered collector's items today.

While Shaker communities continued to grow during the early and mid-19th century, they were in decline by the end of the 1800s. Being celibate, they could only maintain their populations through converts, and this dropped dramatically after the American Civil War. Shaker villages during the war had become havens for men seeking pacifist and religious exemption to avoid President Lincoln's unpopular military draft into the Union Army. By the beginning of the 20th century, the Hancock Shaker community dwindled to a population of just fifty individuals, which were mostly children. Excess land was sold to maintain finances, and many buildings were dismantled for materials.

Sometime around 1818, the Shakers constructed an earthen and stone dam to impound water from Shaker Brook descending mountain wetlands north of Central Village. Using oxen and horses, they built the dam to supply water through underground culverts for irrigation, supply water for laundry, drinking, and livestock, and power machinery. The original reservoir was expanded in 1894 to hold over 2 million gallons of water, transported via an aqueduct under US 20 to the Central Village.

The North Family commune was dissolved shortly after the Civil War in 1867. The Dwelling House was disassembled with materials salvaged for the Center Village. The once vibrant mills were closed and abandoned with only the dams and reservoir left over to provide water to the remaining community.

Stone dam for the upper pond.

Today, the Hancock Shaker Village provides the public with a means to understand the lives of this religious community and their contributions to American culture, while also providing hikers with a visual context for interpreting the North Family ruins.

THE HIKE

The Shaker Mountain Trail is part of the Pittsfield State Forest, offering several hiking options. Exploration of the North Shaker Family stone ruins is an easy, 3-mile out-and-back trek. Should you option to climb Shaker Mountain and loop to Holy Mount, expect a 6.5-mile round-trip hike over moderate-to-strenuous trails.

Before you start your hike, we strongly recommend taking the tour of the Hancock Shaker Village directly across the road from the trailhead parking area. You will profit from a history of the Shaker community, an understanding of how they used the rural landscape, and aid your "mind's eye" in reconstructing the structures from the ruins you will encounter.

Beginning at the pull-off on US 20, the trail commences at the dirt roadway leading north. Along the way, look for green triangular markers with a white dot in the center for direction and interpretation of stone features.

The first historical element will be on your right when the trail hugs the west side of the Shaker Reservoir. As you continue the trail, another path on your right, whose entrance is also on US 20 and east of your parking area, will connect and merge into a single trail along the brook (Blue Trail). Note a series of stone walls on the left that defined pasture areas where Shakers maintained their domestic animals.

Follow along the brook and watch for the stone footings of a bridge that once crossed over the stream leading to the North Family Dwelling House. The bridge ceased to exist by the mid-20th century. This is the route Shakers from the Central Village would have taken to go up the mountain to conduct religious activities.

Waterfall over a breached lower pond dam.

The next stone ruin will be the remnants of the Lower Dam constructed in the early 19th century. This dam would have held water to power the various mills below it, whose stone ruins you can see on the opposite bank of the brook.

Pass a wooden trail bridge for pedestrian passage over Shaker Brook. This was once a formidable wagon overpass connecting the Dwelling House and mills. Do not cross the bridge just yet but continue upstream toward the ruins of the High Dam (c. 1810) and sawmill (c. 1858). Explore along the road to get a closer look at the dam, pond, and sawmill ruins across the waterway.

Retrace your steps back to the pedestrian bridge and cross over. When the trail intersects with the Shaker Mountain Trail, turn left (uphill) to get a closer look at the high dam and sawmill now on your left. If you are having a hard time locating the pit for the waterwheel, that is because the mill straddled the brook. Many of the earliest mill operations employed this strategy, though it was risky business since storms and flooding could destroy the mill in a single episode. To compensate for this, later mills were constructed on the side of streams with water carried through wooden sluices providing energy with less peril. This Shaker sawmill burned down in 1926.

Once again, retrace your steps back to the pedestrian bridge and continue straight on the trail without crossing. The Lower Dam will be on your far right as you hike. Below the dam will be the remains of mills used for various economic activities: grist, thrashing, and wood cutting. In 1845, a carding or fulling mill was constructed here to process wool. These stone features may be hard to see due to vegetation, but the waterwheel pit and tailrace (a watercourse that carries water away from a mill or water wheel) should be unmistakable. Water was most likely transported through wooden sluices that have not survived.

A short distance beyond the mill sites will be the remains of the North Family Dwelling House on your right. Unfortunately, remains of the stone foundation are either covered by vegetation or more likely removed and reused when the site was abandoned in 1867. However, the large depression or cellar hole in front of you is plainly visible.

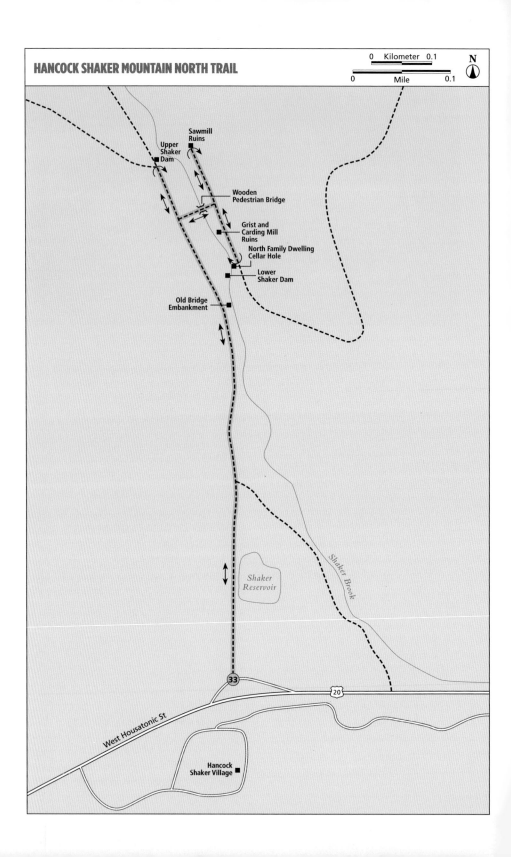

HANCOCK SHAKER MOUNTAIN NORTH TRAIL

0   Kilometer   0.1

0   Mile   0.1

N

Sawmill Ruins

Upper Shaker Dam

Wooden Pedestrian Bridge

Grist and Carding Mill Ruins

North Family Dwelling Cellar Hole

Lower Shaker Dam

Old Bridge Embankment

Shaker Reservoir

Shaker Brook

33

20

West Housatonic St

Hancock Shaker Village

Your tour of the Hancock Shaker Village will help you visualize the three-story wood and brick structure which would have housed 28–40 people and contained ground floor and basement rooms for a large kitchen, dining room, chapel, meeting places, and laundry, with bedrooms on the upper floors.

You have the option of either returning to the trailhead and parking area or continuing up Shaker Mountain Trail to your left. If you decide to go on, note that the trail will be strenuous in some areas and, depending on the time of year, wet. The full hike to the Holy Mount is a 6.5-mile loop; however, you can also go up to the top of the mountain and return via the CCC Trail, which is a shorter 4-mile loop.

On the trail to the mountain summit (Mount Sinai), you will pass the remains of a charcoal hearth and, at the top, the remains of the Feasting Ground, which was not necessarily a place to dine, but a sacred place for singing and dancing. While all the ruins associated with the latter area are no longer visible, the stone wall surrounding this sacred area is still in place. Likewise, Holy Mount and its Feasting Ground on the western rise has a stone wall enclosure as well as a spring cited in the Shaker records. Both trails will return you to the lower level and to the parking area.

MILES AND DIRECTIONS

0.0 Trailhead has no signboard but begin your hike on the dirt road behind the closed vehicle gate.

0.10 Shaker Reservoir on your right. Trail hugs the edge of the pond.

0.42 On right, footing for the old bridge that would have spanned the stream leading to North Family Dwelling House.

0.53 Lower dam on right.

0.53 Come to wooden pedestrian bridge but stay straight uphill.

0.63 Upper Pond dam on right.

0.66 Observe depression that was the millpond. Return downhill to the pedestrian bridge.

0.75 Cross bridge over stream onto Shaker Mountain Trail.

0.77 Turn left at intersection and climb hill for another view of the sawmill.

0.86 Mill ruins on your left. Waterwheel straddled the stream.

0.84 Stone mill dam for Upper Pond. Return downhill toward the pedestrian bridge.

0.89 Continue straight on Shaker Mountain Trail. Do not cross bridge just yet.

0.95 Stone dam for the Lower Pond on right. Note the upright alignment of standing stones on your right as you walk the trail. We are not sure of their function.

1.01 Industrial site foundations on right. Explore depressions.

1.06 North Family Dwelling site is on the right—note cellar hole is only visible remnant of the large community house. Go to the stream and locate the footings to the bridge encountered on the west bank of the waterway.

1.09 Trail splits. Trail to the left ascends the mountain. Option 1: Reverse your steps, cross pedestrian bridge, turn left, and return to the parking area. Option 2: Take trail to the summit and complete longer loop.

1.28 Recross wooden bridge, turn left to return to the trailhead.

2.18 Return to parking lot and trailhead.

34 EYRIE HOUSE RUINS TRAIL

This historic mountaintop resort sits at the summit of Mount Non-otuck overlooking the Connecticut River Valley and town of East-hampton, MA. There are incredible stone ruins to explore. The trail is uphill out and downhill back. There is a tour map available near the summit with photos at each of the ruins to envision what the build-ings looked like before the fire that brought the vacation spot to a close.

Start: Mount Tom North Trailhead, 96 East St., Easthampton, MA
Distance: 3.46 miles out-and-back, then loop
Hiking time: About 2.5 hours
Difficulty: Easy to moderate
Trail surface: Dirt
Seasons: Best in late fall/early spring
Other trail users: None
Canine compatibility: On leash
Land status: Mount Tom State Reservation; City of Easthampton

Nearest town: Easthampton, MA
Fees and permits: None
Schedule: Year-round
Maps: USGS Mount Holyoke, MA, Quadrangle
Trail contact: Mount Tom State Reservation, 125 Reservation Rd., Holyoke, MA 01040; (413) 534-1186; www.mass.gov/locations; City of Easthampton, 50 Payson Ave., Easthampton, MA 01027; (413) 529-1400; www.easthamptonma.gov

FINDING THE TRAILHEAD

The Mount Tom North Trailhead is located on 96 East St., Easthampton, MA. From I-91, take exit 15 (southbound) or 15B (northbound) to MA 141 west. Turn right onto East Street. The trailhead is 2.7 miles on the right. **GPS:** 42.285291, -72.620277

THE HISTORY AND RUINS

The military and social disruption of the American Civil War had just begun, but that didn't impede William Street from building a summit resort on Mount Nonotuck. Opened to the public on Independence Day in 1861, the resort offered prominent vistas of the Connecticut River Valley to the east, north, and west along with recreational activities for both adults and children. William Street was inspired to name his resort perched on top high cliffs, Eyrie House, suggesting the nests, or eyries, of eagles.

Eyrie House offered guests the opportunity to stroll along two wooden promenades with majestic views, climb a lookout tower, play croquet, roller-skate, picnic, or dine indoors. Children were amused by animals in a small petting zoo and by swings over-looking the valley below. A stable and corral were provided for the guests' horses. And all this for a 25-cent wagon ride up the mountain, 25 cents for admission, 50 cents for dinner, and $2 per night's stay. By the 1880s, the hotel expanded from twelve to thirty guest rooms as Eyrie House was hosting 5,000 paying customers a year.

So successful was William Street's entrepreneurship that competitors started to build more modernized mountaintop resorts along the Mount Tom Range. To maintain his clientele, Street needed upgrades. By the turn of the 20th century, he began construc-tion on a new hotel and an inclined railway to transport guests to the summit. While the

Stone foundation of the unfinished new hotel at Eyrie House. CAROL AND LEE WEST

railway was completed, financial constraints delayed the new hotel's construction and business at the innovative mountaintop resort was in steady decline. Then, in 1901, a fire sealed the deal.

When two of his horses died in the hotel's stable, Street decided to cremate the animals in a huge bonfire since there was little soil buildup on the basalt ridge to bury them. Thinking that the blaze had been extinguished, Street retired for the night. Unfortunately, the fire rekindled, and the resulting conflagration speedily grew out of control. Street awakened as the inferno engulfed his resort, including the old and partially built new hotel. All was lost before the flames could be contained and, without fire insurance to rebuild, the Eyrie House closed its doors for good.

Three years later, the State of Massachusetts offered William Street $5,000 for the 100 acres he owned to incorporate Mount Nonotuck into the newly created Mount Tom State Reservation. Though he refused the money, believing that his land was worth more than the state's offer, the property was eventually secured by Eminent Domain. As a result, all that remains today of the once prosperous mountaintop resort are stone foundation ruins of the unfinished new hotel, the original Eyrie House, the pavilion, and the horse stable.

Pavilion and horse stable stone ruins at Eyrie House. CAROL AND LEE WEST

THE HIKE

Start at the Mount Tom North Trailhead on East Street, Easthampton, MA. Parking stalls are limited, though overflow parking is available on Underwood Avenue. If the East Street parking lot is full, continue up the road and turn right onto Underwood Avenue just before the highway overpass. The Metacomet-Monadnock Trail entrance will be on your right with parking along the street on the opposite side of the road. The trail runs along the power line gravel right-of-way. Should you need to take this latter option, hike 0.52 miles to the start of the New England (White) Trail marker on your left. The entrance to the Kestrel Loop Trail will be on your right directly opposite. Follow our directions upslope (though mileage will be different) as you hike the White Trail.

The Kestrel Loop Trail begins behind the trailhead kiosk on East Street. This is a wide handicap accessible path. There are interpretive signages along the way, trail switchbacks to avoid higher angle slopes, and wooden picnic tables accommodating wheelchairs. When you reach the Mount Tom North Trailhead kiosk, proceed on a small path behind it toward the power lines. A wooden rail sign is set at the end of the clearing beginning the New England (White) Trail up to the summit. Arrows direct you to the Eyrie House Ruins (0.7 miles) and other destinations.

Stone ruins of the unfinished new hotel showing cellar archways. CAROL AND LEE WEST

The trail will switchback uphill toward the summit and is well marked. Continue to the John McCook Trail split leading to the Visitor's Center on the right and Eyrie House Ruins to the left (0.3 miles). Hike uphill to the paved Mount Nonotuck Road (which is closed to motor vehicles), then turn left and continue uphill until you reach an old parking lot with a wonderful open vista of the valley below.

After enjoying the scenic view, look for a small path at the northeast end of the parking lot. This footpath will lead you to the Eyrie House Ruins at the mountain's summit. Be sure to take a photo of the posted trail map with location numbers highlighted and a brief history of Eyrie House before taking the path. We will be noting the station numbers in our hike description.

Your first imposing view of the ruins will be on the right as you ascend the footpath. The high stone foundation of the new hotel, which started construction in 1893 will appear above on the right. Resist the temptation to go directly up to the ruins (you will see them soon enough) and continue along the path to Marker #5, then turn right and hike the steeper trail to the summit and Beacon Tower. After viewing the tower, you will see the Signpost #9 indicating the southern stone foundation of the original 1861 Eyrie

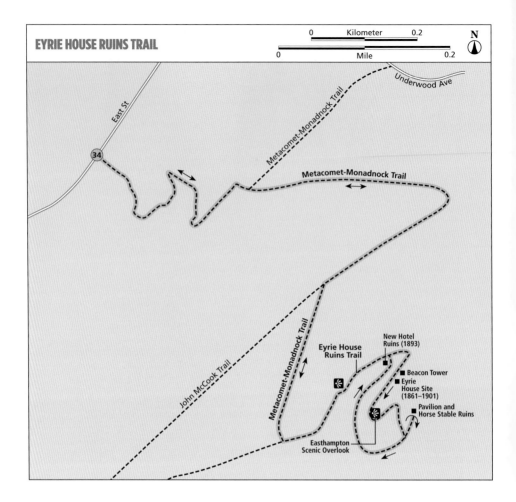

0   Kilometer   0.2

0   Mile   0.2

N

East St

Underwood Ave

Metacomet-Monadnock Trail

34

Metacomet-Monadnock Trail

John McCook Trail

Metacomet-Monadnock Trail

Eyrie House
Ruins Trail

New Hotel
Ruins (1893)

Beacon Tower

Eyrie
House Site
(1861–1901)

Pavilion and
Horse Stable Ruins

Easthampton
Scenic Overlook

House site. Explore behind the tower to see additional stone foundation ruins and get a real appreciation of how large the original structure was.

As you continue down the path, you will be hiking parallel to the South Promenade, which was a wooden walking lane set on the summit's rock outcroppings and destroyed by the 1901 fire. Be sure to enjoy the overlook with the town of Easthampton below (#10).

The path will then curve to the left downhill in a U-turn. Divert off this path when you see another path on the right that also twists downhill. Look closely and you will see the stone ruins of the pavilion and stable below (#11). The slope is too steep to attempt to go down to the ruins from there. Instead, continue along the path to another cutoff on your left, switchbacking farther downslope to the stone ruins. Explore after examining the available photographs of the pavilion. Reimagine the structure from the observed stone foundations. Note the horse stable foundations are lower to the north.

Reverse your steps and this time continue straight on the path, swinging around the summit in a clockwise rotation. Note the retaining wall to your lower left. Follow the path around to the new hotel ruin (#13), which you previously viewed from below.

Explore the stone arches separating rooms of the cellar but be careful not to climb on the stone arches as they are fragile and can collapse.

After enjoying the ruins, take another small path on the far side of the foundation leading downslope, completing a loop around the summit. Turn left and proceed down to the parking lot, Mount Nonotuck Road, and the White Trail back to the trailhead.

MILES AND DIRECTIONS

0.0 Start at the Mount Tom North Trailhead. Take the Kestrel Loop Trail, which accesses the Mount Tom hiking trails.

0.31 Reach the Mount Tom North Trailhead kiosk. Bear right behind the kiosk, crossing under power lines.

0.34 Enter the New England (White) Trail uphill into the forest. Stay on the White Trail following posted directions to Eyrie House Ruins.

0.49 Intersection with John McCook Trail. Bear left uphill on the New England Trail.

0.78 Split in trail. Bear left.

0.99 Reach paved Mount Nonotuck Road. Turn left and proceed uphill.

1.04 White Trail veers to the right off paved road; continue straight uphill.

1.10 Reach old parking lot with wonderful vista of the valley.

1.20 Path leading up the ruins begins at kiosk northeast of the parking lot. Be sure to take a photo of the tour map and continue ascending.

1.28 Northwest corner of Eyrie House Ruins (New Hotel—1893) above on right.

1.32 Take path on your right, which steeply rises uphill toward the Beacon Tower.

1.37 Reach the highest point of Mount Nonotuck at the Beacon Tower (#7).

1.39 Reach the southern foundation wall of the original Eyrie House site (#8).

1.43 Reach the overlook with the town of Easthampton in the distance below (#10). Continue.

1.45 Take trail turning downslope on your right, overlooking the pavilion and horse stable ruins (#11).

1.48 Take dead-end trail on left. Switch back down slope to the pavilion and stable ruins.

1.53 Reach pavilion and stable ruins (#12). After exploring, return downhill to rejoin trail.

1.59 Return to trail; proceed straight walking around the summit.

1.71 After circling the summit ridge, reach the new hotel foundation ruins first viewed from below (#13). Explore the arches and the interior of the cellar.

1.73 Take small path downslope back to trail, completing a loop of the summit. Look over the cliff and you will see the route of the inclined railway.

1.84 Return to the old parking lot. Reverse your hike back to the trailhead.

3.46 Arrive back at the trailhead on East Street.

35 UPTON HERITAGE PARK TRAIL

One of the more interesting and controversial stone ruins in southern New England. Some say that the Upton Stone Chamber was built by Pre-Columbian Irish monks, others claim it was constructed by pagan Druids, and still others contend that Native Americans erected the chamber as an astronomical observatory. And if that were not enough, a further explanation claims that colonial farmers constructed the edifice as a root cellar. Be sure to bring a flashlight if you plan to enter the beehive-shaped chamber. Your imagination can run wild.

Start: Upton Heritage Park Trailhead, 18 Elm St., Upton, MA
Distance: 0.04 miles out-and-back
Hiking time: About 10 minutes
Difficulty: Easy
Trail surface: Grass and dirt
Seasons: Open all seasons
Other trail users: None
Canine compatibility: On leash

Land status: Town Park
Nearest town: Upton, MA
Fees and permits: None
Schedule: Year-round
Maps: USGS Milford, MA, Quadrangle
Trail contact: Town of Upton, 1 Main St., Suite 12, Upton, MA 01568; (508) 529-3019; www.uptonma.gov

FINDING THE TRAILHEAD

From the Massachusetts Turnpike (I-90), take exit 106 (I-495) southbound to exit 54B (West Main Street). Turn right at the end of the exit. West Main Street turns into Hopkinton Road. At 3.5 miles, turn left onto Cedar Mill Lane. At the end of the road, turn right onto Elm Street. Be sure to bear left, remaining on Elm Street where it splits into River Street. Upton Heritage Park will be a driveway on the right between residential houses. **GPS:** 42.175238, -71.597246

THE HISTORY AND RUINS

Everyone loves a mystery, and the controversy over who created the Upton Stone Chamber has interested parties wrangling over multiple interpretations.

The dry-laid stone structure has a 6-foot-high, 14-foot-long passageway leading into the main compartment, which broadens to 12 feet in diameter and 11 feet in height. There are several large, flat stone ceiling slabs enclosing the assembly overhead and remnants of decomposing wooden planks as flooring over the damp earth. The beehive-domed, igloo-shaped Upton Stone Chamber has one of the most interesting narratives of any stone ruin in southern New England. Unfortunately, few artifacts have been recovered from the interior leading to much speculation as to the structure's origin.

In 1946, William Goodwin started it all with his book, "The Ruins of Great Ireland in New England." Goodwin asserted that stone "chambers" throughout the Northeast were not, as previously believed, the work of Euro-American farmers during the Colonial and Early Republic Periods. Rather, he contended, they were erected over a thousand years ago by early Christian Irish Monks who somehow crossed the Atlantic Ocean in leather boats hundreds of years before Columbus sailed. Goodwin tells us that these intrepid religious travelers built a series of "chambers" throughout interior New England. Upon

Top: Upton Stone Chamber with adjacent stone walls.
Bottom: Interior of the Upton Stone Chamber.

The Upton Stone Chamber.

arriving in Upton (sorry), the friars built the "Stone Chamber" featured prominently as a Pre-Columbian Irish ceremonial site in Goodwin's book.

Originally published in 1976, *America B.C.: Ancient Settlers in the New World*, by Barry Fell, a professor of invertebrate zoology, expanded the Pre-Columbian European hypothesis. Promotion for Fell's book reads, in part, "Druids in Vermont, Phoenicians in Iowa before the time of Julius Caesar!" Indeed! To Barry Fell and his supporters, Upton represents an ancient Druid ceremonial center.

Yet another publication toppled these previous Eurocentric explanations. In 1989, James Mavor and Byron Dix published *Manitou: The Sacred Landscape of New England's Native Civilization*. The authors hypothesized that Native Americans constructed the chamber, dating it to 700–750 CE, and that its western-facing aspect was deliberate to mark sunset during the summer solstice and align stars to stone cairns perched on top of Pratt Hill about a mile away. Members of the Mashpee, Wampanoag, and Narragansett tribes have studied the Upton Stone Chamber and concur that it was built by their ancestors for astronomical observations.

The most accepted theory by historians and archaeologists is that Upton's stone ruins have a far more mundane explanation. Instead of ceremonial or astronomical backdrops for the chamber, they see the stone ruin as having an economic function, serving as a root cellar for the storage of produce by Euro-American farmers, after Columbus, not before. In other words, the stone structure was a historical pre-electricity refrigerator where vegetables and meats could be stockpiled. New England farmers built stone cellars into the sides of hills, covering the stone ceiling slabs with earth to create a cave-like chamber whose interior could maintain a constant temperature year-round (warmer in the winter

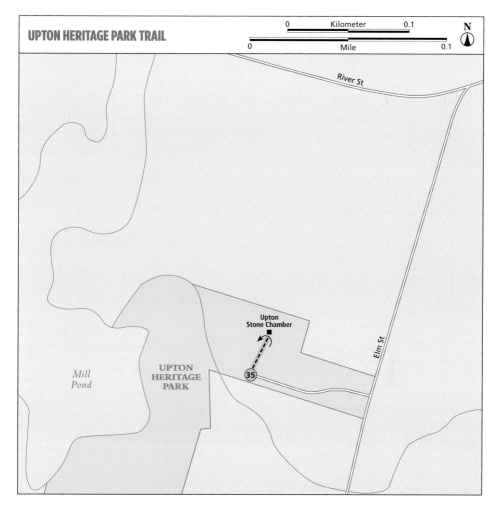

and cooler in the summer), preserving perishable food products for subsistence and marketplaces. These stone cellars have long been associated with historical agricultural landscapes, found in the rocky soils of Europe as well as in America.

Most proponents of Druid, Irish monk, and/or Native American origins agree that the chamber was used by historical farmers but deem that the structure was erected in earlier times for spiritual or astronomical purposes. Colonial farmers, they contend, simply reused already-existing stone structures for agrarian purposes. The problem, of course, is that if archaeologists find historical artifacts associated with the ruins, it can be argued that the stone structures were still built hundreds, if not thousands of years ago, then reused during historical times. But where are the earlier artifacts? Too sacred a place to leave artifacts behind? Well, every religious archaeological site in the world has left artifacts for interpreting belief systems, so why not here?

To further complicate the issue, an archaeological restoration project undertaken by John Milner Associates, a cultural resource consultant, obtained five soil samples from behind the lowest wall stones in the entranceway and from a test pit dug in front of the Upton Stone Chamber. The samples were processed for optically stimulated luminescence dating (OSL) by Shannon A. Mahan, F. W. Martin, and Catherine Taylor (*Quaternary Geochronology*, 2015). Their findings suggest that the chamber dates to 523 years ago (1350–1625 CE). We should, however, point out that OSL has an uncertainty range of 5–10 percent, which, in this case, would bring the structure into the New England Colonial Period.

Still love a mystery, or, more confused than ever? We Americans have "cultural amnesia," that is, we are so focused on the future with our strong beliefs in "progress" and "tomorrow" that we quickly forget our collective historical pasts. Technological and cultural change occurs so rapidly that we fail to recall how people lived generations ago. What may have been commonplace stone structures on the historical landscape have now become "mysterious," especially if associated artifacts are not found or if discounted by alternative theories.

Though more a walk than a hike, enjoy the controversial Upton Stone Chamber and speculate on its origin and purpose.

THE HIKE

The stone ruins are right off the trailhead and parking area, requiring no extensive hiking. From the trailhead, walk across the open grassy area left of the Eagle Scout shed (constructed from toppled trees during Superstorm Sandy in 2012) to the bordering forest. You will find a small path into the woods that leads directly to the stone chamber.

The opening to the ruin is low, but the height of the structure changes quickly to 6 feet, so you can stand once inside the passageway and the "beehive" back section. A flashlight will be necessary in the dark interior. Note the series of stone walls associated with the chamber that would have delineated animal pens and pastures. Today, the stone wall running alongside the chamber serves as the property boundary for the park.

The Old Field Trail is located at Upton Heritage Park by the Mill Pond. To get to the trail, hike downhill through the open park area and the stone wall enclosure into Long Meadow.

MILES AND DIRECTIONS

0.0 Start at the trailhead at Upton Heritage Park kiosk and parking area. Opposite the parking area, cross the field to wooded area left of the wooden Eagle Scout shed. Pass birdhouse and stone slab, taking the small path into the woods.

0.02 Stone chamber will be straight ahead on the right side. Note the large stone walls enclosing old pasture lands. Explore. Return to trailhead or continue downslope to the Old Field Trail.

0.04 Arrive back at the trailhead.

This family-friendly trail follows scenic country pastures to the top of a hill with the stone ruins of a "castle." And a castle combined with a name suggesting the hill may have been used for hanging criminals in the 1600s.

Start: Gibbet Hill Grill and Barn, MA 40, Groton, MA
Distance: 1.56 miles out-and-back
Hiking time: About 45 minutes
Difficulty: Easy, though one steep hill to climb
Trail surface: Dirt
Seasons: Best in late fall/early spring
Other trail users: None
Canine compatibility: On leash
Land status: Gibbet Hill Farm, LLC, and Groton Open Space Association

Nearest town: Groton, MA
Fees and permits: None
Schedule: Year-round
Maps: USGS Ayer, MA, Quadrangle
Trail contact: Gibbet Hill Farm, 61 Lowell Rd., Groton, MA 01450; (978) 448-2900; www.gibbethillfarm .com; Town of Groton Open Space Association, PO Box 9187, Groton, MA 06340; gosamail@gmail.com

FINDING THE TRAILHEAD

From I-495, take exit 80 (Littleton Commons, Groton), MA 119. Travel west for 6.7 miles to Groton Center. Turn right onto Lowell Road (MA 40) and in 0.2 miles Gibbet Hill Grill and Barn will be on your left. As you pull in, the trailhead is on your right. Hikers are permitted to use the back of the parking lot on the left. Go around the pond toward Lowell Street to find the trail. **GPS:** 42.60862, -71.55976

There is also limited parking along MA 40 on Lowell Street. Pass Gibbet Hill Farm and look for stone pillars on your left. There is a small pull-off along the road. Enter the trail at the pillar gate and hike to your right. Be aware that this parking area is closed from dusk to dawn. This entrance will cut 0.25 miles off your trip up to the castle. **GPS:** 42.60673, -71.55915

THE HISTORY AND RUINS

We New Englanders would pronounce it "GIB-bet" Hill, but the British would say "JIB-et" Hill. Either way, in England the term refers to a place where gallows were erected for public executions. However, there are no primary documents that prove anyone was hanged at Gibbet Hill in Groton, MA.

There are historical records that John Lawrence built a farmhouse there in 1645. While the farm has been around for almost 400 years, the property's fame rose when General William Bancroft, a veteran of the Spanish-American War, dreamed of building a home on Gibbet Hill for he and his wife to live out their final days serenely overlooking the town of Groton.

Along with his military title, Bancroft was also the mayor of Cambridge and a prominent businessman. He called his new estate, "Shawfieldmont" and commenced construction in 1906, planning a castle-themed mansion and large stable for his horses. Unfortunately, Bancroft was only able to erect a bungalow, not his entire dream castle and stable, when he ran out of funds.

Main fireplace inside Bancroft's Castle ruins.

Bancroft eventually sold the property to a local physician, Harold Ayers, who envisioned a tuberculosis and mental health sanatorium permitting wealthy clients to partake in healthy fresh air during a quiet convalescence in this pastoral country setting. An advertisement in the August 22, 1915, issue of the *Boston Globe* promised "Absolute Quiet, Pure Air, Atmosphere of Home," amenities for prospective patients. However, Ayers's dream also met a quick demise when the hospital was forced to close its doors in the late 1920s.

Turret of Bancroft's Castle.

Though the "castle" was used by the Groton Hunt Club for social events, the property had been abandoned for years when the structure was destroyed by fire. According to the *Lowell Sun* (July 5, 1932), trespassers were setting off fireworks during a July Fourth celebration, when a spark erupted into massive flames. Once the fire was doused, the only remaining ruins were the stone foundation, fireplace, and castle turret.

After World War II, the property was purchased by Marion Campbell, a writer whose father owned *The Atlantic Monthly* magazine, where she successfully managed a Black

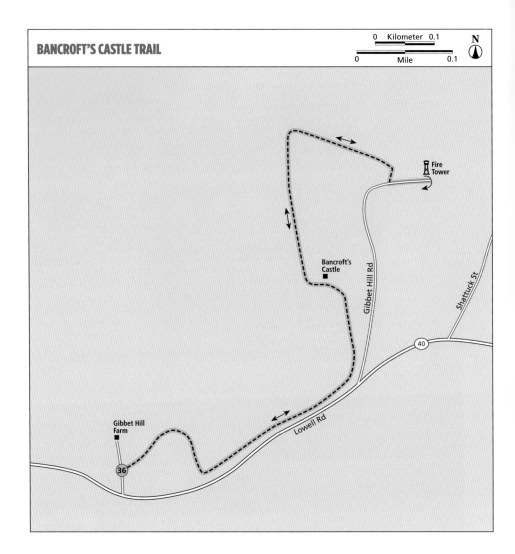

Angus cattle farm. When Marion died, her "trust" decided to sell the farm to a construction company proposing to build seventy-eight houses on the farm. Before the land transfer could be finalized, Steve Webber, a Groton native and successful entrepreneur, stepped in and bought the land to preserve it as an operating farm and open space. The Webber family owns and operates the Gibbet Hill Grill and Barn, and they continue to work with the Groton Open Space Association, consenting to families and hikers use of the trail to view the stone ruins of Bancroft's Castle and enjoy panoramic views of northern Massachusetts and New Hampshire.

THE HIKE

Start at the trailhead sign by the Gibbet Hill Grill and Barn. Walk downhill and along the left side of the pond. As you proceed around the pond, the trail bends to the right toward Lowell Street and follows the north side of the road before bending left up a short, relatively steep slope.

The stone ruins of General William Bancroft's Castle will appear on your right as the hill terraces. Spend some time exploring the turret and inside the castle's impressive ruins.

When finished, return to the front of the castle where you entered and turn right. The trail will bend right and proceed farther uphill. As you walk along pasture fence lines, take time to survey the panoramic view which extends into New Hampshire including the White Mountains peaking in the distance. In the foreground below, you will see the buildings of Gibbet Hill Farm and Groton Center. This is an especially magnificent view during fall foliage.

At a pasture gate, the trail turns sharply to the right, following the fence line. This is a particularly good spot to view Angus cattle in the pasture.

Continue going downslope along the Groton Trails Network by following the green-on-white markers. You will cross a wooden bridge at the bottom of the slope and hike uphill. Through the trees you will see a fire tower on your left. The trail brings you to gravel, and then paved roadway. Turn left (uphill) on the paved portion and to see the fire tower.

The fire tower is one of five in the state of Massachusetts. It rises 68 feet high and is 400 feet above sea level. Originally a wooden construction, the tower was erected three months before the attack on Pearl Harbor in 1941. The tower remains active today. The wood was dismantled and replaced with steel, a cab, and two-way radios. While not a stone ruin, it is impressive to see.

You can continue the Green Trail to its Shattuck Street outlet, or, as we recommend, make an about-face and return to the trailhead. And, by doing so, you get to revel in the "castle" ruins again!

MILES AND DIRECTIONS

0.0   Start at the trailhead at Gibbet Hill Farm.

0.25 Stone pillars at gate entrance on right along MA 40. Trail bends left and uphill.

0.40 Bancroft's Castle on your right. Go within the stone ruins and explore. Return to trail and turn right to continue up Gibbet Hill.

0.48 Panoramic view of Gibbet Hill Farm and Groton Center to your left.

0.54 Reach pasture gate. Follow trail with the fence line on your left.

0.72 Cross the wooden bridge over wetlands and continue uphill.

0.76 Reach gravel road; turn right.

0.78 Reach paved road; turn left uphill to fire tower. Retrace steps back to the trailhead.

1.56 Arrive back at the trailhead and parking lot.

37 TRAIL THROUGH TIME

This five-star loop trail combines Native American, colonial farming, stone quarries, and industrial history in one tour. Appropriately named a "Trail Through Time" (TTT), the hike provides a diversity of stone ruins with excellent maps, well-maintained and clearly marked trails, and informational kiosks. The TTT is a not-to-be-missed experience for stone ruin enthusiasts.

Start: End of Wheeler Lane, Acton, MA

Distance: 2.36-mile loop

Hiking time: About 2 hours

Difficulty: Easy

Trail surface: Dirt

Seasons: All seasons

Other trail users: None

Canine compatibility: On leash

Land status: Nashoba Conservation Trust

Nearest town: Acton, MA

Fees and permits: None

Schedule: Year-round

Maps: USGS Westford, MA, Quadrangle

Trail contact: Nashoba Conservation Trust, PO Box 188, Peppermill, MA 01463; www.nashobatrust.org

FINDING THE TRAILHEAD

From I-495, take exit 80 (Littleton Common), onto Great Road (MA 119) southbound. Travel for about 6.5 miles passing Lake Nagog (MA 119 joins MA 2A). Turn left onto MA 27 (V-turn) for 1.5 miles, turning right on Wheeler Lane. The

Trail Through Time Trailhead at Nashoba Brook.

trailhead and parking area are at the end of Wheeler Lane. Traveling west on MA 2 coming out of Boston, connect on to MA 2A at the five-point rotary located at West Concord. MA 2A will be the second turn as you swing onto the rotary. Take MA 2A for 3 miles, turning right onto MA 27. Follow the directions above to the trailhead at the end of Wheeler Lane. **GPS:** 42.512856, -71.405289

THE HISTORY AND RUINS

There is so much history to review in the stone ruins of the TTT. Fortunately, the trail's kiosks do an excellent job providing multi-cultural histories. So, please take the time to read through the signage as they go into far more detail than we have space for here, which merely presents an overview in the order stone ruins are encountered on the trail.

WHEELER HOMESTEAD

Originally built by Thomas Wheeler Jr., c. 1720–1730s, the house stood until it was demolished in the 20th century. While residing at the homestead, Thomas and his family operated two mills, one for cutting wood and the other for grinding flour, along Nashoba Brook. The family also managed a working farm with barns, pens, pasture areas, and outbuildings. Each of these economic and residential activities have left stone ruins telling their history.

Stone foundation and cellar hole of the Thomas Wheeler House.

NASHOBA BROOK STONE CHAMBER

This stone ruin is a classic colonial root cellar. Moses Wood operated a farm at this site in 1774 and most likely built the structure to preserve produce, including potatoes and apples, for subsistence and outside markets. Since Moses Wood was a blacksmith, and a Revolutionary War veteran, it has been suggested that the "chamber" was used as a foundry. For this to be ascertained, there would have to be more archaeological evidence beyond hand-wrought nails found during below-ground testing of the site in 2008.

Interior of the Nashoba Brook Stone Chamber.

Historical documents record that a later property owner, Samuel Tuttle, received income from the renting of the structure as an icehouse. Amazingly, there are seven enormous, flat slabs of stone spanning the L-shaped roof.

The kiosk suggests that Native Americans built the chamber for ceremonial purposes thousands of years ago and that colonial farmers used this earlier-built structure during historical times as root cellars and icehouses. However, it stretches probability to invoke two cultures, at two different time periods, for two different purposes using the same structure. Considering historical records and similar stone ruins associated with farming families in the area, Occam's razor would have that Euro-American settlers constructed the "chamber" for economic reasons.

PENCIL FACTORY

American industrialized pencil manufacturing came of age in the early 1800s and was a recognized specialty in the Concord, MA, region. Among others, the family of Henry David Thoreau were pencil makers with the poet learning the trade from his father.

Although the French were producing high-quality pencils earlier than the Americans, pencil-making in the Concord area received a boost in 1812 when David Munroe began mixing locally available plumbago (lead) with adhesives into grooves cut into cedar casings. One of Munroe's employees was cabinetmaker Ebenezer Wood, who operated a two-man saw used to cut cedar slabs. Wood's inventiveness helped mechanize and increase pencil production in Munroe's mill, hence making the latter a very rich man.

Ebenezer Wood also produced a high-quality plumbago ground on millstones powered by the waters of Nashoba Brook. Other area pencil factories preferred Wood's lead for their quality graphite. So, when you use a modern pencil with their hexagonal and octagonal shapes, think of and credit Ebenezer Wood, for he constructed that casing type—a 19th-century achievement that has never needed improvement.

NATIVE STONE MOUNDS

As you cross Nashoba Brook, be on the lookout for clustered stone mounds on hilly terraces. These "stone piles" have been interpreted as sacred ceremonial landscapes constructed and used by local Native Americans for thousands of years. Each of these stone clusters (Princess Pine, Plaintain, and Blueberry) are said to have their own individual arrangements signifying ceremonial meaning, such as memorials, astronomical, and ritual centers. Kiosks at these specific areas provide Native American perspectives on the origin of the stone mounds.

Many New England historical archaeologists have also interpreted these stone ruins as part of British American agricultural practices, such as stone wall building and the removal of stone from fields and pasture lands. Whatever the interpretation, these stone mounds are significant cultural resources, deserving preservation and respect, so please do not touch or climb on any of these stone features.

PEST HOUSE

Behind the "Plaintain Stone Piles" are the ruins of a large dwelling foundation with a deep cellar hole referred to as the "Pest House." For such an extensive structure, it is interesting to note that there are no land deeds associating a house to this area. The land was held by an absentee landowner, Dr. Jonathan Davies, in the late 18th century, who lived and practiced medicine in Cambridge, MA.

Native American stone mound.

Stone foundation and cellar hole of the Nashoba Brook Pest House.

In 1792, an outbreak of smallpox infected the Boston area and when news reached Concord, civic leaders decided to build a facility away from the town center to inoculate and quarantine smallpox victims in an effort to contain the deadly disease. The "Pest House" along the TTT may have housed over one hundred people with a central chimney stack providing heat to adjacent rooms.

WHEELER COMPLEX

The Wheeler farm, gristmill, and sawmill provided important economic products for the residents of the Towne of Concord. In the 1730s, Thomas Wheeler Jr. petitioned Concord's selectmen to survey a road connecting his farm to the town. The deal was that the town would survey the land for the road and Thomas would build a bridge and causeway over Nashoba Brook.

Now, called the "Old Road to Concord," an archaeological survey conducted in 2008 concluded that a portion of today's Yellow Trail is this original 18th-century thoroughfare. The double-walled stone ruins and the roadbed width suggest a vibrant corridor of transportation where wagonloads of flour, lumber, and farm produce would have been carried to Concord's markets.

The Old Road to Concord and the Wheeler Homestead are also the site of Thomas Wheeler Jr.'s sawmill and gristmill. The natural topography of this portion of Nashoba Brook drops 10 feet in elevation, providing appropriate surge for water-powered industry.

By 1832, Thomas took advantage of an earlier stone and earthen dam constructed by the Blood family, who were related to the Wheelers by marriage. (Robbins Mill Pond is named after subsequent property owners.) Thomas acquired land through a lottery and traded land already in the family to accumulate hundreds of acres encompassing the mill complex bordering lands along Nashoba Brook which he desired for farming.

If Ebenezer Wood was a gifted inventor, Thomas Wheeler Jr. was a creative engineer. Wheeler erected fieldstone-lined canals to supply downstream sluices and a gate to control water flow to the two operating mills. The industrial system he designed divided water flow from the stone and earthen dam to canals feeding two smaller streams: one directed to his gristmill and one providing power to the sawmill.

THE HIKE

The Wheeler Lane Trailhead has a wooden arched kiosk area with the history and map of the TTT. Please do not park on the road. There are instructions at the kiosk for overflow parking.

Since this is a loop trail, the hiker can proceed either south or east on the Yellow Trail and return to the Wheeler Lane Trailhead. We recommend starting on the trail heading south and looping in a counterclockwise direction.

After reviewing the kiosk information, follow the path through the arch, taking a right and another right onto the Yellow Trail. The first of the stone ruins will be on the kiosk.

This is the location of the original Wheeler Family farmhouse. Note that the exposed stone-lined cellar hole represents a partial cellar with the house much larger than the rectangular imprint. The large flat stone laying before the foundation (trail side) is the front door of the house. Between the cellar hole and the parking lot is a low-lying wall which may have been a kitchen shed/creamery based on its proximity to the well.

Archaeological surveys conducted during the restoration of the house foundation discovered that the cellar floor was lined with large flat slabs of stone. A paved cellar is a rarity in New England and may have been associated with food storage.

After viewing the Wheeler farmhouse, continue right on the Yellow Trail. Note the large double stone walls lining the old roadway. This was a corridor to drive domestic animals to barns and pastures. As the trail nears the wetlands, the hiking path narrows becoming stony with exposed roots, so proceed carefully. There are wooden walkways to assist crossing wetland areas.

A path off the trail leads to a kiosk with the "Nashoba Brook Stone Chamber" behind it. While explanations for this structure vary, it is a classic L-shaped root/ice cellar. Historical records list the Wood and Tuttle families on property to the south of the Wheeler farm. Explore and speculate, then return to the Yellow Trail, turning right.

Additional wooden walkways appear crossing Nashoba Brook. Stone walls greet you as the trail follows the east side of the brook, leading to the intersection with the Blue Trail. However, for now stay straight on the Yellow Trail to the three-sided kiosk for the Pencil Factory. From there go right toward the wetlands and walk over the factory's earthen/stone dam. Stone ruins of the pencil factory are below on your left.

Return to the kiosk and venture left, connecting with the Blue Trail. The trail will advance amid numerous stone walls and provide a shortcut to rejoin the Yellow Trail farther uphill. (You can also continue southbound on the Yellow Trail as it loops around stone-walled pasture areas and horseshoes to the north intersecting with the Blue Trail. Both trails lead to the same location.)

Once rejoining the Yellow Trail, turn left continuing among old pasturelands. The Red Trail will intersect on your right—but stay straight on the Yellow Trail. (Should you wish, the Red Trail will lead to the southbound Green Trail where you can visit a stone quarry.)

Continuing the Yellow Trail, turn left onto the Green Trail to observe Native American stone mounds. This is a loop trail that will reconnect to the Yellow Trail. Stone mounds will be on the right along the upper slope of the hill as you hike. When the Green Trail reunites with the Yellow Trail, a kiosk will provide an explanation of how Native Americans built and used the stone mounds for ceremonial purposes.

Once back on the Yellow Trail, turn left continuing downhill. On the far side of a stone wall on the right will be another kiosk for the Plantain Stone Piles Cluster. After reading the kiosk information, take the Green Trail leading back along the stone wall to the Pest House ruins. Explore and return on the same path, back to the Yellow Trail.

From the Yellow Trail, turn right and continue passing the Blueberry Stone Piles Cluster. There is another Red Trail intersection on the right, but once again stay straight on the Yellow Trail.

When a stone-lined water canal along Nashoba Brook appears on your left, you will be approaching the "Old Road to Concord," linking Wheeler's farm and mills to the "Towne of Concord." Note the double stone walls on both sides of the old roadbed, as well as the width of the roadbed. Turn to the left and continue along the Yellow Trail, crossing Nashoba Brook. As you cross the footbridge, observe the stone piers supporting the earliest bridge.

The trail proceeds uphill returning to the trailhead at Wheeler Lane. However, when you reach the rise where the Yellow Trail veers left, turn right to the picnic area and walk toward the Robbins Mill ruins.

Cross a bridge over the headrace (a waterway that feeds water to a mill or water wheel or turbine) of the mill leading to other northward trails. Observe Robbins Mill from the bridge. Note the stonework and the gate to control water flow that would have been engineered by Thomas Wheeler Jr.

At this point, you can picnic and return to the trailhead or continue over the bridge to the Red Trail, which heads north crossing the brook following the east side of Robbins Mill Pond to Roof Slab Quarry.

MILES AND DIRECTIONS

0.0 Start at the trailhead kiosk and parking area at the end of Wheeler Lane, Acton, MA. Walk through kiosk, turn right, and right again onto the Yellow Trail.

0.02 Wheeler house foundation on right.

0.17 Cross the stone wall. Trail narrows.

0.45 Cross the stone wall.

0.50 Wooden walkway begins.

0.52 Bear right; stay on TTT.

0.58 Nashoba Brook Stone Chamber.

0.62 Stay to the right and continue TTT (Yellow Trail).

0.71 Second wooden bridge/walkway crossing Nashoba Brook.

0.88 Turn right at trail intersection.

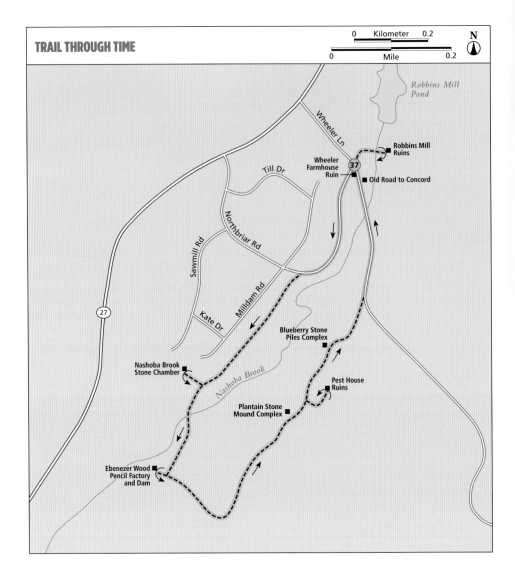

0   Kilometer   0.2

N

0   Mile   0.2

Robbins Mill Pond

Robbins Mill Ruins

Wheeler Ln

Wheeler Farmhouse Ruin

37

Old Road to Concord

Till Dr

Northbriar Rd

Sawmill Rd

Millidam Rd

27

Kate Dr

Blueberry Stone Piles Complex

Nashoba Brook Stone Chamber

Pest House Ruins

Nashoba Brook

Plantain Stone Mound Complex

Ebenezer Wood Pencil Factory and Dam

0.90 Pencil Factory ruins and kiosk. Go right and cross bridge, walking on dam. Factory ruins to your left.

0.99 Return to kiosk. Retrace trail steps to your left.

1.04 Bear right onto the Blue Trail, hiking uphill.

1.15 Intersection with the Yellow Trail; turn left.

1.27 Cross stone wall.

1.37 Intersection with the Green Trail. Stay left on the Yellow Trail.

1.41 Take the Green Trail on left. Native American stone mounds on your right.

1.54 Kiosk intersection with the Yellow Trail. Turn left, downhill.

1.60 Wooden walkway.

1.63 Take the path on the left to see the Native American kiosk.

1.66 Return to the Yellow Trail. Turn left uphill and cross a stone wall.

1.68 Plantain Stone Piles. Take the Green Trail on right to Pest House foundation.

1.73 Arrive at Pest House ruins. Return to the Yellow Trail by same path.

1.81 Arrive at the Yellow Trail. Continue right.

1.89 Wooden walkway.

1.95 Blueberry kiosk.

1.99 Cross stone wall.

2.00 Intersection with the Red Trail. Bear left, staying on the Yellow Trail.

2.17 Note stone-lined water canal on left.

2.19 Cross wooden bridge; the Old Road to Concord kiosk.

2.29 Arrive back to the trailhead. Turn right toward open picnic area.

2.32 Reach bridge over Robbins Mill ruins. Note the stone-lined canal and gate. Return toward the trailhead.

2.36 Arrive back at the trailhead and parking area.

38 BREAKHEART RESERVATION TRAILS

An early farmstead, a water-powered mill, a private hunting and fishing lodge, and the conservation and recreation efforts of Civilian Conservation Corps (CCC) projects have changed the landscape and consigned stone ruins as testaments to their various land uses. Breakheart Reservation's interpretive trail guide is appropriately entitled, "Stories in Stone," though we would add "Stories in Stone Ruins."

Start: Forest Street entrance, Saugus, MA
Distance: 3.18-mile loop
Hiking time: About 1.5 hours
Difficulty: Easy to moderate
Trail surface: Dirt, portions paved
Seasons: All seasons
Other trail users: Motor vehicles on paved areas
Canine compatibility: On leash
Land status: Massachusetts State Park

Nearest town: Saugus, MA
Fees and permits: None
Schedule: Year-round
Maps: USGS Boston North, MA, Quadrangle
Trail contact: Massachusetts Department of Conservation and Recreation, 177 Forest St., Saugus, MA 01906; (781) 233-0834; www .mass.gov

FINDING THE TRAILHEAD

Route 1 (Broadway) northbound out of Boston, take the Lynn Fell Parkway exit. Turn left and follow for less than a quarter mile. Forest Street will be on your right. Travel to the end of Forest Street to the trailhead and parking area by the Visitors' Center. Traveling Route 1 southbound, take the exit merging onto Lynn Fell Parkway to Forest Street on the right. **GPS:** 42.483393, -71.027893

THE HISTORY AND RUINS

Breakheart Reservation became a Massachusetts State Park in 1934 but the story doesn't start there. Stone and ceramic artifacts recovered from Indigenous archaeological sites in the park date to over 8,000 years ago, bearing witness to the area's antiquity and land stewardship by Native Americans.

The hilly, forested terrain of the Breakheart Reservation shows up in historical records within a hundred years of European settlement in the Boston area. Declared as Common Land, the expanse west of the Saugus River was subdivided among English settlers in 1706. Termed the "Six Hundred Acres," the land remained relatively undeveloped, primarily used as woodlots for fuel and building materials.

Today's Forest Street entrance is the site of the Hitchings family farmstead. The land for the most part was too rugged and stony for plowing but made excellent pasturelands for grazing livestock with dairy farming and apple cultivation as the most important economic activities. Through time, the Hitchings and other families made use of the abundant supply of local stone as foundations for houses, barns, and other agricultural outbuildings.

Top: CCC-built stone stairway at the Flume.
Bottom: Catchment Pond at the Flume.

Stone and cement ruins of the old hunting lodge.

The changes in the landscape and the industrial ruins at the terminus of the Mill Site Trail date to 1814 when the Linen and Duck Manufacturing Company of Boston set up a factory along the Saugus River, producing sailcloth for ships. Based on the sizes of the stone and earthen dam, sluice, and mill structure, the operation appears to have been economically viable.

Overall, the Saugus River became an important source for water-powered commerce supporting sawmills, gristmills, cider presses, and especially for the Saugus Iron Works, the earliest (1646–1670) large-scale integrated forge in the Americas. The Iron Works were owned and operated by Jonathan Winthrop the Younger (see Bluff Point Trail chapter) and is listed as a National Historic Site open to the public.

More than 200 years later, in 1891, Benjamin Johnson, a well-to-do attorney from Lynn, MA, along with other affluent hunting and fishing enthusiasts, obtained the mortgage to a series of forested hilly woodlots originally part of the "Six Hundred Acres." The cadre built an impressive hunting lodge, hired a caretaker to continue farming activities and keep trespassers out of their private domain, and funded construction of wildlife-friendly projects. For example, the partners dammed up two spring-fed marshes, creating upper and lower ponds that they stocked with fish. They called their hunting, fishing, swimming, and hiking paradise "Breakheart Hill Forest." As a result of conserving the property for their sportsmen's interest, they inadvertently saved the land from other types of economic development into the 20th century.

The purchase of Breakheart Hill Forest by the state coincided with Franklin Roosevelt's creation of the CCC during the Great Depression of the 1930s. The CCC employed young men to rebuild the nation's infrastructure and upgrade national and

Trailhead at Breakheart Reservation.

state parklands, including Breakheart Reservation. For six years, the CCC constructed roads and trails, planted trees and shrubs, and repaired the pond dams. They also built the "Flume" designed to prevent soil erosion between the two ponds by directing overflow water from the upper pond downhill through a series of stone-lined channels and pools to the lower pond, resulting in a seldom-seen series of stonework in southern New England.

In part due to the early efforts of the CCC, Breakheart Reservation today is a delightful and well-maintained park with activities for the whole family. The hiking trails offer lakeside paths as well as unique historical ruins.

THE HIKE

We propose a 3-mile loop starting and finishing at the Forest Street entrance by the Visitors' Center, which we encourage you to stop at to see their exhibits on the history and people who occupied Breakheart Reservation.

The trail starts at the stone pillar entrance to the park. Take the Saugus River (Yellow) Trail on your right, then Lodge Trail on your left. A short hike uphill will take you to the hunting lodge ruins on the right above the Rhododendron Grove. Return downhill to the Saugus River Trail and turn left.

Take the Mill Site (Blue) Trail on your right and hike for a tenth of a mile to arrive at the 1814 water-powered mill ruins. Locate the mill dam, search for stone ruins, and follow the sluice trench on your right along the Saugus River. Retrace your steps back to the Saugus River (Yellow) Trail, then turn right.

Stone pillar at Breakheart Reservation Trailhead.

This portion of the trail gets a bit narrow and stony as it skirts the south border of the river and wetlands. Steep hills on your left; wetlands on your right. Keep your eyes open for a wildlife blind and cabins associated with Camp Nihan Education Center on the far riverbank. This is the most rugged part of the hike bordering the wetland and steep rocky slopes.

As the trail bends to the left, the woodland opens approaching the gas pipeline corridor. The gas pipeline has no trail access, so simply cross, bearing right, to connect with the Saugus-Fox Link Trail. This takes you to Pine Tops Road. Turn right and continue along the paved portions of the road. While Pine Tops Road is open to motor vehicles, it is heavily used as a hiking, dog walking, and running trail.

As you walk Pine Tops Road in a counterclockwise loop, note the various attractions along the way: Bark Place Dog Park, a private golf course, Chimney site and Pine Tops Picnic areas, and Peach Lake (Lower Pond). Continue to Flume Road at an uphill bend on the right. Take this dirt road (with a gate restricting motor vehicles), following a terrace on the east side of Peach Lake. When the trail descends rapidly, the "Flume" will be on your left. The Flume is a scenic cascade of falling water over stone dams and channels. Though built by the CCC in the 1930s, it still functions today.

To get a better perspective of the Flume, follow the Orange Trail uphill along the Flume's northern border. Climb the stone stairway connecting to Silver Lake Trail, which you will follow to the left. Hike around the northern side of the lake, passing a couple of scenic viewpoints. When you come to the intersection with double orange markers, bear left reconnecting with Pine Tops Road.

Turn right and stay on Pine Tops Road as it swings around Breakheart Hill to the Visitors' Center and parking area. When you arrive, cross Forest Street toward the "Exercise Center" and "Amphitheater" signs. Follow the boardwalk and locate a bench next to a stone wall foundation. The stone ruins you see are associated with the old farmstead, including house (wooded area on your left) and barn foundations (downslope on your right).

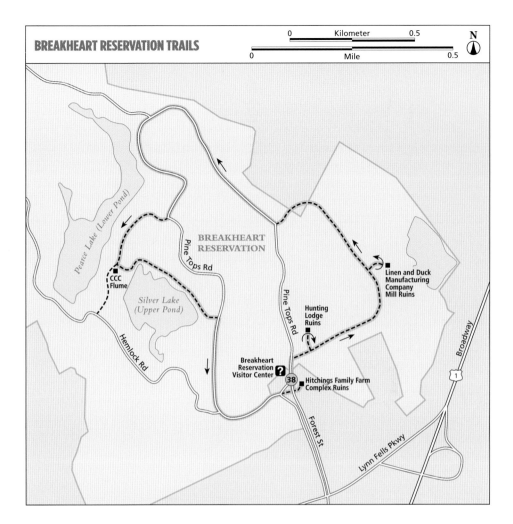

MILES AND DIRECTIONS

0.0 Start at the Forest Street entrance by the Visitors' Center. Trailhead will begin by the stone pillars at Pine Tops Road.

0.03 Turn right onto Saugus River (Yellow) Trail.

0.10 Intersection with Lodge Trail, turn left uphill toward the Rhododendron Grove.

0.15 Cement stairs to the hunting lodge ruins on right. Return, reconnecting with the Saugus River (Yellow) Trail and turn left.

0.42 Turn right on Mill Site (Blue) Trail.

0.47 Bear right and continue uphill. Take small path with the millpond on your left.

0.56 Mill sluices, headrace, and dam. Venture uphill to the right and walk on top of the sluiceway to see how the water would have flowed to the waterwheel. Return.

0.69 Arrive back to Blue Trail. Turn left to rejoin the Yellow Trail.

0.83 Arrive back to Saugus (Yellow) Trail, continue to your right.

0.89 Cross stone wall. Note river on the right and large outcropping of bedrock upslope on the left. Trail narrows, becoming stony.

1.21 Reach gas pipeline crossing. Turn right and straight across to the Saugus-Fox Link Trail. The gas pipeline has no trail access, so do not walk along right-of-way.

1.28 Take steep pathway on right to Pine Tops Road.

1.32 Turn right on paved Pine Tops Road. Be alert for traffic as you hike.

1.54 Reach Bark Place Dog Park on right.

1.58 Reach Pine Tops Picnic Area on left.

2.13 Turn right onto Flume Road (dirt) at top of the hill.

2.36 Flume on left. Explore. Follow orange markers uphill, climbing stone stairs, connecting with Silver Lake Trail.

2.43 Turn left on Silver Lake (Blue) Trail.

2.50 Silver Lake Trail turns right (orange and blue markers), hiking along the north shore of Silver Lake (Upper Pond).

2.59 Reach scenic lake overview on right.

2.74 Look for double orange markers. Turn left returning to Pine Tops Road.

2.76 Reach Pine Tops Road (paved). Turn right.

2.99 Hemlock Road on right but remain on Pine Tops Road as it bends to the left.

3.17 Complete the loop and reach parking area by Visitors' Center. Cross the road to the Exercise Stations and Amphitheater for stone foundations of the farmhouse and barn. Complete hike by returning to the parking area.

Stone gatepost at Canonchet Farm.

39 CANONCHET FARM HISTORY TRAIL

Canonchet Farm is a green space unlike any other in Rhode Island. Initially inhabited by the Narragansett Tribe, the district later became home to some of the earliest colonial settlers. The farm offers easy walk-through fields and quarries where stone walls in all shapes and sizes appear along a well-maintained trail. There is also a large glacial erratic and some pleasant panoramas of the Pettaquamscutt River.

Start: Narragansett Community Center, 53 Mumford Rd.
Distance: 3.18 miles out-and-back
Hiking time: Under 2 hours
Difficulty: Easy, though roots and boulders to navigate
Trail surface: Dirt and stone
Seasons: Best in late fall/early spring
Other trail users: None
Canine compatibility: On leash
Land status: Town of Narragansett

Nearest town: Narragansett, RI
Fees and permits: None
Schedule: Year-round
Maps: USGS Narragansett Pier, RI, Quadrangle
Trail contact: Town of Narragansett Parks and Recreation, 25 Fifth Ave., Narragansett, RI 02882; (401) 789-1044; Friends of Canonchet Farm, PO Box 418, Narragansett, RI 02882; www.canonchet.org

FINDING THE TRAILHEAD

From Route 1 northbound take the exit for Wakefield, and turn right onto Narragansett Avenue East, which turns into Mumford Road. In a half mile, turn left at Schoolhouse Road and then take a quick right. The Narragansett Community Center will be on your left across from Sprague Park on your right. Southbound on Route 1, take the Old Tower Hill Road exit and turn left onto Peckham Avenue. After you cross the highway bridge, Peckham Road will turn left and merge onto Narragansett Avenue. Follow the above directions to the Community Center. **GPS:** 41.44264, -71.46535

THE HISTORY AND RUINS

The Canonchet Farm History Trail takes you on a journey into the past, going by Native American sites where the Narragansett tribal members hunted, fished, and grew maize, beans, and squash along the well-drained soils of Pettaquamscutt Cove and Narrows River. The farm was also home to 17th-century colonial settlers, as well as Governor William Sprague's 19th-century mansion.

Canonchet was a powerful Narragansett sachem, who led his warriors into battle during King Philip's War in 1675–1676. Prior to the Native American uprising in New England, the land was conveyed to English settlers as part of the original Pettaquamscutt Purchase of 1658. John Porter, Samuel Wilson, Thomas Mumford, Samuel Wilbore, and John Hull exchanged 16 British pounds and assorted trade goods with three Narragansett sachems (Quassuchquansh, Kachanaquant, and Quequaquenuet) for land on the west shore of Narragansett Bay. Further English-Narragansett transactions expanded the acquisition to 12 square miles. Within four years, English farmers bought property at

Pettaquamscutt and established a fortified house. The community thrived with many houses built along the river while cultivated fields lay inland.

However, King Philip's War brought on devastating Native American attacks to the settlement, leaving the Pettaquamscutt abandoned and destroyed. It would not be until the 18th century that the English rebounded. Fortunes were then made in raising livestock, quarrying, and intensive farming, and by exploiting African captives for free labor. The region's stone walls are the remnants of the work Africans and Native Americans performed toiling for the English landlords.

In the late 1800s, Governor William Sprague and his wife, Kate Chase, purchased the land and built a large mansion and stable whose ruins are part of the South County Museum property bordering the Canonchet Farm History Trail.

THE HIKE

Though there are other options, we recommend starting at the Narragansett Community Center Trailhead on Mumford Road behind the Senior Center and across from Sprague Park, where you can also pick up a trail map. As you enter the woods you have an option to follow the "new" path shortcutting the "old" path to your left. The original ("old") trail will lead you to a rise that was once the bed of a trolley system connecting the towns of East Greenwich, Narragansett, Wakefield, and Peace Dale. There are no ruins simply changes in the landscape indicative of the streetcar line.

Either path will reconnect you to the Canonchet History (Red) Trail. A wooden bridge crosses Crooked Brook, which has been built over the original stone bridge. As you cross the wooden bridge, take a moment and look down to your left to view abutment stones laid to support horse-pulled wagons.

As the trail turns to the left at the junction of the South County Museum, you hike along an old farming road with a large stone wall on your right. Note the barway (passage into a field or yard, closed by bars) which was an entrance to Governor William Sprague's mansion.

Continuing down the trail, follow the loop (a footpath) to the left to a series of well-built stone walls on the southern portion of Pettaquamscutt River (Cove). If you hike during the late fall through early spring, there is a wonderful view of the river/cove area. Note the large barway between stone walls that allowed wagons to access the salt marsh to collect hay during the spring thaw. The trail will also take you by a double stone wall and return you to the start of your loop. Turn left and cross between stone walls.

With stone walls on your left, come to another barway and a path leading down to the Chaffee Wildlife Preserve. Stay straight on the History (Red) Trail.

Proceeding along the trail, the stone wall bends to the right through a sassafras grove. Keep an eye open for steplike stones projecting from the wall making it easier for farmers to cross over it. Soon you will come upon an upright stone column along the right edge of the trail. This supported a gate for the quarry entry. Note the iron ring and braces for the gate. The companion stone has fallen and is covered by vegetation. However, you can determine which side of the trail the gate swung based on the metal attachments. Also, note the drill holes to split granite for the gatepost. You will see the same patterns at the stepped quarry farther up the trail.

Look for a path on your left leading downslope from the Red Trail. Take the path, which is a continuation of the Canonchet Trail circling back to the wider trail near a

Stone gatepost at Canonchet Farm.

large glacial erratic. The path will bend to the right and lead to a stepped-stone quarry. This 18th-century granite quarry was a relatively small operation, but it has all the classic features of larger New England quarries. The stepped appearance is the result of cutting away granite in long blocks. (Consider the stone gatepost.) Quarried stone could be used for multiple purposes including foundations, bridges, and fences. Note the drill holes and their spacing created by "feature and wedges" to split the granite—an excellent example of early quarrying methods and their archaeological visibility.

CANONCHET FARM HISTORY TRAIL

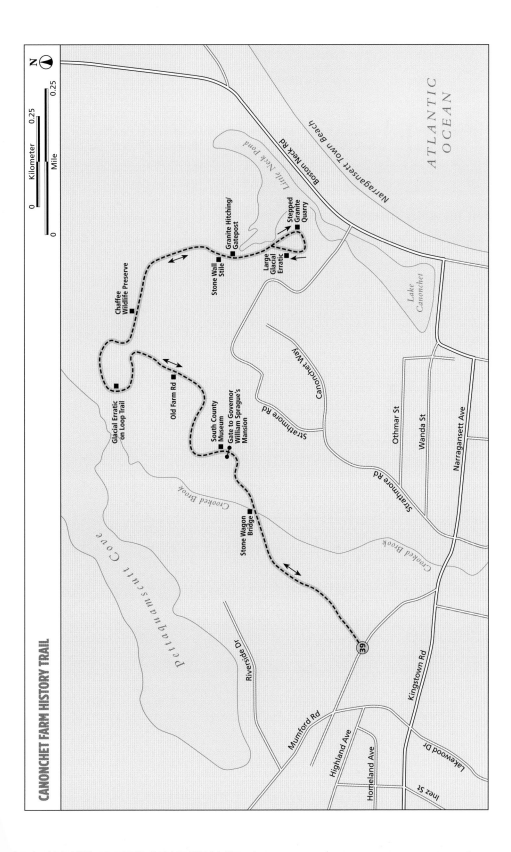

The trail takes you over the quarry leading back to the wider trail. Turn right toward a large glacial erratic. After the quarry loop, we recommend you retrace your steps back to the trailhead.

There is no need to return to the loop adjacent to the Pettaquamscutt River unless you want another panoramic view of the salt marsh. When you return to the signage for the South County Museum, you can bear to the right and return to the trailhead, or we further recommend you turn left and enter the museum property. There you can visit Sprague's Stable foundation built from granite and Narragansett stone in 1900 and see Robinson's Family Cemetery with its stone wall enclosure.

MILES AND DIRECTIONS

0.0   Begin at the trailhead at Narragansett Community Center.

0.04 Bear to the right onto "new" trail and follow red markers.

0.16 Wooden planks by vernal pool.

0.33 Stone bridge, historical marker H-2.

0.42 Stone wall on right, perpendicular to trail.

0.51 Cross the stone wall; trail turns sharply to the right.

0.61 Trail turns sharply to the left at the South County Museum path. Stay on Canonchet Trail.

0.73 Barway at H-4 marker.

0.82 Bear left onto "CT" marker. Trail becomes a footpath.

0.96 H-5—view of stone wall.

1.0   H-6A marker—trail follows the stone wall to your left.

1.04 Reconnect with wide trail. Turn left crossing the stone wall.

1.07 H-6B marker "Fish and Wildlife Preserve" sign.

1.13 "Field" sign on right. Stay left on Canonchet Trail.

1.19 H-7 stone stile—stepping-stones projecting outward used for crossing over wall.

1.26 Cross stone wall on wooden planks.

1.28 Stone gatepost, H-8.

1.32 Note quarried stones lining the trail on your right.

1.44 Divert to the path on your left, downslope. Note the appearance of a large glacial erratic uphill on the right.

1.51 Following the small pathway, a stepped-stone quarry will appear. Note the drill holes used to split the granite and the spacing between drill holes. Continue over the stones.

1.56 Return to the wide trail. Turn right toward the glacial erratic.

1.59 Glacial erratic. Continue downslope on the trail over bedrock outcropping and retrace your steps to the trailhead. On the way back, turn left at the South County Museum sign and tour the museum, Sprague's Stable, and the Robinson's Family Cemetery.

3.18 Arrive back at the trailhead.

40 CANONCHET-HOXIE PRESERVE TRAILS

Canonchet Preserve has a rugged, rocky landscape, defined by stone walls and old foundations providing some of the best examples of colonial and pre-colonial stonework in Rhode Island. Tour 18th-century house and barn foundations, a water-powered sawmill with intact dam system, Native American sacred landscapes, and even a huge glacial erratic. There are a total of 5 miles of marked trails near the Rhode Island–Connecticut border.

Start: Hoxie Preserve at Canonchet Preserves
Distance: 1.96 miles out-and-back
Hiking time: About 1 hour
Difficulty: Easy, though roots and boulders to navigate
Trail surface: Dirt and stone
Seasons: Best in late fall/early spring
Other trail users: None
Canine compatibility: On leash
Land status: The Nature Conservancy and Hopkinton Land Trust

Nearest town: Hopkinton, RI
Fees and permits: None
Schedule: Year-round
Maps: USGS Ashaway, RI-CT, Quadrangle
Trail contact: Hopkinton Land Trust, 1 Townhouse Rd., Hopkinton, RI 02833; (602) 730-LAND; HopkintonLandTrust@gmail.com; The Nature Conservancy, (401) 331-7110; ri@tnc.org

FINDING THE TRAILHEAD

Going southbound on I-95, take exit 2 in Hopkinton, RI (Woodville Alton Road); turn right. Coming northbound, turn left on exit 1, keeping right at the fork. Follow signs for Hopkinton, merging onto RI 3, Nooseneck Hill Road. The entrance to the Canonchet Preserve will be on your right on Main Street, across from a large white farmhouse. **GPS:** 41.481845, -71.747044

THE HISTORY AND RUINS

The Canonchet Preserve lies within the homeland of the Narragansett Tribe, whose ancestors lived and subsisted there for thousands of years. Utilizing the natural resources of the area, Native Americans hunted wild game, gathered plant products, and conducted sacred ceremonies. As on many of the southern New England trails available to the hiker, stone mounds of these sacred landscapes can still be seen. Canonchet (Cononchet, Quanonchet) was a Narragansett sachem and leader of Native American warriors in the Great Swamp Fight during King Philip's War (1675).

Later, British settlers developed farmsteads on this land, and with the advance of the Industrial Revolution, sought waterpower here to cut wood and grind corn. These economic activities have left manifestations in stone ruins within the preserve.

The Foster family built a sawmill on the South Fork of Canonchet Brook by the time of the American Revolution. The Hoxie family, as main proprietors of the land into the 19th century, farmed, did blacksmithing and masonry, and even operated a tollgate on what is today RI 3. The Hoxies served as teachers and members of the Town Council

Stone foundation of barn ruin at Canonchet Preserve.

for over 25 years. They continued to expand their farm into the early 20th century by purchasing parcels from their neighbors, increasing their holdings to over 200 acres. In 2010, descendants transferred ownership of 117 acres of Hoxie property to The Nature Conservancy.

THE HIKE

The trailhead begins on RI 3 (Main Street) with the Yellow Trail leading to the stone ruins. While it is a relatively easy walk, the trail is strewn with stone boulders and exposed tree roots, so exercise caution as you hike. Be sure to read the history and archaeological etiquette posted on the trailhead kiosk.

From the trailhead, walk to your right and upslope to the start of the Yellow Trail. Though the Yellow Trail intersects with the White Trail a few times, stay on the Yellow throughout the hike. Begin by crossing a small brook and stone causeway coming to a T-intersection. Bear left and continue the Yellow Trail. At the next intersection, bear left (Yellow Trail) with a stone wall stretching parallel on the left.

Keep alert and you will encounter what appears to be a high stone wall to your right. These ruins are the eastern extent of a stone dam impounding water for Foster's sawmill. Follow the dam to the sawmill. Before crossing the stone bridge over Canonchet Brook, take the unmarked path on your right for a good view of the mill ruins. Return to the Yellow Trail, cross the stone bridge, and take another short path on your right for an alternative view of the mill. This perspective will give you an appreciation of the narrow wheelhouse and its tailrace.

Returning to the Yellow Trail, continue to your right. The trail will then veer to the left and scattered within the wooded area on the right you will see stone mounds, which the Narragansett Tribal Nation has interpreted as a ceremonial stone landscape. Please be respectful in this area and stay on the trail as you pass.

Soon, a large glacial erratic and additional mounded stones appear upslope. The Yellow Trail then descends downslope, crossing a small brook, turns upslope, and bends to the left. Cross a stone barway and on your left a small path leads to a stone foundation. This is a small house structure, yet the cellar is deep and overlooks the wetlands.

Back to the Yellow Trail, turn left once again and continue upslope. Pass through two additional barways connecting multiple pastures coming to a right turn in the trail. At that bend, a small path on the left will lead to the lower level of a large barn ruin. Walk inside the floor of the barn and note stone pillars used to support the upper floor levels for wagons. The barn would have had a loft for hay storage. Also, note that the lower level was subdivided into various workstations and animal stalls.

Come out of the ruins you entered and continue to your right around the lower end of the structure. Behind the barn, find an impressive root cellar dug into the slope for the preservation of produce. Look left beyond the root cellar to see the smaller entrance to a second root cellar. This was clearly a very productive farming enterprise, storing food for market as well as family subsistence.

From the second root cellar, climb up over the rocks or retrace your steps back to the Yellow Trail turning left. Either way will take you to the top of the slope and the ruins

Colonial "saltbox" house ruin showing center stack and cellar hole.

CANONCHET-HOXIE PRESERVE TRAILS

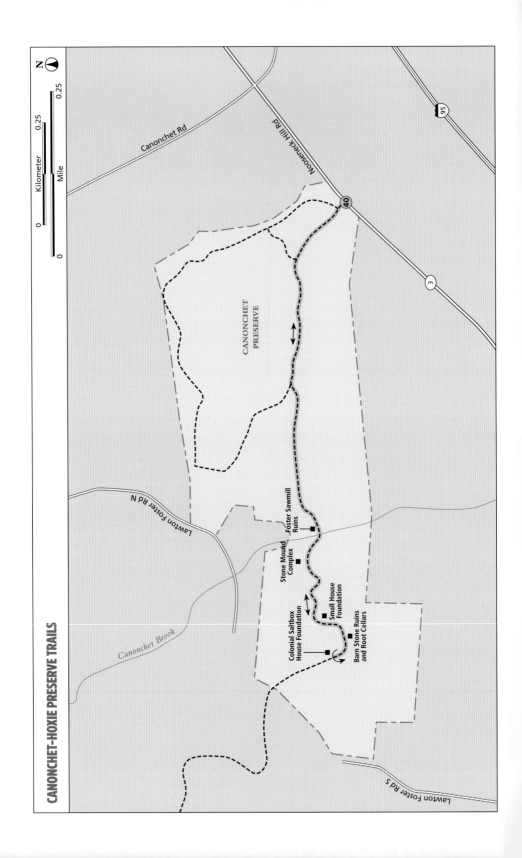

N

Kilometer
0   0.25

Mile
0   0.25

Canonchet Rd

Nooseneck Hill Rd

95

40

3

CANONCHET PRESERVE

Canonchet Brook

Lawton Foster Rd N

Foster Sawmill Ruins

Stone Mound Complex

Colonial Saltbox House Foundation

Small House Foundation

Barn Stone Ruins and Root Cellars

Lawton Foster Rd S

Stone ruins of Foster's Sawmill along Canonchet Brook.

of the main farmhouse. The extent of the stone foundation suggests one of the largest house ruins you will probably ever see in southern New England. A classic colonial saltbox with a center chimney stack. Note the large flat stone centered along the foundation serving as the stepping-stone to the front door.

Explore. The cellar is divided into two sides with separate stone steps leading to the basement. The house would have been two-and-a-half stories high with a peaked roof. To the right of the house, note the level landscape, probably the family's garden.

The house foundation is just shy of a mile out from the trailhead. There are no significant stone ruins farther on the trail, so either extend your hike by completing the full loop of the Yellow Trail, or simply retrace your steps back to the parking lot. Either way, the stone ruins associated with the Canonchet Preserve are well worth visiting.

MILES AND DIRECTIONS

- 0.0 Begin at the Canonchet Yellow Trail trailhead.
- 0.11 First intersection with the White Trail. Bear left, staying on the Yellow Trail.
- 0.32 Second intersection with the White Trail. Bear left, downslope on the Yellow Trail.
- 0.35 Cross the stone wall; mill dam on your right.
- 0.54 Marker 3 with stone dam in the background.
- 0.55 Marker 4, Foster's sawmill. Take the small dirt path along the brook for a better look at the stone ruins.

0.57 Return to the Yellow Trail, turn right, cross the stone bridge, and take another small path to the ruins to locate the waterwheel pit.

0.63 Return to the Yellow Trail; continue right.

0.65 Trail veers left and follows the stone wall.

0.71 Stone mounds on your right.

0.73 Marker 5, large glacial erratic. Continue downslope left.

0.75 Cross small brook.

0.77 Pass through the stone wall barway.

0.79 Marker 6; turn off trail to your left to small cellar hole to a house foundation. Return to the Yellow Trail and proceed left.

0.82 Pass through another stone wall barway.

0.84 Continue upslope through yet another barway. Note stone mounds on your right.

0.88 Marker 7, a large barn foundation. Take the path left and enter the lower level of the barn. Note stone pillars and work compartments. Continue around the back side of the structure.

0.95 Locate the first root cellar behind the barn.

0.96 Locate the second root cellar behind left. Continue upslope over the rocks or retrace your steps back to Marker 7, whichever you are comfortable doing—either way leads to the Yellow Trail and the house foundation.

0.98 Marker 8, sizable stone house foundation. Note the large flat stepping-stone for the front door with chimney stack behind. Explore. Return the way you came to the trailhead.

1.96 Arrive back at the trailhead.

HIKE DIFFICULTY

EASY

1. Putnam Memorial State Park Trail
2. Lovers Leap State Park Trails
4. Lighthouse Village and Jessie Gerard Trails
5. Tunxis Trail, Caseville
7. Falls Trail, Keith Mitchell Park
11. Valley Falls Park Trails
12. Dividend Pond Trails
13. Farmington Canal Heritage Trail and Farmington River Trail
14. Gay City State Park Trails
17. Salt Meadow Trail, Stewart B. McKinney National Wildlife Refuge
18. Westwoods Trail
19. Ironwoods Preserve Trail
20. Papermill Trail
22. Mount Archer Woods Trail
25. Bluff Point State Park Trails
26. Coogan Farm Trail
27. Natchaug State Forest Trail, Nathaniel Lyon
28. Natchaug State Forest, Ashford Woods
29. Tri-State Trail
30. Becket Quarry Trail
31. Keystone Arch Bridges Trail
32. Old Mill Trail
33. Hancock Shaker Mountain North Trail
35. Upton Heritage Park Trail
36. Bancroft's Castle Trail
37. Trail Through Time
39. Canonchet Farm History Trail
40. Canonchet-Hoxie Preserve Trails

EASY/MODERATE

6. Walt Landgraf and Elliot Bronson Trails
9. Suburban Park Trail
15. The Preserve Trail
16. Canfield-Meadow Woods Trail

23. Mattabesett Trail, Mica Ledges
34. Eyrie House Ruins Trail
38. Breakheart Reservation Trails

MODERATE
8. Little Laurel Lime Ridge Trail
10. Sweetheart Mountain Trail
21. Hartman Park Trails
24. Mattabesett Trail, Mount Higby

MODERATE/DIFFICULT
3. Henry Buck Trail

NATIONAL PARKS OF SOUTHERN NEW ENGLAND

Adams National Historic Park, Massachusetts
Appalachian National Scenic Trail, Connecticut, Massachusetts
Boston African American National Historic Site, Massachusetts
Boston Harbor Islands National Recreation Area, Massachusetts
Cape Cod National Seashore, Massachusetts
Frederick Law Olmsted National Historic Site, Massachusetts
John F. Kennedy National Historic Site, Massachusetts
Longfellow National Historic Site, Massachusetts
Lowell National Historical Park, Massachusetts
Minute Man National Historical Park, Massachusetts
New Bedford Whaling National Historical Park, Massachusetts
Roger Williams National Memorial, Rhode Island
Salem Maritime National Historic Site, Massachusetts
Saugus Iron Works National Historic Site, Massachusetts
Springfield Armory National Historic Site, Massachusetts
Weir Farm National Historic Site, Connecticut

STATE ARCHAEOLOGY AND HISTORICAL PRESERVATION OFFICES

CONNECTICUT

Office of State Archaeology, 354 Mansfield Rd., University of Connecticut, Storrs, CT 06269-1176; (860) 617-6884

State Historic Preservation Office, CT Department of Economic and Community Development, 450 Columbus Blvd., Suite 5, Hartford, CT 06103; (860) 500-2393

MASSACHUSETTS

Massachusetts Historical Commission, 1 Ashburton Place, Boston, MA 02108; (800) 392-6090

RHODE ISLAND

Rhode Island Historical Preservation and Heritage Commission, 150 Benefit St., Providence, RI 02903; (401) 222-2678

BIBLIOGRAPHY

Atwell, Sarah. "Hike to the Pest House." www.patch.com.

Betts, M.W., and M. G. Hrynick. *The Archaeology of the Atlantic Northeast.* Toronto: University of Toronto Press, 2021.

Burge, Kathleen. "Chamber of mystery." *Boston Globe,* July 12, 2012.

Burke, Carol, and Ronald. "History of Valley Falls Park." www.tankerhoosen.info.

Butler, Jo-Ann. www.rebelpuritan.blogspot.com.

Cahill, R. *New England's Ancient Mysteries.* Salem, MA: Old Saltbox Publishing House, 1993.

Clew, Harry T. "New Yorkers are victims of tragedy." *Hartford Courant,* November 1, 1954.

Cruson, D. *Putnam's Revolutionary War Winter Encampment.* Cheltenham, Gloucester: History Press, 2011.

Feder, Kenneth L. *A Village of Outcasts: Historical Archaeology and Documentary Research at the Lighthouse Site.* New York: McGraw-Hill, 1993.

Fell, Barry. *American B.C.: Ancient Settlers in the New World.* Muskogee, OK: Artisan Publishers, 2008.

Friends of the Keystone Arches, Inc. www.keystonearches.com.

Gavalis, Amy. "The Canton Ski Club." www.nelsap.org.

Goodwin, William. *The Ruins of Great Ireland in New England.* Boston: Meador Press, 1946.

Goudsward, D. *Ancient Stone Sites of New England and the Debate over Early European Exploration.* Jefferson, NC: McFarland & Company, 2006.

Ives, Timothy. *Stones of Contention.* Nashville, TN: World Encounter Institute, 2021.

Kerber, J. *A Lasting Impression: Coastal, Lithic, and Ceramic Research in New England Archaeology.* Westport, CT: Praeger, 2002.

Lavin, L. *Connecticut's Indigenous Peoples: What Archaeology, History, and Oral Traditions Teach Us.* New Haven, CT: Yale University Press, 2013.

Leff, David K. "Byzantine church or Stonemason Doodling?" www.davidkleff.typepad.com.

Leskovitz, Frank J. "Science Leads the Way," Murder and the Berkshire Cultural Center, www.gombessa.tripod.com.

Linda. "Wandering out to the CT-MA-RI Tri-State Marker." www.thedistractedwanderer.com.

Madison Land Conservation Trust. "The Ironwoods Preserve." www.madisonlandtrust.org.

Madison Land Conservation Trust. "Papermill Trail." www.madisonlandtrust.org

Mahan, Shannon A., F.W. Martin, and C. Taylor. "Construction ages of the Upton Stone Chamber: Preliminary findings and suggestions for future luminescence research." *Quaternary Geochronology,* vol. 30, Part B, 2015.

Marteka, Peter. "Discover mysterious stone structures and Ice Age-era boulders at Hartman Park," *Hartford Courant*, November 17, 2020.

Mavor, James W., and Bryon E. Dix. *Manitou: The Sacred Landscape of New England's Native Civilization*. Rochester, VT: Inner Traditions, 1989.

MHC Reconnaissance Survey Town Report: Chester. Associated Regional Report, 1982.

Mills, Lewis Sprague. *Legends of Barkhamsted Lighthouse and Satan's Kingdom in New Hartford*. Hamden, CT: Shoestring Press, 1961.

Owen, Ryan W. "Groton's Castle of broken dreams—Bancroft Castle on Gibbett Hill." www.forgottennewengland.com.

Russell, H. S. *Indian New England before the Mayflower*. Lebanon, NH: University Press of New England, 2014.

Rzasa, Peter J., and Barbara J. Rzasa. *Little Laurel Lime Ridge Park: Colonial Lime Kiln, Marble Quarries, Charcoal Pits, Seymour, Connecticut*. Unpublished manuscript, 2013.

Sanford, R. M., M. Shaughnessy, et al. *Reading Rural Landscapes: A Field Guide to New England's Past*. Thomaston, ME: Tilbury House, 2015.

Snow, D. R. *The Archaeology of New England*. Cambridge, MA: Academic Press, 1980.

Streeter, Jim. "History Revisited: A hurricane devastates a Groton colony." *The Day*, September 21, 2017.

Thompson Historical Society. "The Great 1891 East Thompson 4-Engine Wreck Site." www.thompsonhistorical.org.

Trocchi, Jim. "The Farmington Canal." *Newsletter of the Friends of the Office of State Archaeology*, Fall 2007.

Trustees. "Becket Historical Quarry and Forest." www.thetrustees.org.

Walter, Carl E. "Map of the Farmington Canal in Avon, Connecticut," 2016.

HIKE INDEX

Waterfall at Keystone Arch Bridges Trail.

THE TEN ESSENTIALS OF HIKING

American Hiking Society

American Hiking Society recommends you pack the "Ten Essentials" every time you head out for a hike. Whether you plan to be gone for a couple of hours or several months, make sure to pack these items. Become familiar with these items and know how to use them.

1. Appropriate Footwear
Happy feet make for pleasant hiking. Think about traction, support, and protection when selecting well-fitting shoes or boots.

2. Navigation
While phones and GPS units are handy, they aren't always reliable in the backcountry; consider carrying a paper map and compass as a backup and know how to use them.

3. Water (and a way to purify it)
As a guideline, plan for half a liter of water per hour in moderate temperatures/terrain. Carry enough water for your trip and know where and how to treat water while you're out on the trail.

4. Food
Pack calorie-dense foods to help fuel your hike, and carry an extra portion in case you are out longer than expected.

5. Rain Gear & Dry-Fast Layers
The weatherman is not always right. Dress in layers to adjust to changing weather and activity levels. Wear moisture-wicking cloths and carry a warm hat.

6. Safety Items (light, fire, and a whistle)
Have means to start an emergency fire, signal for help, and see the trail and your map in the dark.

7. First Aid Kit
Supplies to treat illness or injury are only as helpful as your knowledge of how to use them. Take a class to gain the skills needed to administer first aid and CPR.

8. Knife or Multi-Tool
With countless uses, a multi-tool can help with gear repair and first aid.

9. Sun Protection
Sunscreen, sunglasses, and sun-protective clothing should be used in every season regardless of temperature or cloud cover.

10. Shelter
Protection from the elements in the event you are injured or stranded is necessary. A lightweight, inexpensive space blanket is a great option.

Find other helpful resources at AmericanHiking.org/hiking-resources